Financial and Accounting Guide for Not-for-Profit Organizations

Seventh Edition
2009 Cumulative Supplement

D1414386

Update Service

BECOME A SUBSCRIBER!
Did you purchase this product from a bookstore?

If you did, it's important for you to become a subscriber. John Wiley & Sons, Inc. may publish, on a periodic basis, supplements and new editions to reflect the latest changes in the subject matter that you *need to know* in order to stay competitive in this ever-changing industry. By contacting the Wiley office nearest you, you'll receive any current update at no additional charge. In addition, you'll receive future updates and revised or related volumes on a 30-day examination review.

If you purchased this product directly from John Wiley & Sons, Inc., we have already recorded your subscription for this update service.

To become a subscriber, please call **1-877-762-2974** or send your name, company name (if applicable), address, and the title of the product to:

mailing address:
Supplement Department
John Wiley & Sons, Inc.
One Wiley Drive
Somerset, NJ 08875

e-mail: **subscriber@wiley.com**
fax: **1-732-302-2300**
online: **www.wiley.com**

For customers outside the United States, please contact the Wiley office nearest you:

Professional & Reference Division
John Wiley & Sons Canada, Ltd.
22 Worcester Road
Etobicoke, Ontario M9W 1L1
CANADA
Phone: 416-236-4433
Phone: 1-800-567-4797
Fax: 416-236-4447
E-mail: canada@wiley.com

John Wiley & Sons, Ltd.
The Atrium
Southern Gate, Chichester
West Sussex PO 19 8SQ
ENGLAND
Phone: 44-1243-779777
Fax: 44-1243-775878
E-mail: customer@wiley.co.uk

John Wiley & Sons Australia, Ltd.
33 Park Road
P.O. Box 1226
Milton, Queensland 4064
AUSTRALIA
Phone: 61-7-3859-9755
Fax: 61-7-3859-9715
E-mail: brisbane@johnwiley.com.au

John Wiley & Sons (Asia) Pte., Ltd.
2 Clementi Loop #02-01
SINGAPORE 129809
Phone: 65-64632400
Fax: 65-64634604/5/6
Customer Service: 65-64604280
E-mail: enquiry@wiley.com.sg

Financial and Accounting Guide for Not-for-Profit Organizations

Seventh Edition
2009 Cumulative Supplement

Malvern J. Gross, Jr., CPA
Retired Partner, PricewaterhouseCoopers LLP

John H. McCarthy, CPA
Retired Partner, PricewaterhouseCoopers LLP

Nancy E. Shelmon, CPA
Partner, PricewaterhouseCoopers LLP

WILEY

John Wiley & Sons, Inc.

Published by John Wiley & Sons, Inc., Hoboken, New Jersey.

Published simultaneously in Canada.

For general information on our other products and services, or technical support, please contact our Customer Care Department within the United States at 800-762-2974, outside the United States at 317-572-3993 or fax 317-572-4002.

Wiley also publishes its books in a variety of electronic formats. Some content that appears in print may not be available in electronic books.

For more information about Wiley products, visit our Web site at http://www.wiley.com.

Library of Congress Cataloging-in-Publication Data:
Financial and accounting guide for not-for-profit organizations /
Malvern J. Gross, Jr., ... [et al.].—7th ed.
   p. cm.
  Malvern J. Gross's name appears as main author entry in earlier ed.
  Includes index.
  ISBN 978-0-470-28659-3 (supplement)
  1. Nonprofit organizations—Accounting. I. Gross, Malvern J.
    HF5686.N56G76 2005
    657.98–dc22

                            2005000045

Printed in the United States of America

10 9 8 7 6 5 4 3 2 1

About the Authors

Malvern J. Gross, Jr., was the author of the first edition of this text and a significant contributor to many of the subsequent editions. He is a retired partner of Price Waterhouse (a predecessor to PricewaterhouseCoopers LLP) and a nationally recognized authority on accounting and financial reporting for not-for-profit organizations. He was chairman of the AICPA Subcommittee on Nonprofit Organizations that wrote the 1978 landmark Statement of Position for Certain Nonprofit Organizations and of the Accounting Advisory Committee to the Commission on Private Philanthropy and Public Needs. He was a member of the committee that wrote the second edition of *Standards of Accounting and Financial Reporting for Voluntary Health and Welfare Organizations* and a coauthor of the *Museum Accounting Handbook*. He served as an advisor to the Financial Accounting Standards Board in the early phases of its work on setting accounting standards for not-for-profit organizations and to the New York State Charities Registration Office, as well as an adjunct professor of accounting at Lehigh University, his alma mater. After retirement from Price Waterhouse, he was president of a not-for-profit organization, the National Aeronautics Association. He now lives in the San Juan Islands off the state of Washington.

 John H. McCarthy is Senior Vice President for Administration and Finance at Northeastern University. Jack is also affiliated with Harvard University's Hauser Center for Nonprofit Organizations and a lecturer at the Kennedy School of Government. He served as the National Leader of PricewaterhouseCoopers' Education & Nonprofit Practice before his retirement from the firm in 2005. He was a coauthor of the sixth and seventh editions of this text. He is a coauthor of *Understanding Financial Statements: A Strategic Guide for Independent College & University Boards*, published by the Association of Governing Boards of Universities and Colleges, 2nd edition (2007), as well as several publications by PricewaterhouseCoopers including: *The Changing Role of the Audit Committee: Leading Practices for Colleges, Universities and Other Not-for-Profit*

Educational Institutions (2004); *A Foundation for Integrity* (a 2004 guide for codes of conduct, conflicts of interest, and executive compensation); *Meeting the Challenges of Alternative Investments* (2004); *Understanding Underwater Endowment Funds (2003)*; and *Financial Reporting and Contributions: A Decision Making Guide to FASB Nos. 116–117* (1996) among others. He is a CPA who, for 37 years, served PricewaterhouseCoopers' education and not-for-profit clients, including many of the most prestigious institutions in the United States. He graduated from Boston College and holds an MBA from the University of Michigan Business School.

Nancy E. Shelmon is a senior partner of PricewaterhouseCoopers LLP and is the firm's West Region Leader for the Education and Not-for-Profit Industry within the United States. She is a frequent speaker at AICPA and state CPA conferences on financial reporting and accounting issues affecting not-for-profit organizations and is currently a member of the AICPA Not-for-Profit Expert Panel. She is currently chair of the planning committee for the AICPA's annual Not-for-Profit Conference. She has been serving education and not-for-profit clients for over 30 years and has been involved with some of the most widely respected organizations in North America. She serves on the board of directors of the Los Angeles Urban League and Executive Service Corps of Southern California. In addition to being a CPA, she is also a Certified Fraud Examiner. She holds her accounting degree from the University of Minnesota.

Contributors

We also want to recognize the past contributions of **Richard F. Larkin,** who was a coauthor of the fourth, fifth, and sixth editions of *Financial and Accounting Guide for Not-for-Profit Organizations*. Prior to his retirement from PricewaterhouseCoopers, he served as a technical director for the Education & Nonprofit practice. We are very grateful to Dick for his efforts on prior editions of this Guide.

The seventh edition of this Guide represents the collaborative efforts of many PricewaterhouseCoopers professionals who work with our not-for-profit and higher education clients throughout the United States. The authors wish to very gratefully acknowledge the contributions of the following PricewaterhouseCoopers partners, directors, and managers to this Guide: Emily Bernhardt, Ted Budge, Amy Cloud Barrett, Ralph DeAcetis, Diane Duncan, John Edie, Kaye Ferriter, Kevin Fordyce, Martha Garner, Elaine Garvey, Paul Hanley, Julie Henderson, Sandra Johnson, Elisabeth Lippuner, Riva Mirvis, Brian Neumann, Christos Poulios, Robert Spear, Gwen Spencer, Jessica Vroman, Nancy Leparto, Lori Scott, and Frederick Wentzel, Jr. Their assistance has been invaluable.

Contents

Note to the Reader: Chapters or sections not in the main bound volume, *Financial and Accounting Guide for Not-for-Profit Organizations, Seventh Edition* (978-0471-72445-2) are indicated by "(New)" after the title. Material from the main bound volume that has been updated for *this* supplement is indicated by "(Revised)" after the title. Material new to or modified in *this* supplement is indicated by an asterisk (*) in the left margin in the contents and throughout the supplement.

CONTENTS

■ xi ■

Preface

This supplement updates the seventh edition of *Financial and Accounting Guide for Not-for-Profit Organizations*. This supplement includes all of the changes we have made to the seventh edition since it was published in 2005.

We have further revised several chapters in this supplement to reflect the most current information. The highlights of these changes follow:

- We have updated Appendix D, "Summary of Emerging Accounting, Tax, and Regulatory Issues for Not-for-Profit Organizations in 2008," which highlights accounting, financial reporting, tax, and regulatory compliance issues, including their potential impact.

- Chapter 26 on investments includes the Alternative Investments Practice Aid issued by the Alternative Investments Task Force established by the Audit Issues Task Force of the Auditing Standards Board. In addition, we have included a comprehensive white paper on this topic (useful for management, the board, and the auditors) as Appendix E.

- Another white paper, helping management and the Board to understand the FAS 159 choices, has been included as Appendix G.

- Chapter 28 discusses some of the IRS's proposed revisions to Form 990 and provides a web site where you may obtain the most recent status and information.

Nancy Shelmon
Los Angeles, California
February 1, 2009

CHAPTER ONE

Responsibilities for Fiscal Management

§ 1.8 Conclusion   1

§ 1.8   CONCLUSION

p. 12. Add the following as the second paragraph in *section 1.8:*

In addition to this guidance, the treasurer is encouraged to develop networks and relationships with other not-for-profit organizations and trade associations to improve financial understanding and communication. Many professional associations and industry associations have publications, web sites, conferences, and seminars dedicated to education and enrichment for business officers in nonprofit organizations. Other web sites are dedicated to sharing public information about not-for-profit organizations. Keeping abreast of current issues and trends will only enhance the value the treasurer brings to the organization.

PART ONE

Key Financial Concepts

CHAPTER FIVE

Fixed Assets and Depreciation

§ 5.1 GENERAL PRINCIPLES—WORKING DEFINITIONS

p. 51. Insert new *subsection (c)* **before** *section 5.2:*

(c) Capitalization of Fixed Assets—Change in Estimate (New)

Sometimes an organization will have occasion to consider a change in the estimated future benefits of an asset, the pattern of consumption of the benefits associated with an asset, or new information about the future benefits that are associated with an asset. Then the organization may change the depreciation or amortization associated with the asset. This change is considered a change in accounting estimate effected by a change in accounting principle, as defined by Financial Accounting Standards Board (FASB) Statement of Financial Accounting Standards (SFAS) 154, *Accounting for Changes and Error Corrections, a Replacement of APB Opinion No. 20 and FASB Statement No. 3,* and should be accounted for in the period of change if the change affects only the reporting period or in the period of change and future periods if the change affects both.

§ 5.7   IMPAIRMENT OR DISPOSAL OF LONG-LIVED ASSETS

pp. 58–59. Replace current *subsection (c)* **with the following:**

(c)   Consideration of Retirement Obligations

Note: This section is amended for the issuance of Financial Accounting Standards Board Interpretation No. 47, *Accounting for Conditional Asset Retirement Obligations* (FIN 47).

SFAS 143, *Accounting for Asset Retirement Obligations,* describes the accounting and reporting for legal obligations associated with the retirement of tangible long-lived assets and the associated retirement costs. This statement applies to all entities, including not-for-profit organizations. SFAS 143 and FIN 47 require recognition of a liability for the fair value of an asset retirement obligation or any conditional asset retirement obligation (CARO) when the organization has sufficient information to make a reasonable estimate by applying an expected present value technique. A CARO is defined in FIN 47 as: "A legal obligation to perform an asset retirement activity in which the timing and (or) method of settlement are conditional on a future event that may or may not be within the control of the entity." Uncertainty associated with the settlement date and method of settlement does not preclude recognition for the CARO as the legal obligation to perform the retirement activities exist.

The fair value of the liability for the asset retirement obligation should be recognized when incurred. When initially recognizing the liability for an asset retirement obligation, the organization should capitalize the asset retirement cost (ARC) by increasing the carrying amount of the related long-lived asset by the same amount as the liability. Thus, over the life of the long-lived asset, there is an annual charge to expense to depreciate the asset and the ARC. There is also an annual charge to expense to accrete the asset retirement obligation. When the asset retirement obligation is ultimately settled, the liability should approximate this cost.

Examples of situations where an asset obligation and ARCs might need to be recorded by a not-for-profit organization would include, among others:

- The removal of an underground fuel storage tank
- The dismantling of a cogeneration plant
- A requirement to undo modifications made to leased property
- A gift of a building with stipulation from the donor that after ten years the building is to be destroyed and the land converted into a garden
- The legal requirement to remove or abate asbestos in buildings

The calculation to estimate an asset retirement obligation is complex. For each asset retirement obligation, the entity must determine a settlement date, a settlement method, and a settlement cost using a current valuation. Then the current cost must be inflated to the estimated settlement date using a reasonable inflation rate. Finally, the inflated cost must be reported at its present value using a credit-adjusted risk-free rate of return. On an annual basis, the valuation of the asset retirement obligation must be updated and adjusted as necessary.

The five steps to evaluate asset retirement obligations for older assets, new assets, or on an ongoing basis are the same:

1. Take an inventory of long-lived assets that have asset retirement obligations.
2. Gather information from legal advisors, facilities management, and others.
3. Using the information gathered from others, measure the obligation.
4. Develop written policies and procedures to codify accounting for FIN 47/SFAS 143 transactions.
5. Develop financial reports and disclosures.

For many organizations with a fiscal year-end June 30, 2006, the effect of implementing FIN 47 was presented as a cumulative effect of a change in accounting principle in the statement of activities.

CHAPTER SIX

Investment Income, Gains and Losses, and Endowment Funds

§ 6.1   ACCOUNTING PRINCIPLES

(h)   Display of Investment Income When a "Spending Formula" Is Used

p. 67. Add the following as last paragraph in *subsection (h):*

The National Conference of Commissioners on Uniform State Laws (NCCUSL) has approved a comprehensively revised version of UMIFA, called the Uniform Prudent Management of Institutional Funds Act, or UPMIFA. This new law, if adopted by the various state and territorial legislatures, is anticipated to have widespread implications for nonprofit organizations, including:

- Elimination of the historic dollar-value limitation on spending (the so-called "underwater funds" rule)
- Broadening the scope covered by the statute, which is intended to apply to trusts, governmental agencies, and any other type of entity dedicated to charitable purposes, as well as nonprofit organizations

- Comprehensive incorporation of modern portfolio investment standards by providing for diversification of assets, pooling of assets, total return investment, and whole portfolio management

- An endorsement of the concept of intergenerational equity via an optional provision that allows states to find that an organization spending more than 7 percent of its endowment in one year is acting imprudently

UPMIFA was approved by 300 state law commissioners on July 13, 2006, at NCCUSL's annual meeting. The act will now go to the American Bar Association for approval; after that, it will be introduced into the legislature of each jurisdiction. If signed into law, UPMIFA will replace UMIFA, which has been the standard in 48 states for the past three and one-half decades.

While UPMIFA adds only one word to UMIFA's title, the underlying change in the law is major in both structure and significance. UMIFA had gone unchanged over its entire 34-year existence. If adopted, UPMIFA will likely reshape the landscape of nonprofit fund management and investment.

Under UPMIFA, the rules governing expenditures from endowment funds could be modified to give a governing board more flexibility in making investment and expenditure decisions within the general standard of prudence, so that the board can cope with fluctuations in the value of the endowment.

*The web site www.upmifa.org, provides an up-to-date status of which states have passed UPMIFA as well as comparisons of the versions passed in different states.

UPMIFA eliminates the concept of "historical gift value," and relies on a "prudence" standard, which specifies that spending above 7 percent creates a rebuttable presumption of imprudence:

> The appropriation for expenditure in any year if an amount greater than seven percent of the fair market value of an endowment fund, calculated on the basis of market values determined at least quarterly and averaged over a period of not less than three years immediately preceding the year in which the appropriation for expenditure was made, creates a rebuttable presumption of imprudence. [Section 4 (d)]

The Act also includes a process for releasing or modifying restrictions on a gift, and specifies appropriate circumstances for doing so:

> If an institution determines that a restriction contained in a gift instrument on the management, investment, or purpose of an institutional fund is unlawful, impracticable, impossible to achieve, or wasteful, the institution, [60 days] after notification to the [Attorney General], may release or modify the restriction, in whole or part, if:
>
> 1) the institutional fund subject to the restriction has a total value of less than [$25,000]; 2) more than [20] years have elapsed since the fund was established; and 3) the institution uses the property in a manner the institution reasonably determines to be consistent with the charitable purposes expressed in the gift instrument. [Section 6 (d)]

*In August 2008, the FASB issued Staff Position FAS 117-1, *Endowments of Not-for-Profit Organizations: Net Asset Classification of Funds Subject to an Enacted Version of the Uniform Prudent Management of Institutional Funds Act, and Enhanced Disclosures for All Endowment Funds*. This FASB Staff Position (FSP) provides guidance concerning: (1) the disclosures that not-for-profit organizations should make with regard to their endowments, and (2) the effect of a state's adoption of the model Uniform Prudent Management of Institutional Funds Act of 2006 (UPMIFA) on the classification of net assets related to donor-restricted endowment funds of not-for-profit organizations within that state. The key provisions of the FSP are as follows.

Expanded Disclosure Requirements for All Endowments. FSP proposes a number of new disclosures that would be required for endowments of all not-for-profit organizations, not just endowments held in states where UPMIFA has been enacted. These include:

- A description of the governing board's interpretation of the law that underlies the net asset classification of donor–restricted endowment funds
- A description of endowment spending policies
- A description of endowment investment policies, including the organization's return objectives and risk parameters, how those

objectives relate to the organization's endowment spending policies, and the strategies employed for achieving those objectives

- An endowment reconciliation by financial statement net asset
  class that shows cumulative investment returns in the permanently restricted net asset class that relate to the organization's
  interpretation of relevant law, rather than what is required by
  explicit donor stipulation

- The composition of an organization's endowment by net asset
  classification at the end of the period, in total and by type of
  endowment fund, showing donor–restricted endowment funds
  separately from board–designated endowment funds

- A reconciliation of the beginning and ending balances of the
  organization's endowment, in total and by net asset class,
  including, at a minimum, the following line items:

  ○ Investment return, separated into investment income and net
    appreciation or depreciation of investments

  ○ Contributions

  ○ Amounts appropriated for expenditure

  ○ Reclassifications

  ○ Other changes

- Disclosure of how much (if any) of additions of investment
  return to permanently restricted net assets in the current period
  are the result of the organization's interpretation of relevant law,
  beyond that required by explicit donor stipulations

- Planned appropriation for expenditures, if known, for the year
  following the most recent period for which the organization
  presents financial statements

The FSP provides an illustrative example of such disclosures.

PwC Observations: In substance, the changes brought about by
UPMIFA merely provide organizations with short-term spending flex-
ibility to deal with market declines that result in underwater situations.
While the amount of assets associated with an endowment fund might

fluctuate, the accountability to the donor for a permanent endowment remains unchanged.

Apart from the new disclosure requirements that apply to all organizations with endowments, the FSP may also impact net asset accounting depending on the relevant state UPMIFA law. In light of the short time frame for implementation, not-for-profit organizations should start preparing for the proposed FSP's expanded disclosure requirements as quickly as possible.

CHAPTER SEVEN

Affiliated Organizations, Pass-Through Transactions, and Mergers

§ 7.3 MERGERS OF NOT-FOR-PROFIT ORGANIZATIONS

(b) FASB-Proposed Exposure Draft—Combinations of Not-for-Profit Organizations

p. 89. Insert the following to replace the material after the second paragraph:

Proposed FASB Staff Position No. SOP 94-3-a and AAG HCO-a, *Omnibus Changes to Consolidation and Equity Method Guidance for Not-for-Profit Organizations*, was issued by the FASB staff, with a comment deadline of November 30, 2007.

This FASB Staff Position (FSP) makes several changes to the guidance on consolidation and the equity method of accounting in AICPA Statement of Position 94-3, Reporting of Related Entities by

Not-for-Profit Organizations, and the AICPA Audit and Accounting Guide, Health Care Organizations. This FSP:

a. Eliminates the temporary control exception to consolidation that currently exists for certain relationships between not-for-profit organizations, and makes two related changes:

   1. Amends the definition of majority voting interest in the board of another entity in SOP 94-3 and the health care Guide

   2. Conforms the categorization of sole corporate membership in SOP 94-3 to that in the health care Guide

b. Confirms the continued applicability to not-for-profit organizations of the guidance on consolidation of special-purpose entities in the following EITF Issues:

   1. No. 90-15, "Impact of Nonsubstantive Lessors, Residual Value Guarantees, and Other Provisions in Leasing Transactions"

   2. No. 96-21, "Implementation Issues in Accounting for Leasing Transactions Involving Special-Purpose Entities"

   3. No. 97-1, "Implementation Issues in Accounting for Leasing Transactions, Including those Involving Special-Purpose Entities"

c. Requires that not-for-profit organizations apply the guidance on the equity method of accounting in the following pronouncements to their investments in for-profit partnerships, limited liability companies (LLCs), and similar entities unless those investments are reported at fair value:

   1. AICPA Statement of Position 78-9, Accounting for Investments in Real Estate Ventures

   2. EITF Issue No. 03-16, "Accounting for Investments in Limited Liability Companies"

   3. FSP SOP 78-9-1, Interaction of AICPA Statement of Position 78-9 and EITF Issue No. 04-5

This FSP eliminates the exception to consolidation for related but separate not-for-profit organizations if control is likely to be temporary. Consolidation of one not-for-profit organization by another not-for-profit organization shall be required, permitted, or prohibited, depending on whether there is control, an economic interest, or both, and depending on the nature of the control, in accordance with the guidance in paragraphs 11–13 of SOP 94-3 and paragraphs 11.11–11.13 of the health care Guide, regardless of whether that control is likely to be temporary.

> 8. An organization shall be deemed to have a majority voting interest in the board of another entity whenever it has the direct or indirect ability to appoint individuals that together constitute a majority of the votes of the fully constituted board (that is, including any vacant board positions). Those individuals are not limited to the organization's own board members, employees, and officers.
>
> 9. Sole corporate membership of one not-for-profit organization in another generally shall be considered a controlling financial interest unless the sole corporate member's economic interest in the controlled entity is limited by state law or contractual agreement.

SOP 94-3

RELATIONSHIP TYPE	PAR.	EXISTING GUIDANCE	AMENDED GUIDANCE
Controlling financial interest through ownership of a majority voting interest	10	Consolidation is required unless control does not rest directly or indirectly with the majority owner (no temporary control exception).	No change, except sole corporate membership interests are now included here.
Control through majority voting interest in the board of another entity (by means other than ownership), coupled with an economic interest	11	Consolidation is required unless control is likely to be temporary, in which case consolidation is prohibited. (Currently includes sole corporate membership interests, which the health care Guide deems a controlling financial interest.)	Consolidation is required (no temporary control exception). (This FSP also clarifies the definition of majority voting interest.)

SOP 94-3 (*continued*)

Relationship Type	Par.	Existing Guidance	Amended Guidance
Control through other means, coupled with an economic interest	12	Consolidation is permitted unless control is likely to be temporary, in which case consolidation is prohibited. Disclosures are required if not consolidated.	Consolidation is permitted. Disclosures are required if not consolidated (no temporary control exception).

Health Care Guide

Relationship Type	Par.	Existing Guidance	Amended Guidance
Controlling financial interest through ownership of a majority voting interest or sole corporate membership	11.10	Consolidation is required unless control does not rest directly or indirectly with the majority owner or sole corporate member (no temporary control exception).	No change.
Control through majority voting interest in board of another entity (by means other than ownership or sole corporate membership), coupled with an economic interest	11.11	Consolidation is required unless control is likely to be temporary, in which case consolidation is prohibited.	Consolidation is required (no temporary control exception). (This FSP also clarifies the definition of majority voting interest.)
Control through other means, coupled with an economic interest	11.12	Consolidation is permitted unless control is likely to be temporary, in which case consolidation is prohibited. Disclosures are required if not consolidated.	Consolidation is permitted. Disclosures are required if not consolidated (no temporary control exception).

*PwC Observations: The proposed FSP clearly indicates that not–for–profit organizations should apply the SPE consolidation guidance in EITF Issues 90-15, 96-21 and 97-1. However, the applicability of Topic D-14, which is referenced in Issue 90-15, is not clear. It also is unclear whether FASB intends for the SPE guidance to apply only to leasing SPEs, or for it to have broader applicability to other types of SPE relationships. The final FSP is likely to provide clarity with respect to those questions.

- Affected not-for-profits that do not wish to use the equity method might consider electing fair value measurement for these investments using the instrument-by-instrument option allowed under FAS 159.

In November 2008, the FASB substantially completed redeliberations of its October 2006 exposure drafts, *Not-for-Profit Organizations: Mergers and Acquisitions*, and *Not-for-Profit Organizations: Goodwill and Other Intangible Assets Acquired in a Merger or Acquisition* (the goodwill Exposure Draft), and directed the staff to begin drafting a final Statement. That Statement will provide guidance on accounting for both mergers of not-for-profit organizations and acquisitions by not-for-profit organizations. It also will amend FASB Statement No. 142, *Goodwill and Other Intangible Assets*, to make that Statement fully applicable to not-for-profit organizations.

The Board affirmed its decision that a merger of two or more not-for-profit organizations involves the creation of a newly formed entity as of the merger date. It clarified that in applying the carryover basis of accounting, the merged entity's statement of activities and statement of cash flows for its first period should (1) reflect the combined amounts of the merging entities' net assets (in total and by classes of net assets) and cash as of the merger date in its opening amounts and (2) include activity from the merger date through the end of the fiscal period. The opening amounts should be adjusted to conform the individual accounting policies of the merging entities at the merger date.

In addition, the Board decided to:

1. Require that a newly merged public not-for-profit organization include specified pro forma premerger information as supplementary information.

2. Require certain disclosures for mergers of not-for-profit organizations and acquisitions by not-for-profit organizations. (A draft of those disclosures is available on the FASB's web site.)

3. Require that:

   (a) Previously recognized goodwill assigned to a reporting unit predominantly supported by contributions and returns on investments be written off as a change in accounting principle and presented as proposed in paragraphs 63 and 64 of the goodwill exposure draft (which are based on Statement 142).

   (b) All other previously recognized goodwill be subject to a transitional impairment evaluation and presentation requirements as proposed by the goodwill exposure draft and, subsequently, to the provisions of Statement 142.

4. Require that all not-for-profit organizations apply the final Statement in the first fiscal year beginning after December 15, 2009, and not provide a delayed effective date for small organizations.

5. Prohibit early adoption of the final Statement.

CHAPTER EIGHT

Contributions, Pledges, and Noncash Contributions

§ 8.2   GIFTS-IN-KIND

(a)   Fixed Assets (Land, Buildings, and Equipment) and Supplies

*p. 109. Insert the following new paragraph before *subsection (b)*:

The noncash contribution of physical assets must be valued under the provisions of FAS 157 (fiscal years beginning after November 15, 2008), *Fair Value Measurements,* and an organization must look at the "highest and best use" of the physical asset and what is the most advantageous market. How the organization is planning on utilizing the physical asset is irrelevant. The perspective has to be that of a willing market participant—an unbiased, impartial, independent party who is a hypothetical buyer in the market for this physical asset—and what would they be willing to pay to acquire the physical asset based on what they would view as the most profitable use of the asset. FAS 157 includes examples of such situations and should be referred to in order to better understand this concept.

Unless the contributed physical asset represents "other investments" that are carried at fair value by the organization on a recurring basis, the contribution is measured at fair value only at initial recognition and therefore no additional disclosures under FAS 157 are required. However, if the organization reports alternative investments at fair value under the Audit Guide, then the disclosures under FAS 157 for recurring measurements would be required.

§ 8.3   SUPPORT NOT CURRENTLY EXPENDABLE

(b)   Pledges (Promises to Give)

(iii) Discounted to Present Value.

*p. 117. Insert the following new paragraphs before *subsection (iv)*:

After the effective dates of FAS 157, *Fair Value Measurements*, and FAS 159, *The Fair Value Option for Financial Assets and Financial Liabilities, Including an Amendment of FASB Statement No. 115*, (fiscal years beginning after November 15, 2007), organizations will have a choice as to how pledges will be valued on a going forward basis.

Under FAS 159, pledges are considered financial assets, as they are assets that are expected to be settled in cash, and therefore the organization will have a choice as to whether to apply the provisions of FAS 157 to pledges receivable. As FAS 116 requires organizations to measure each pledge individually, the decision of the organization as to whether to apply the provisions of FAS 157 to pledges must be made on an individual pledge-by-pledge basis.

Under FAS 116, the initial discount rate used to value a pledge is used throughout the life of the pledge and is not changed to reflect changes in the current market condition. As such, an argument could be made that in future years the recorded value of the pledges does not truly reflect their market value.

For a pledge (or pledges) that an organization elects to apply the provisions of FAS 157, the fair value of the pledge will continue to be measured using the income approach. However, unlike the approach in FAS 116 where the discount rate does not change, under FAS 157 the discount rate would change to reflect the rate a willing market participant would demand if they were to purchase the pledge. One potential rate would be the market participant's endowment or investment return (as this would be the return the willing market participant would expect for their financial assets). Under FAS 157, when pledges are revalued annually, a two-year pledge will likely be valued using a different discount rate than that used for a ten-year pledge.

If the organization elects to apply the provisions of FAS 157 to their outstanding pledges, then the additional disclosure requirements will need to be incorporated into the organization's footnotes—the pledges will become recurring fair value measurements, which must be included in the FAS 157 tabular disclosures each year. If the measurement of pledges is determined to require Level 3 inputs (as is likely the case), the disclosure requirements would be even more extensive.

Therefore, organizations must weigh the simplified record keeping against the expanded disclosure requirements.

(d) Split-Interest Gifts

(iii) Accounting for Split-Interest Gifts.

*p. 125. Insert the following new paragraphs before *subsection (iv)*:

Whether the organization serves as trustee will dictate whether the fair value option is available for split-interest agreements. For those split-interest agreements where a third-party serves as the trustee, the organization's beneficial interest in the trust should already be measured at fair value, and therefore FAS 157 is not applicable (from the organization's aspect).

If the organization is the trustee, then the organization has the option to measure the trust obligation at fair value, utilizing the FAS 157 methodology. Similar to the considerations for pledges, electing this option may simplify record keeping, as the organization would remeasure its obligations at fair value by adjusting the discount rates to reflect market conditions. However, the organization must weigh the advantages of simplified record keeping against the additional administrative burden associated with fair value disclosures, as it is likely that this calculation will require Level 3 inputs and would result in extensive additional disclosures.

CHAPTER NINE

Accounting Issues Relating to Fundraising

§ 9.1   ACCOUNTING FOR GIFTS

(e)   Pass-through Gifts

p. 147. Delete first sentence in fourth complete paragraph beginning with *"The FASB currently . . . "*.

p. 147. Insert as fourth complete paragraph:

In October 2006, the FASB issued two exposure drafts related to its long-standing not-for-profit combinations project. The first exposure draft, "Not-for-Profit Organizations, Mergers, and Acquisitions," would eliminate the use of the pooling-of-interests method of accounting and would instead require the application of the acquisition method. The second exposure draft, "Not-for-Profit Organizations: Goodwill and Other Intangible Assets Acquired in a Merger or Acquisition," proposes guidance for intangible assets acquired after a merger or acquisition.

PART TWO

Financial Statement
Presentation

CHAPTER ELEVEN

Accrual-Basis Financial Statements

§ 11.1 SIMPLE ACCRUAL-BASIS STATEMENTS

p. 171. Replace with revised Exhibit 11.2:

EXHIBIT 11.2

Example of a Simple Accrual-Basis Balance Sheet

CAMP SQUA PAN, INC.
BALANCE SHEET
DECEMBER 31, 20X1 and 20X2

ASSETS	20X1	20X2
Current assets:		
Cash	$ 13,107	$ 9,997
U.S. treasury bills at market	10,812	—
Accounts receivable	1,632	853
Prepaid insurance	2,702	1,804
Total current assets	28,253	12,654

Exhibit 11.2

Example of a Simple Accrual-Basis Balance Sheet *(continued)*

CAMP SQUA PAN, INC.
BALANCE SHEET
Dесемвеr 31, 20X1 and 20X2

Fixed assets, at cost:		
Land	13,161	13,161
Buildings	76,773	76,773
Furniture	22,198	23,615
Automobiles	13,456	14,175
Canoes and other equipment	12,025	12,675
	137,613	140,399
Less: Accumulated depreciation	(71,242)	(76,629)
Net fixed assets	66,371	63,770
Total assets	$ 94,624	$ 76,424

LIABILITIES AND NET ASSETS

Current liabilities:		
Accounts payable and accrued expenses	$ 4,279	$ 3,416
Camp deposits	18,275	1,610
Total current liabilities	22,554	5,026
Deferred compensation payable	11,820	12,650
Total liabilities	34,374	17,676
Unrestricted net assets:		
Original YMCA contribution	50,000	50,000
Accumulated excess of income over expenses	10,250	8,748
Total net assets	60,250	58,748
Total liabilities and net assets	$ 94,624	$ 76,424

§ 11.2 ACCRUAL-BASIS STATEMENTS—FUNDRAISING ORGANIZATION

p. 175. Replace with revised Exhibit 11.4:

EXHIBIT 11.4

Example of a Simple Accrual-Basis Balance Sheet for a Typical United Fund Drive

UNITED FUND DRIVE OF RICHMOND HILL, INC.
BALANCE SHEET

	January 31,	
ASSETS	20X1	20X2
Cash	$ 38,727	$ 59,805
Pledges receivable, less allowance for uncollectible pledges of $31,161 in 20X1 and $39,192 in 20X2	168,516	229,517
Total assets	$ 207,243	$ 289,322
LIABILITIES AND NET ASSETS		
Allocated to agencies	$ 557,862	$ 645,284
Less payments to date	(361,536)	(389,517)
Net unpaid	196,326	255,767
Payroll taxes and accounts payable	3,615	8,715
Total liabilities	199,941	264,482
Net assets (unrestricted)	7,302	24,840
Total liabilities and net assets	$ 207,243	$ 289,322

§ 11.3 ACCRUAL-BASIS STATEMENTS— INTERNATIONAL ORGANIZATION

p. 176. Replace with revised Exhibit 11.5:

EXHIBIT 11.5

Example of a Comparative Statement of Income, Expenses, and Changes in Net Assets
for a Large International Not-for-Profit Organization

CHILDREN OVERSEAS INC.
CONSOLIDATED STATEMENT OF ACTIVITIES IN UNRESTRICTED NET ASSETS
(IN THOUSANDS)

	For the Year Ended June 30,	
	20X1	20X2
Income:		
Pledges for children	$ 9,210	$ 9,073
Gifts for special purposes	1,372	1,514
Contributions and bequests	450	661
Government grants	155	82
Investment and miscellaneous income	44	74
Unrealized gain (loss) on investments	(44)	92
Total income	11,187	11,496
Expenses (Exhibit 11.6)		
Aid and services to children	8,649	8,206
Supporting operations	2,081	2,353
Fundraising	454	583
Total expenses	11,184	11,142
Change in unrestricted net assets	3	354
Net assets, beginning of year	1,449	1,452
Net assets, end of year	$ 1,452	$ 1,835

p. 178. Replace with revised Exhibit 11.7:

EXHIBIT 11.7

Example of a Balance Sheet for a Large International Not-for-Profit Organization

CHILDREN OVERSEAS INC.
CONSOLIDATED BALANCE SHEET
(IN THOUSANDS)

	June 30,	
ASSETS	20X1	20X2
Cash	$ 563	$ 704
Investments, at market	1,066	1,331
Accounts receivable:		
Estimated unpaid pledges and gifts due from foster parents	155	135
Foreign government grants	24	18
U.S. government grants	3	3
Other receivables	—	22
Prepaid expenses	73	35
Land, building, equipment, net of accumulated for depreciation of $85 in 20X1 and 20X2	60	65
Total assets	$ 1,944	$ 2,313
LIABILITIES AND NET ASSETS		
Liabilities:		
Accounts payable and accrued payroll taxes	$ 84	$ 48
Estimated statutory severance pay liability	92	101
Unremitted gifts for special purposes	316	329
Total liabilities	492	478
Unrestricted net assets	1,452	1,835
Total liabilities and net assets	$ 1,944	$ 2,313

CHAPTER TWELVE

Multiclass Financial Statements

§ 12.2 PREPARATION OF STATEMENT OF CASH FLOWS

p. 187. Replace with revised Exhibit 12.3:

EXHIBIT 12.3

Sample Performing Arts Organization Statement of Financial Activity ($000)
Year Ended June 30, 20X2

	Unrestricted	Temporarily Restricted	Permanently Restricted	Total
Operating revenue				
Ticket sales	$ 857			$ 857
Other performance fees	128			128
Concessions	103			103
Investment income	21	$ 2		23
Gains/losses on investments	55		$ 4	59
Net assets released from				
restrictions	188	(188)	—	—
Total operating revenue	1,352	(186)	4	1,170
Operating expenses:				
Regular season productions	815			815

EXHIBIT 12.3

Sample Performing Arts Organization Statement of Financial Activity ($000)
Year Ended June 30, 20X2 *(continued)*

	Unrestricted	Temporarily Restricted	Permanently Restricted	Total
Ballet school	201			201
Other production	378			378
Production administration	497			497
Management and general	390			390
Total operating expenses	2,281			2,281
Deficiency from operations	(929)	(186)	4	(1,111)
Support:				
Annual giving	584	39		623
Grants	140	125		265
Endowment gifts			4	4
Governments	200	30		230
Donated services and				
materials	43			43
Less: Fundraising costs	(36)			(36)
Net support	931	194	4	1,129
Change in net assets:				
Unrestricted	2			2
Temporarily restricted		8		8
Permanently restricted			8	8
Total change in net assets	2		8	18
Net Assets:				
Beginning of year	211	44	69	324
End of year	$ 213	$ 52	$ 77	$ 342

(Complete comparative prior year information can be presented on a separate page,
or a total column for the prior year added at the right side of this page.)

pp. 192–194. Replace with revised Exhibit 12.6:

Exhibit 12.6

Worksheet for Statement of Cash Flows—Direct Method

	Current	Prior	[Dr. (Cr.)] Balance Sheet Changes
Balance Sheet [A]		[B]	
Cash	$ 116	$169	$ (53)
Short-term investments	154	151	3
Accounts receivable, net of allowance	70	28	42
Grants receivable	28	6	22
Long-term investments, at market value	180	156	24
Property and equipment, net of depreciation	155	140	15
Rent and other deposits	4	9	(5)
Other assets	11	13	(2)
Accounts payable and accrued expenses	$ 111	$ 66	(45)
Deferred season subscription revenue	206	193	(13)
Current portion of mortgage	30	30	0
Mortgage payable, 8%, due 20X3	29	59	30
Total net assets	342	324	(18)
			0

[C]	Unrestricted	Temporarily Restricted	Permanently Restricted	Total
Income Statement:				
Operating revenue:				
Ticket sales	$ 857		[D]	$ (857)
Other performance fees	128			(128)
Concessions	103			(103)
Investment income	21	$2		(23)
Gains/losses on investments	55		$4	(59)

EXHIBIT 12.6

Worksheet for Statement of Cash Flows—Direct Method *(continued)*

	Current	Prior	[Dr. (Cr.)] Balance Sheet Changes
Net assets released from restrictions	188	(188)	0
Operating expenses:			
Regular season productions	815		815
Ballet school	201		201
Other productions	378		378
Production administration	497		497
Management and general	390		390
Total operating expenses	2,281		2,281
Interest			
Support:			
Annual giving	584	39	(623)
Grants	140	125	(265)
Endowments gifts		4	(4)
Governments	200	30	(230)
Donated services and materials	43		(43)
Less: Fundraising costs	(36)		(36)
Change in net assets	2	8	8	18
			0

Noncash financing and investing items (memo):

[E]		[G]	[H]	[I]		[J]		
Reclassifications		**Gross-up**				**[Source (Use)]** **Statement of Cash Flows**		
Within **B/S or** **P/L**	**Between** **B/S &** **P/L**	**Subtotal**	**Purchases**	**Sales**	**Operating**	**Investing**	**Financing**	**Other**
		(53)						(53)
[1](3)		0						
	[6](42)	0						

EXHIBIT 12.6

Worksheet for Statement of Cash Flows—Direct Method *(continued)*

[E]		[G]			[H]	[I]		
Reclassifications		Gross-up			[Source (Use)] Statement of Cash Flows			
Within B/S or P/L	Between B/S & P/L	Subtotal	Purchases	Sales	Operating	Investing	Financing	Other
	[7](22)	0				[(84)		
[13]	[8](59)	(32)	84	(116)		-[116		
	[9](10)20[10]	25				(25)		
	[11]5	0						
	[12](7)9[13]	0						
	[14]45	0						
	[15]13	0						
[2]30		30						(30)
[2](30)		0						
	[16]18	0						
	[15](13)	(870)			870			
	[6]42]-	(189)			189			
	]							
		(23)			23			
	[8]59	0						
-[[4](43)	[10](20)]							
[[5]36	[11](5)]-	2,190			(2,190)			
[[3](5)	[13](9)]							
	[14](45)]							
[3]5		5			(5)			
	[12]7]							
	[9]10]							
	[7]22]-	(1,079)			1,079			
		(4)					4	
	]							
[4]43		0						
[5](36)		0						
	[16](18)	0						
0	0				(34)	+7	+(26)	=(53)
[F]								
	[9]10			Equipment				$10
	[12]7			Life insurance				7

EXHIBIT 12.6

Worksheet for Statement of Cash Flows—Direct Method *(continued)*

1. To group change in short-term investments (other than those that are cash equivalents; these are included with cash) with change in long-term investments.

2. To move change in long-term portion of mortgage to the line related to the actual payment made—that is, the current portion. (This entry is really just a formality, and need not be made.)

3. To break interest paid (requires separate disclosure) out of operating expenses. Number obtained from general ledger.

4. To offset noncash donation against the expense reflecting use of the donated item. (Note: This does not appear as part of the supplemental disclosure of noncash transactions, since it is an operating item, not financing or investing.) Number obtained from contribution records.

5. To include fundraising costs (reported as an offset against contributions) with other cash expenses.

6. To adjust performance fee revenue for change in related receivables.

7. To adjust grant revenue for change in related receivable.

8. To reclassify gain on sale of investments to the investment line.

9. To reduce contribution revenue and the change in fixed assets by the amount of donated fixed assets. (This is one of the supplemental noncash items disclosed, since it is an investing transaction.) Number obtained from contribution records.

10. To reclassify depreciation expense to the fixed assets line. Number obtained from general ledger.

11. To adjust operating expenses for the change in prepaid expenses.

12. To reduce contributions, and change in other assets, by the amount of the donated life insurance policy. Number obtained from contribution records. This is also a separate disclosure item.

13. To adjust operating expenses for the change in other assets. Note that this entry cannot be made until after entry 12 since this is really a plug to zero out the change in other assets, *after* reflecting the change due to the life insurance policy, which must be treated separately since it is a noncash item.

14. To adjust operating expenses by the change in payables and accruals.

15. To adjust ticket sale revenue by the amount of the change in deferred ticket revenue.

16. To offset the two changes in total net assets numbers.

These entries are illustrative only; not all will be required for every organization, and additional entries will be required for many organizations.

pp. 196–197. Replace with revised Exhibit 12.7:

EXHIBIT 12.7

Worksheet for Reconciliation to Operating Cash Flows

Balance Sheet	Current	Prior	[B]	[Dr. (Cr.)] [Balance Sheet Changes
Cash	$116	$169		$ (53)
Short-term investment	154			3
Accounts receivable, net of allowance	70	28		42
Grants receivable	28	6		22
Long-term investments, at market value	180	156		24
Property and equipment, net of depreciation	155	140		15
Rent and other deposits	4	9		(5)
Other assets	11	13		(2)
[A]				
Accounts payable and accrued expenses	$111	$66		(45)
Deferred season subscription revenue	206	193		(13)
Current portion of mortgage	30	30		0
Mortgage payable, 8%, due 20X3	29	59		30
Total net assets	342	324		(18)
				0

Items to reconcile to operating cash flows:
  Gain on sales
  Depreciation
  Noncash contributions:
    Equipment
    Life insurance
    Services and materials
Expense representing use of donated
  services and materials
Nonexpendable gift
  Financing cash flow—nonexpendable gift
  (Steps C, D not used)

EXHIBIT 12.7

Worksheet for Reconciliation to Operating Cash Flows *(continued)*

[E]	[F]	[G]	[H]		[I]		[J]
Reclassifications			Gross-up		[Source (Use)] Statement of Cash Flows		
Within B/S or P/L	Between B/S & P/L	Subtotal	Purchases	Sales	Operating	Financing Investing	Other
		(53)					(53)
[1](3)		—					
		42			(42)		
		22			(22)		
[1]3	[8](59)	(32)	84	(116)		32	
	[9](10)20[10]	25				(25)	
		(5)			5		
	[12](7)	(9)			9		
		(45)			45		
		(13)			13		
[2]30		30				(30)	
[2](30)		—					
		(18)			18		
	[8]59	59			(59)		
	[10](20)	(20)			20		
	[9]10	10			(10)		
	[12]7	7			(7)		
[4](43)							
		0					
[4](43)							
		4					
[17]4					(4)		
[17](4)		(4)				4	
0	0	0	—	—	(34)	+ (19)	= (53)
						[F] − (26)	
						[I] − 7	
						(19)	

§ 12.3 "CLASS" FINANCIAL STATEMENTS EXPLAINED

p. 207. Replace with revised Exhibit 12.11:

EXHIBIT 12.11

Example of a Columnar Statement of Income, Expenses, and Changes in Net Assets

THE McLEAN COMMUNITY SERVICE CENTER STATEMENT OF INCOME, EXPENSES,
AND CHANGES IN NET ASSETS
For the Year Ended August 31, 20X1

	Unrestricted	Temporarily Restricted	Permanently Restricted	Total
Income:				
Contributions and gifts	$ 85,000	$24,000	$ 25,000	$134,000
Service fees	110,000			110,000
Investment income from endowment	20,000			20,000
Gains on sale of investments	40,000		6,000	46,000
Other	13,000			13,000
	268,000	24,000	31,000	323,000
Net assets released from restrictions	23,000	(23,000)		
Total income	291,000	1,000	31,000	323,000
Expenses:				
Program services	163,000			163,000
Administration	43,000			43,000
Fundraising	12,000			12,000
Total expenses	218,000			218,000
Excess of income over expenses	73,000	1,000	31,000	105,000
Reclassification of unrestricted net assets to meet terms of challenge grant	(25,000)		25,000	
Change in net assets	48,000	1,000	56,000	105,000
Net assets, beginning of year	82,000	10,000	225,000	317,000
Net assets, end of year	$130,000	$11,000	$281,000	$422,000

Financial Statements of Not-for-Profit Organizations—Review Points

(b)   Balance Sheet

(i) Net Assets.

p. 225. Replace first bullet with the following:

- The amount of temporarily and/or permanently restricted net assets must equal or exceed pledges receivable (normally).

p. 225. Replace second bullet with the following:

- If the unrestricted net assets caption includes a subcaption for equity in fixed assets, this caption should equal (or at least approximate) the net of fixed assets minus long-term debt used to finance fixed assets.

PART THREE

Accounting and Reporting Guidelines

CHAPTER THIRTEEN

Voluntary Health and Welfare Organizations

§ 13.2   ACCOUNTING FOR CONTRIBUTIONS

(g)   Timing of Reporting of Gifts

(ii) Pledges.

p. 236. Replace fourth sentence in *subsection (ii)* with the following:

The discount is then accreted (or built up) to fair value over the period between the time the pledge is made and the time it is due to be paid.

§ 13.5 ACCOUNTING FOR ASSETS

(a) Carrying Value of Investments

p. 237. Replace third sentence of second paragraph with the following:

The audit guide for *Not-for-Profit Organizations* states (in paragraph 8.11 and Appendix 6-A of Chapter 6) that these other investments should be reported in accordance with whichever one of the old audit guides was applicable to the type of organization concerned.

(b) Fixed-Asset Accounting

(i) Reason for Depreciation.

p. 237. Replace *subsection (i)* with the following:

In discussing the question of depreciation accounting, the *Not-for-Profit Organizations Audit Guide* stated:

> Paragraph 149 of FASB Concepts Statement No. 6, *Elements of Financial Statements*, describes depreciation as a "systematic and rational" process for allocating the cost of using up assets' service potential or economic benefit over the assets' useful economic lives. FASB Statement No. 93, *Recognition of Depreciation by Not-for-Profit Organizations*, requires all not-for-profit organizations to recognize depreciation for all property and equipment except land used as a building site and similar assets and collections. Depreciation should be recognized for contributed property and equipment as well as for plant and equipment acquired in exchange transactions.

§ 13.6 NET ASSETS

(a) Appropriations

p. 238. Replace second sentence of second paragraph with the following:

The expense must be included in the Statement of Support, Revenue and Expenses, and Changes in Net Assets (also called the Statement of Activities).

§ 13.7   FINANCIAL STATEMENTS

p. 239. Replace *Statement 2* with the following:

2.   Statement of Support, Revenue and Expenses, and Changes in Net Assets, or Statement of Activities (Exhibit 13.2)

(c)   Reporting of Expenses

(iii) Supporting Services.

FUNDRAISING EXPENSES

p. 247. Replace first sentence of second paragraph with the following:

Fundraising expenses are normally recorded as an expense in the Statement of Support, Revenue and Expenses, and Changes in Net Assets at the time they are incurred.

(e)   Appreciation of Investments

p. 253. Replace second sentence of *subsection (e)* with the following:

This means that the organization must reflect appreciation (or depreciation) on its Statement of Support, Revenue and Expenses, and Changes in Net Assets (also called the Statement of Activities).

(g)   Statement of Functional Expenses

p. 256. Replace third sentence of *subsection (g)* with the following:

In order to arrive at the functional expense totals shown in the Statement of Support, Revenue and Expenses, and Changes in Net Assets (also called the Statement of Activities), an analysis must be prepared that shows all of the expenses going into each program category.

p. 257. Replace with revised Exhibit 13.4:

EXHIBIT 13.4

Analysis of the Various Program Expenses Showing the Natural Expense Categories Making Up Each of the Functional or Program Categories

NATIONAL ASSOCIATION OF ENVIRONMENTALISTS STATEMENT OF FUNCTIONAL EXPENSES
FOR THE YEAR ENDED DECEMBER 31, 20X2

	Total All Expenses	Program Services				Supporting Services		
		National Environment Magazine	Clean-up Month Campaign	Lake Erie Project	Total Program	Management and General	Fundraising	Total Supporting
Salaries	$170,773	$24,000	$68,140	$60,633	$152,773	$15,000	$3,000	$18,000
Payroll taxes and employee benefits	22,199	3,120	8,857	7,882	19,859	1,950	390	2,340
Total compensation	192,972	27,120	76,997	68,515	172,632	16,950	3,390	20,340
Printing	84,071	63,191	18,954	515	82,660	1,161	250	1,411
Mailing, postage, and shipping	14,225	10,754	1,188	817	12,759	411	1,055	1,466
Rent	19,000	3,000	6,800	5,600	15,400	3,000	600	3,600
Telephone	5,615	895	400	1,953	3,248	2,151	216	2,367
Outside art	14,865	3,165	11,700	—	14,865	—	—	—
VOLUNTARY HEALTH AND WELFARE ORGANIZATIONS								
Local travel	1,741	—	165	915	1,080	661	—	661
Conferences and conventions	6,328	—	1,895	2,618	4,513	1,815	—	1,815
Depreciation	13,596	2,260	2,309	5,616	10,185	3,161	250	3,411
Legal and audit	2,000	—	—	—	—	2,000	—	2,000
Supplies	31,227	—	1,831	28,516	30,347	761	119	880
Miscellaneous	6,027	115	4,378	—	4,493	1,445	89	1,534
Total	$391,667	$110,500	$126,617	$115,065	$352,182	$33,516	$5,969	$39,485

CHAPTER FOURTEEN

Colleges and Universities

§ 14.1 AUTHORITATIVE PRONOUNCEMENTS

(a) AICPA Audit Guide

p. 263. Replace second sentence of *subsection (a)* **with the following:**

Then, in 1996, the American Institute of Certified Public Accountants (AICPA) issued a new audit guide (most recently published in 2007) for all not-for-profit organizations, superseding the previous audit guides and authoritative sources that had been used by colleges and universities up to that time, namely, *Not-for-Profit Organizations*.

§ 14.2 THE PRINCIPAL FINANCIAL STATEMENTS

p. 264. Replace *Statement 2* **with the following:**

2. Statement of Activities (Exhibit 14.2)

(b) Statement of Revenues, Expenses, and Changes in Net Assets

p. 266. Change title of *section (b)* to Statement of Activities and replace first paragraph with the following:

The Statement of Activities summarizes all of the activity of the institution for the entire period that affects a change in its net assets (net worth). Exhibit 14.2 shows the Statement of Activities for Mary and Isla College.

§ 14.3 ACCOUNTING PRINCIPLES

(b) Unrestricted Gifts

p. 268. Replace paragraph in *subsection (b)* with the following:

Additional discussion on accounting for contributions is in Chapter 9 of this book and in Chapters 5 and 6 of the AICPA *Audit Guide for Not-for-Profit Organizations*. All unrestricted gifts, donations, and bequests are recorded as unrestricted revenue in the Statement of Activities in the year received. While the board is free to designate any portions of such unrestricted gifts or bequests as "board-designated endowment" or for other designated purposes, such gifts must, nonetheless, be reported in the unrestricted class of net assets. These amounts may also then be segregated and separately identified within the unrestricted net asset class presentation on the statement of financial position in order to indicate the nature of the board designation.

(c) Temporarily Restricted Gifts

p. 269. Replace paragraph in *subsection (c)* with the following:

Gifts restricted by the donor for a particular purpose or restricted by time (i.e., the gift is due to be received in future periods) are reported in their entirety in the temporarily restricted class in the Statement of Activities, until either the purpose or the time restriction is satisfied. Note, however, that an institution may elect to recognize as "unrestricted revenues" gifts that are secured and expended for the restricted purpose in the same operating period. If an organization adopts this policy, it must be disclosed in the accounting policies footnote.

(d) Permanently Restricted Gifts

p. 269. Replace second sentence in *subsection (d)* **with the following:**

Further discussion of the treatment of appreciation and depreciation on endowments is included in Chapter 6 of this book.

(e) Pledges

p. 269. Replace last sentence in *subsection (e)* **with the following:**

Further discussion of accounting for pledges is in Chapters 8 and 9.

(f) Investment Income, Gains, or Losses on Investments

* p. 269. Replace *subsection (f)* **with the following:**

All investment income (dividends and interest) must be reported as revenues directly in the class of net assets appropriate to any restrictions of the revenue. All investment income must be reported as revenue in the year in which earned.

In August 2008, FASB Staff Position No. FAS 117-1 (FSP 117-1), *Endowments of Not-for-Profit Organizations: Net Asset Classification of Funds Subject to an Enacted Version of the Uniform Prudent Management of Institutional Funds Act, and Enhanced Disclosures for All Endowment Funds* was issued. This FSP provides guidance on the net asset classification of endowment funds (both donor-restricted and board designated) for an organization that is subject to an enacted version of the Uniform Prudent Management of Institutional Funds Act of 2006 (UPMIFA). This FSP also expands the disclosures required by organizations regarding their endowment funds.

A significant classification change within FSP 117-1 is that all income not classified as permanently restricted net assets shall be recorded as temporarily restricted net assets until such funds are appropriated by the organization for expenditures.

Additional discussions regarding FSP 117-1—the accounting aspects and the disclosure requirements—are further discussed in Chapter 6 of this book.

The provisions of FSP 117-1 are effective for fiscal years ending after December 15, 2008. Earlier application is permitted provided that annual financial statements for that fiscal year have not been previously issued.

(h) Carrying Value of Investments

p. 270. Replace fifth sentence in *subsection (h)* with the following:

The AICPA *Audit Guide for Not-for-Profit Organizations* states in paragraphs 8.03 and 8.35 that these other investments should be reported in accordance with whichever one of the audit guides is applicable to the type of organization concerned.

*For those investments that are carried at fair value, FAS 157 modifies how fair value is calculated—from entrance price to exit price. This is further discussed in Chapter 6 of this book, but an organization has to determine what information is available for determining the fair value (using the FAS 157 definition), or whether management must develop a model to estimate the fair value of the investment.

FAS 159 allows management to elect to report certain financial assets and liabilities at fair value (such as real estate investments) utilizing the FAS 157 criteria. If fair value is elected for an individual financial asset/liability, then that election can not be changed for the life of the financial asset/liability.

FAS 157 also increases the amount of disclosure that is required for all items recorded at fair value. The expanded disclosures could be extensive, depending on the inputs utilized by the organization.

(j) Fixed-Asset Accounting

p. 271. Replace third sentence in *subsection (j)* with the following:

This is discussed further in Chapter 5 of this book and in Chapter 9 of the AICPA *Audit Guide for Not-for-Profit Organizations.*

(l) Tuition Revenue

p. 271. Replace first paragraph in *subsection (l)* with the following:

Accounting for tuition revenue is fairly straightforward: prepayments are deferred and amortized over the period of instruction; and unpaid amounts for which a student (or other payor) is contractually liable are receivables, offset by an appropriate allowance for estimated uncollectible amounts.

(m) Expenses

p. 272. Replace first paragraph in *subsection (m)* **with the following:**

Like all not-for-profit organizations, colleges and universities are required to report expenses on a functional basis (program, management, and fundraising) to comply with SFAS 117 and the AICPA *Audit Guide for Not-for-Profit Organizations.* Reporting by natural categories (personnel, occupancy, travel, supplies, etc.) is not required, but this information is often of interest to management and the governing board. The functional expenses may be presented either on the face of the statement of activities or in a separate schedule or footnote.

p. 272. Add a new *section 14.4, "New Accounting Rules:"*

§ 14.4 NEW ACCOUNTING RULES (NEW)

In June 2006, the Emerging Issues Task Force (EITF) issued EITF 06–2, "Accounting for Sabbatical Leave and Other Similar Benefits Pursuant to FASB Statement No. 43."

Institutions may provide its employees with a sabbatical leave benefit under which an employee receives compensated time off. This sabbatical leave is generally provided after a specified period of service. Sabbatical leaves also generally consist of two types: (1) the employee is required to "engage in research or public service to enhance the reputation of or otherwise benefit the employer," or (2) no effort is required by the employee and the sabbatical leave is essentially a vacation.

The issue that arises is whether or not the sabbatical leave benefit should be accrued over the period in which it is earned.

If the institution requires the employee to engage in research or public service, then the sabbatical leave is not to be accrued over the vesting period, as the employee is required to expend efforts and in accordance with the matching principle, the employee is being paid during the sabbatical period in which they are conducting the research or providing public service.

On the other hand, if the employee is not required to expend any efforts on behalf of the institution, then just as with "normal" vacation policies, the amount of the sabbatical will be accrued during the vesting period.

CHAPTER FIFTEEN

The External Financial Statement Reporting Model for Public Colleges and Universities and Other Not-for-Profit Organizations Reporting under the GASB

§ 15.6 BASIC FINANCIAL STATEMENTS

(a) Statement of Net Assets

(iii) Capital Asset Impairment.

p. 288. Replace last paragraph before *subsection (b)* **with the following:**

Impaired capital assets that will no longer be used by public colleges or universities should be reported at the lower of the carrying value or fair value. Impaired capital assets that will continue to be used by institutions should be measured using the method that best reflects their diminished service utility. Statement No. 42 does not require a write-down when the impairment of the assets is considered temporary; only permanent impairments are recognized. Impairment losses should be reported as a program expense, special item, or extraordinary item per Statement No. 34. The impairment loss to be recognized should be net of any insurance recovery associated with events or changes in circumstances resulting in impaired capital assets. Restoration or replacement of the capital asset using the insurance recovery should be reported as a separate transaction. Statement No. 42 does not permit the reversal of impairment in future years.

§ 15.7 FOOTNOTE DISCLOSURES

(d) Deposit and Investment Risk

p. 297. Add the following new paragraphs in *subsection (d):*

Statement No. 40 also requires disclosures of deposit and investment policies related to the identified risks.

Statement No. 40 generally requires that investment disclosures be organized by investment type. The financial statements should also contain accounting policies related to the risks covered by this Statement, that is, credit risk, interest rate risk, and foreign currency risk, as relevant to the institution's deposit and investment holdings.

The Statement requires the disclosure of credit quality ratings of investments in debt securities. Obligations of the U.S. government or obligations explicitly guaranteed by the U.S. government are excluded from this requirement based on the rebuttable presumption that they do not have credit risk.

Organizations should disclose, by amount and issuer, investments in any one issuer that equal or exceed 5 percent of total investments. Again, U.S. government obligations (or those explicitly guaranteed) are excluded from this requirement, as are mutual funds, external investment pools, and pooled investments.

Statement No. 40 requires the disclosure of interest rate risk using one of the methods described in paragraph 15. In addition, investments that are considered highly sensitive to interest rate changes must be specifically disclosed.

If organizations hold deposits or investments that are exposed to foreign currency risk, the balances should be disclosed in U.S. dollars organized by denomination and investment type.

The GASB Implementation Guide Q&A is helpful to use when working through the disclosure requirements of this Standard.

p. 297. Insert the following new *subsection (e)* before *section 15.8:*

(e) Termination Benefits (New)

The GASB issued its Statement No. 47, *Termination Benefits*, in June 2005. This Statement requires governments to disclose a description of the termination benefit arrangement, the cost of the termination benefits (required in the period in which the government becomes obligated if that information is not otherwise identifiable from information displayed on the face of the financial statements), and significant methods and assumptions used to determine termination benefit liabilities, regardless of whether they are provided as a result of a voluntary or involuntary termination of employment. These requirements do not apply if the terminated benefit results in an obligation of either a defined benefit pension plan (DBPP) or a defined benefit other postemployment benefit plan (DBOPBP).

Under Statement No. 47, the government is required to:

- Segregate voluntary and involuntary, health care and non–health care related, termination benefits expense, and liabilities from all other salaries and benefits expense and liabilities.

- Record a liability and expense for termination benefits under voluntary terminations (e.g., early retirement incentives) when the offer is accepted.

- Record a liability and expense for termination benefits under involuntary terminations when a plan of termination has been approved by those with the authority to commit the government to the plan and that plan has been communicated to the employees.

- Exclude from these considerations any obligations that would be satisfied through any DBPPs or DBOPBPs.

- Disclose a description of the termination benefit arrangement and the cost of the termination benefits for the year the liability and expense are recognized.

- Disclose the change in actuarial accrued liability that is attributable to the termination benefits for any DBPPs or DBOPBPs, if any.

GASB Statement No. 47:

- Generally prescribes new reporting requirements, rather than amending previous guidance, although this Statement supersedes paragraphs 6, 7, 8b, 12, 17, and 18 of National Council on Governmental Accounting (NCGA) Interpretation 8, *Certain Pension Matters*, and amends paragraph 5 of NCGA Interpretation 6, *Notes to the Financial Statements Disclosure*; paragraph 8 of GASB Statement No. 1, *Authoritative Status of NCGA Pronouncements and AICPA Industry Audit Guide*; paragraph 2 of GASB Statement No. 10, *Accounting and Financial Reporting for Risk Financing and Related Insurance Issues*; paragraph 2 and footnote 2 of GASB Statement No. 12, *Disclosure of Information on Postemployment Benefits Other Than Pension Benefits by State and Local Governmental Employers*; paragraphs 12 and 44 of GASB Statement No. 25, *Financial Reporting for Defined Benefit Pension Plans and Note Disclosures for Defined Contribution Plans*; paragraphs 5 and 11 of GASB Statement No. 26, *Financial Reporting for Postemployment Healthcare Plans Administered by Defined Benefit Pension Plans*; footnotes 2 and 3 and paragraphs 5, 6, and 39 of GASB Statement 27; paragraph 81 of GASB Statement No. 34, *Basic Financial Statements—and Management's Discussion and Analysis—for State and Local Governments*; paragraphs 9 and 46 of GASB Statement No. 43, *Financial Reporting for Postemployment*

Benefit Plans Other Than Pension Plans; paragraphs 8 and 40 of GASB Statement 45; and paragraphs 5, 6, 9, 11, and 14 and footnote 7 of GASB Interpretation No. 6, *Recognition and Measurement of Certain Liabilities and Expenditures in Governmental Fund Financial Statements*.

- Is effective for FY 2005–2006. Depending on materiality, the cumulative effect of applying this Statement should be reported as a restatement of beginning net assets for the liability at June 30, 2005, associated with termination plans or benefits that are in effect as of June 30, 2005.

- Does not apply to any defined contribution benefit plans, 403(b) plans, or 457(b) plans.

p. 297. Insert the following new *subsection (f)* before *section 15.8*:

(f)   Postemployment Benefits Other than Pensions (New)

In addition to pensions, many institutions provide other postemployment benefits (OPEB) as part of the total compensation offered to attract and retain the services of qualified employees. In April 2004, the GASB issued its Statement No. 43, *Financial Reporting for Postemployment Benefit Plans Other than Pension Plans*, to establish uniform financial reporting standards for OPEB plans. Statement No. 43 supersedes the interim guidance included in Statement No. 26, *Financial Reporting for Postemployment Healthcare Plans Administered by Defined Benefit Pension Plans*. The approach followed in Statement No. 43 generally is consistent with the approach adopted in Statement No. 25, *Financial Reporting for Defined Benefit Pension Plans and Note Disclosures for Defined Contribution Plans*, with modifications to reflect differences between pension plans and OPEB plans. In July 2004, the GASB issued Statement No. 45, *Accounting and Financial Reporting by Employers for Postemployment Benefits Other Than Pensions*, which establishes standards for the measurement, recognition, and display of OPEB expense/expenditures and related liabilities (assets), note disclosures, and, if applicable, RSI in the financial reports of employers.

The standards in Statement No. 43 apply for OPEB trust funds included in the financial reports of plan sponsors, as well as for stand-alone financial reports on OPEB plans or other parties that administer them.

Statement No. 43 also provides requirements for reporting of OPEB funds of multiple-employer plans when the fund used to pay benefits or premiums and to accumulate assets is not a trust fund.

The GASB issued Statement No. 45 to address how institutions should account for and report costs and obligations related to post-employment health care and other nonpension benefits. Statement No. 45 improves the relevance and usefulness of financial reporting by (a) requiring systematic, accrual-basis measurement and recognition of OPEB cost over a period that approximates employees' years of service and (b) providing information about actuarial accrued liabilities associated with OPEB and whether and to what extent progress is being made in funding the plan. Annual OPEB cost for most institutions will be based on actuarially determined amounts that, if paid on an ongoing basis, generally would provide sufficient resources to pay benefits that come due. The disclosure requirements include information about the plan in which an employer participates, the funding policy followed, the actuarial valuation process and assumptions, and, for certain institutions, the extent to which the plan has been funded over time.

The measurement and disclosure requirements of Statement No. 43 and Statement No. 45 are related, and disclosure requirements are coordinated to avoid duplication when an OPEB plan is included as a trust or agency fund in an employer's financial report.

Statements No. 43 and 45 are effective in three phases based on an institution's total annual revenues in the first fiscal year ending after June 15, 1999:

a. Institutions with total annual revenues of $100 million or more, are required to implement Statement No. 43 for financial statement periods beginning after December 15, 2005 and Statement No. 45 for financial statement periods beginning after December 15, 2006.

b. Institutions with total annual revenues of $10 million or more but less than $100 million are required to implement Statement No. 43 for financial statement periods beginning after December 15, 2006 and Statement No. 45 for financial statement periods beginning after December 15, 2007.

c. Institutions with total annual revenues of less than $10 million are required to implement Statement No. 43 for financial statement periods beginning after December 15, 2007 and Statement No. 45 for financial statement periods beginning after December 15, 2008.

*p. 297. Insert the following new *subsection (g)* before *section 15.8:*

(g)   GASB Statement No. 50 *Pension Disclosures* (New)

GASB Statement No. 50, *Pension Disclosures—an Amendment of GASB Statement Nos. 25 and 27*, is effective for fiscal years ending June 30, 2008, and later and more closely aligns the financial reporting requirements for pensions with those for other postemployment benefits (OPEB) and, in doing so, enhances information disclosed in notes to financial statements or presented as required supplementary information (RSI) by pension plans and by employers that provide pension benefits.

This Statement amends GASB Statement No. 25 to require defined benefit pension plans and defined contribution plans to disclose in the notes to financial statements the methods and assumptions used to determine the fair value of investments, if the fair value is based on other than quoted market prices.

This Statement also amends GASB Statement No. 27 to require cost-sharing employers to include, in the note disclosure of the required contribution rates of the employer(s) in dollars and the percentage of that amount contributed for the current year and each of the two preceding years, how the contractually required contribution rate is determined (for example, by statute or by contract, or on an actuarially determined basis) or that the cost-sharing plan is financed on a pay-as-you-go basis. In addition, if a cost-sharing plan does not issue a publicly available stand-alone plan financial report prepared in accordance with the requirements of GASB Statement No. 25, as amended, and the plan is not included in the financial report of another entity, each employer in that plan should present as RSI the schedules of funding progress and employer contributions for the plan (and notes to these schedules). Each employer also should disclose that the information presented relates to the cost-sharing plan as a whole, of which the employer is one participating employer, and should provide information helpful for understanding the scale of the information presented relative to the employer.

*p. 297. Insert the following new *subsection (h)* before *section 15.8:*

(h)   GASB No. 53, *Accounting and Financial Reporting for Derivative Instruments* (New)

GASB No. 53, *Accounting and Financial Reporting for Derivative Instruments,* was issued in June 2008.

Certain paragraphs of GASB Statement No. 40 will be amended by GASB 53 (effective for periods beginning after June 15, 2009). GASB 53 requires governmental entities to measure most derivative instruments at fair value. Some exclusions apply as discussed in paragraphs 4 through 6. The change in fair value of a derivative instrument should be reported as investment gains or losses, while the change in fair value of a hedging derivative instrument should be reported as a deferral on the statement of net assets. Governments are also required to include summary information about its derivative instruments as well as its use of hedging derivative instruments in the footnotes.

Generally, derivative instruments that are considered investments should follow GASB Statement No. 40 disclosure guidelines. Hedging derivative instrument disclosures should include the basis for investing in the instrument, significant terms, the net cash flows of the hedging derivative instruments, and the risks associated with such instruments.

§ 15.8   MANAGEMENT'S DISCUSSION AND ANALYSIS

p. 297. Delete first sentence in *section 15.8* and replace with the following:

Management's discussion and analysis (MD&A) was for the first time required through Statement No. 34, which asked financial managers to share with users information about the transactions, events, and conditions that are reflected in the institution's financial report and about the fiscal policies that govern its operations.

p. 297. In second sentence, replace *"government's"* with *"institution's".*

p. 298. Revise third bullet to read as follows:

- An analysis of significant changes that occur in various funds

p. 298. Add new bullet before fourth bullet:

- An analysis of significant variances between budgeted activities and actual results of activities only in the case of the general fund (Ref. No. 34 ¶11.2)

p. 298. Add new *sections 15.8A and 15.8B* before *section 15.9:*

§ 15.8A   REQUIRED SUPPLEMENTAL INFORMATION OTHER THAN MD&A (NEW)

In addition to the MD&A, Statement No. 34 requires institutions to present as Required Supplementary Information (RSI) budgetary comparison schedules for governmental funds and information about infrastructure assets reported using the modified approach. Statement No. 41, *Budgetary Comparison Schedules—Perspective Differences—An Amendment of GASB Statement No. 34*, provides a clarification on the budgetary presentation requirements for institutions whose structure of financial information for budgetary purposes differs from the fund structure defined in Statement No. 34.

Statement No. 34 requires budgetary comparison schedules for the general fund and for each major special revenue fund that has a legally adopted annual budget. The budgetary comparison schedule should present (a) the original or first complete appropriated budget; (b) the final legally authorized budgets for the reporting period; and (c) actual inflows, outflows, and balances, stated on the institution's budgetary basis. Variance between the original and final budget and between final budget and actual amounts may be reported.

Institutions that are not able to present budgetary information comparisons for the general fund and each major special revenue fund because of perspective differences are required by Statement No. 41 to present budgetary comparison schedules based on the fund, organization, or program structure that the institution uses for its legally adopted budget.

Statement No. 34 provides that infrastructure assets eligible under the modified approach are not depreciated. All expenditures made for these eligible infrastructure assets (except for additions and improvements) should be expensed in the period incurred. Additions and improvements to the eligible assets should be capitalized. In order to be eligible to the modified approach of reporting, infrastructure assets must meet certain requirements, namely: (a) the institution manages the eligible infrastructure assets using an asset management system that has the characteristics set forth in paragraph 23 of Statement No. 34; and (b) the institution documents that the eligible infrastructure assets are being preserved approximately at (or above) a condition level established and disclosed by the institution.

Paragraphs 132 and 133 of Statement No. 34 require institutions to present two schedules for all infrastructure assets eligible to the modified approach: (a) the assessed condition for at least the three most recent complete condition assessments that were performed at least every three years; and (b) the estimated annual amount. The said schedules should be accompanied by disclosures on (a) the basis for the condition measurement and the measurement scale used; (b) the condition level at which the infrastructure asset is intended to be preserved; and (c) factors that affect significantly the information reported in the schedules.

§ 15.8B   STATISTICAL SECTION (NEW)

NCGA Statement 1, *Governmental Accounting and Financial Reporting Principles*, provides guidance on the preparation of the statistical section. Statement No. 44, *Economic Condition Reporting: The Statistical Section—An Amendment of NCGA Statement 1*, amends portions of NCGA 1. The statistical section presents detailed (typically in ten-year trends) information that assists users in utilizing the basic financial statements, notes to basic financial statements, and RSI to assess the economic condition of an institution. The statistical section is a required part of a comprehensive annual financial report (CAFR), although institutions are not required to prepare a statistical section if they do not present their basic financial statements within a CAFR. The provisions of Statement No. 44 are effective for statistical sections prepared for periods beginning after June 15, 2005.

In order to clarify that the requirements are applicable to all types of state and local governmental entities that prepare a statistical section,

Statement No. 44 establishes the objectives of the statistical section and the five categories of information it contains: financial trends information, revenue capacity information, debt capacity information, demographic and economic information, and operating information. The more specific requirements of this Statement should be adapted by each type of institution in order to meet their overarching objectives.

Statement No. 44 adds new information that users have identified as important and eliminates certain previous requirements. For instance, an institution's statistical section should now include trend information on governmental fund balances and principal employers. However, institutions are no longer required to present in their statistical sections information that users have identified as less useful, such as special assessment levies and collections, construction activity, and bank deposits. Additionally, statistical sections do not have to include a separate schedule of debt service ratios; the most useful information from that schedule will be presented with the changes in fund balances information.

The most significant new information added to the statistical section is the government-wide, accrual-based information required by Statement No. 34. The statistical section will include ten-year trend information about net assets and changes in net assets. The debt information presented in the statistical section will also be more comprehensive due to the inclusion of information from the government-wide financial statements and notes. Finally, Statement No. 44 further improves the understandability and usefulness of the statistical section information by requiring institutions to augment their schedules with notes regarding sources, methodologies, and assumptions, and to provide narrative explanations of (a) the objectives of statistical section information, (b) unfamiliar concepts, (c) relationships between information in the statistical section and elsewhere in the financial report, and (d) atypical trends and anomalous data that users would not otherwise understand.

CHAPTER SIXTEEN

Health Care Providers

§ 16.3   FINANCIAL STATEMENTS

(c)   Statement of Operations

(ii) Extraordinary Items, Discontinued Operations, and Effect of Changes in Accounting Principle.

p. 308. Add the following new paragraph:

After the effective date of FAS 154 (fiscal years beginning after December 15, 2005), *Accounting Changes and Error Corrections*, voluntary changes in accounting principles will no longer be reported via a cumulative-effect adjustment to change in net assets of the period of change.

(d) Statement of Cash Flows

p. 309. Replace third major bullet with the following:

- Equity transfers, restricted investment income for long-lived assets, and restricted contributions (including contributions restricted for purchase of long-lived assets) will need to be "transferred" to the financing category by adjusting them out of operating cash flows and increasing (or decreasing, as appropriate) the financing category by that same amount.

§ 16.4 ACCOUNTING PRINCIPLES

(h) Investments

p. 320. Add the following new *subsection (iii)*:

(iii) Framework for Assessing the Accounting for Alternative Investments Held by a Not-for-Profit Health Care Organization (New). The accounting for investments held by enterprises in all industries is often challenging due to the broad range of available investment alternatives, the variety of legal forms of investment entities, and the nature of the rights they convey to the investors. The authoritative accounting literature can be quite complex, and for some, it may be further complicated by specialized industry accounting practices.[8.1] Generally, the current accounting guidance follows a hierarchy where consolidation accounting is considered first, equity method of accounting second, and the accounting for equity securities with readily determinable market values and debt securities is considered third. To the extent the conditions at one of these levels are met, then subsequent analysis at the

---

8.1. Some industries have industry-specific accounting guidance for investments. For example, organizations within the scope of the AICPA industry audit and accounting guides *Not-for-Profit Organizations* or *Investment Companies* have the ability to mark all investments to market in certain circumstances based on those guides; employee benefit plans and SFAS 60 insurance enterprises have the ability to mark investments to market based on specialized FASB standards. A nonprofit HCO should not base its accounting for investments on specialized guidance developed for other industries unless the investments are held by a subsidiary that falls within the scope of that guidance and it is appropriate to carry those specialized industry practices forward in consolidation.

remaining lower levels in the hierarchy are not considered necessary. As an example, to the extent that an investment fails to meet the requirements for consolidation accounting, but does meet the requirements for the equity method of accounting, then consideration of the accounting for equity securities with readily determinable market values and debt securities is not needed nor permitted, and the equity method should be applied. In those instances where an investment falls through each of the methods in the hierarchy and is not covered by any other specific accounting guidance or specialized industry accounting practices, then the cost method should generally be applied.

The determination of where a particular investment falls within the accounting hierarchy requires careful analysis of the investment, particularly with respect to the rights of the investor. The following framework is designed to assist not-for-profit health care organizations (HCOs) with working through their evaluation of the hierarchy of accounting literature for investments. It is important to note that there may be investment structures that do not appear to clearly fall within the accounting hierarchy. In some instances, it may be acceptable for HCOs to apply the existing guidance applicable to a similar structure by analogy. In other instances, HCOs may find that the terms used in the accounting guidance may not be sufficiently defined to easily apply the guidance to an investment. In those instances, a reasonable interpretation of the guidance within the spirit of the overall principle may be acceptable.

1. SHOULD THE HCO'S INVESTMENT BE ACCOUNTED FOR USING THE CONSOLIDATION METHOD?

The first step in analyzing an HCO's investments or financial interests in other entities is to determine whether consolidation is required, which is generally the case if the investor has a controlling financial interest. Chapter 11 of the *AICPA Audit and Accounting Guide for Health Care Organizations* ("HCO Guide"), paragraphs 11.10 through 11.16, goes through various scenarios and provides guidance for determining whether the investor has a controlling financial interest. The primary source for the HCO Guide's conclusions is ARB No. 51, *Consolidated Financial Statements*, as amended by FASB Statement No. 94, *Consolidation of all Majority Owned Subsidiaries*. Additionally, for investments in partnerships and similar entities (such as limited liability companies that are the functional equivalent of a limited partnership), the guidance in EITF Issue No. 04-5, *Determining Whether a General Partner, or the General Partners as a Group, Controls a Limited Partnership or Similar Entity When the Limited Partners Have Certain Rights* (EITF 04-5), and FSP No. SOP 78-9-1, *Interaction of AICPA Statement of Position 78-9 and EITF Issue No. 04-5*, should be considered. The scope exception provided in FASB Interpretation No. 46 (FIN 46), *Consolidation of Variable Interest Entities*, applies to all not-for-profit entities, including HCOs subject to the HCO Guide, unless a not-for-profit entity is used by a business enterprise in a manner to circumvent the provisions of FIN 46.

2. Should the HCO's investment be accounted for using the equity method?

If consolidation accounting is not applicable, the next step is to determine whether the equity method of accounting is appropriate. The significant factor in making this determination is the amount of influence that the investor has over the operating and financial policies of the investee.

A. Noncontrolling investments in common stock or "in-substance" common stock (as defined by EITF Issue No. 02-14, *Whether an Investor Should Apply the Equity Method of Accounting to Investments Other than Common Stock*) of corporations and corporate joint ventures should consider the guidance in APB Opinion No. 18, *The Equity Method of Accounting for Investments in Common Stock* (APB 18), and FASB Interpretation No. 35, *Criteria for Applying the Equity Method of Accounting for Investments in Common Stock* (FIN 35), paragraph 4 (HCO Guide, Chapter 11, paragraph 17), which requires the application of the equity method when the investor has the ability to significantly influence the operating and financial policies of the investee. APB 18 indicates a presumption that in the absence of evidence to the contrary, the investor has the ability to exercise significant influence when it owns (directly or indirectly) 20 percent or more of the outstanding voting securities of the investee. FIN 35 sets forth indicators which should be considered in determining whether or not an investor is able to exercise significant influence.

B. Noncontrolling investments in general and limited partnerships should follow the guidance in the AICPA's Statement of Position 78-9, *Accounting for Investments in Real Estate Ventures* (SOP 78-9), paragraphs 6 through 10.

   (i) Noncontrolling general partnership investments follow the equity method because a general partner is presumed to have the ability to significantly influence the operating and financial policies of the investee.

   (ii) Noncontrolling limited partnership investments generally follow equity method of accounting unless the interest in the partnership is so minor that the limited partner may have virtually no influence over partnership operating and financial policies. If a partner has virtually no influence, then the equity method of accounting should not be used. EITF Topic No. D-46, *Accounting for Limited Partnership Investments*, discusses the SEC staff's view that generally investments of more than 3 to 5 percent are considered more than minor. However, depending on the circumstances, it is possible that this threshold (i.e., the level of ownership where an investment is so minor that the limited partner has virtually no influence) may be lower than a 3 percent investment. Therefore, each partnership's governing documents should be analyzed to determine what rights the limited partners have, and what ability the investor has to influence the investee's operating and financial policies. The facts and circumstances to consider when making this evaluation may include:

   • Whether decisions regarding changes to the partnership require a simple majority, supermajority, or unanimous vote

   • The voting interest of each limited partner, that is, one vote per limited partner or votes based on investment amount/units held

   • The size of the HCO's investment as compared to other limited partners

- To what extent the rights of the limited partners are participating rights or protective rights

  The guidance provided in EITF 04-5 should be considered when evaluating the level of influence held by the limited partners.

C. Noncontrolling investments in limited liability companies (LLCs) should follow the guidance in EITF Issue No. 03-16, *Accounting for Investments in Limited Liability Companies* (EITF 03-16).

Under the provisions of EITF 03-16, the application of the equity method of accounting to an LLC depends on its structure and its similarity to partnership or corporate forms of organization.

(i) An investment in an LLC that maintains a "specific ownership account" for each investor similar to a partnership capital structure should be viewed as similar to an investment in a limited partnership for purposes of determining whether a noncontrolling interest in an LLC should be accounted for using the cost equity method. The usage of specific ownership accounts is often a by-product of how the LLC is designed to be taxed. An LLC will be established with specific ownership accounts generally when the members prefer that the LLC be taxed like a partnership. An LLC will be established without specific ownership accounts (i.e., "unitized") if it elects to be treated like a corporation for tax purposes. However, only LLCs with units specifically called for in the underlying governing legal or offering documents should be considered unitized.

(ii) Investments in LLCs that do not maintain "specific ownership accounts" (e.g., the investments are unitized rather than providing ownership accounts for each investor) are to be accounted for like investments in common stock and apply the equity method as appropriate if there is evidence of substantive rights that indicate the ability of the investor to exert significant influence over the operating and financial policies of the company (e.g., where the ownership level is greater than 20 percent). See section 2A, above.

(iii) EITF 03-16 does not apply to investments in LLCs that are required to be accounted for as debt securities pursuant to paragraph 14 of FASB Statement No. 140, *Accounting for Transfers and Servicing of Financial Assets and Extinguishment of Liabilities* (SFAS 140). LLCs are sometimes formed in connection with certain securitizations. The interests in these LLCs are subject to the income and impairment recognition established by EITF Issue No. 99-20, *Recognition of Interest Income and Impairment on Purchased and Retained Beneficial Interests in Securitized Financial Assets.*

D. In EITF 03-16, some Task Force members indicated that in determining whether the equity method of accounting should be applied to investments in other entities with specific ownership account structures, it may be appropriate to analogize to the guidance in that issue. Therefore, the equity method of accounting may be applied to noncontrolling investments in other organizational forms (i.e., those other than corporations, partnerships, or LLCs discussed in 2A, 2B, and 2C above) with specific ownership account structures, unless the investment is so minor that the investor has virtually no influence. However, this accounting should be adopted as a matter of accounting policy, consistently applied to all applicable investments, and the policy disclosed in the financial statements if material. If such a policy is not elected or the investment does not have a specific ownership account structure, the guidance in APB 18 should still be considered.

3. Should the HCO's investment be accounted for using the guidance in FASB Statement No. 124, *Accounting for Certain Investments Held by Not-for-Profit Organizations* (SFAS 124)?

If the HCO's investment does not follow the consolidation or equity methods of accounting or the specific guidance addressed above, the next step in analyzing the accounting treatment is to review the scope provisions of SFAS 124 (HCO Guide, Chapter 4). That Statement applies to noncontrolling investments in equity securities with readily determinable fair values that are not accounted for under the equity method and all investments in debt securities. Investments within the scope of SFAS 124 should be recognized at fair value and subsequently marked to market each period. Investment return (including unrealized and realized gains and losses) not restricted by donors or by law shall be classified as changes in unrestricted net assets in accordance with the HCO Guide, Chapter 4. All debt and equity securities should be evaluated for other-than-temporary impairment.

A. Does the HCO investment meet the definition of a *debt* or *equity security?*

SFAS 124 defines a *security*, *equity security*, and *debt security* as:

Security
A share, participation, or other interest in property or in an enterprise of the issuer or an obligation of the issuer that (a) either is represented by an instrument issued in bearer or registered form or, if not represented by an instrument, is registered in books maintained to record transfers by or on behalf of the issuer, (b) is of a type commonly dealt in on securities exchanges or markets or, when represented by an instrument, is commonly recognized in any area in which it is issued or dealt in as a medium for investment, and (c) either is one of a class or series or by its terms is divisible into a class or series of shares, participations, interests, or obligations.

Equity security
Any security representing an ownership interest in an enterprise (for example, common, preferred, or other capital stock) or the right to acquire (for example, warrants, rights, and call options) or dispose of (for example, put options) an ownership interest in an enterprise at fixed or determinable prices. However, the term does not include convertible debt or preferred stock that by its terms either must be redeemed by the issuing enterprise or is redeemable at the option of the investor.

Debt security
Any security representing a creditor relationship with an enterprise. It also includes (a) preferred stock that by its terms either must be redeemed by the issuing enterprise or is redeemable at the option of the investor and (b) a collateralized mortgage obligation (CMO) (or other instrument) that

is issued in equity form but is required to be accounted for as a nonequity instrument regardless of how that instrument is classified (that is, whether equity or debt) in the issuer's statement of financial position. However, it excludes option contracts, financial futures contracts, forward contracts, and lease contracts.

- Thus, the term *debt security* includes, among other items, U.S. Treasury securities, U.S. government agency securities, municipal securities, corporate bonds, convertible debt, commercial paper, all securitized debt instruments, such as CMOs and real estate mortgage investment conduits (REMICs), and interest-only and principal-only strips.

- Trade accounts receivable arising from sales on credit by industrial or commercial enterprises and loans receivable arising from consumer, commercial, and real estate lending activities of financial institutions are examples of receivables that do not meet the definition of *security;* thus, those receivables are not debt securities (unless they have been securitized, in which case they would meet the definition).

B. As noted above, preferred stock that is redeemable by the issuing enterprise or at the option of the investor is included within the definition of debt securities regardless of whether it has a readily determinable fair value. However, common stock or residual equity of an entity, even if it has redemption features, is not considered a debt security and is within the scope of SFAS 124 only if it meets the definition of an equity security with a readily determinable fair value.

C. If it is determined that the investment meets the definition of an equity security described in A above, does the investment have a readily determinable fair value as defined by SFAS 124?

SFAS 124 defines *readily determinable fair value* in paragraph 3:

a. The fair value of an equity security is readily determinable if sales prices or bid-and-asked quotations are currently available on a securities exchange registered with the Securities and Exchange Commission (SEC) or in the over-the-counter market, provided that those prices or quotations for the over-the-counter market are publicly reported by the National Association of Securities Dealers Automated Quotations systems or by the National Quotation Bureau. Restricted stock does not meet that definition.

b. The fair value of an equity security traded only in a foreign market is readily determinable if that foreign market is of a breadth and scope comparable to one of the U.S. markets referred to above.

c. The fair value of an investment in a mutual fund is readily determinable if the fair value per share (unit) is determined and published and is the basis for current transactions.

When analyzing the applicability of SFAS 124 for each HCO investment, the actual nature of the investments underlying the actual form of the initial investment should not be used as a basis for determining the overall accounting treatment of the investment. During its deliberations of SFAS 124, the Board considered many of the same concerns that were examined for business enterprises in FASB Statement No. 115, *Accounting for Certain Investments in Debt and Equity Securities* (SFAS 115). The FASB Staff Implementation Guide to SFAS 115 within question 5 addresses this issue in relation to an investment within a limited partnership that meets the definition of an equity security but does not have a readily determinable fair value, however substantially all of the partnership's assets consist of investments that have a readily determinable fair value. The FASB staff asked whether in that scenario it would be appropriate to "look through" the form of the investment to determine the applicability of SFAS 115. The response provided was that a "look through" was inappropriate and in the scenario described, SFAS 115 would not apply to that investment.

With respect to the application of the guidance in paragraph 3c of SFAS 124 to mutual funds, the words *mutual fund, published,* and *basis for current transactions* have not been specifically defined or clarified further in accounting literature and are therefore subject to interpretation by clients.

The term *mutual fund* is the popular name for an open-end management investment company as defined in the Investment Company Act of 1940 (the 1940 Act). Mutual funds registered with the SEC under the 1940 Act are the most common form of investment companies. Investors typically purchase mutual fund shares from the fund itself (or through a broker for the fund), not from a secondary market such as the NYSE or

NASDAQ. The price investors pay for the mutual fund shares is the fund's per-share net asset value (NAV). Mutual fund shares are redeemable; investors sell the shares back to the fund at their approximate NAV, less applicable fees, and have normal settlement provisions. Mutual funds generally sell and redeem their shares on a continuous (i.e., daily) basis. Larger mutual fund NAVs are published daily in the popular press such as the *Wall Street Journal*, but NAVs for less active or small mutual funds are readily available from brokers. The mutual funds described above would typically be accounted for under the guidance provided by SFAS 124, as they meet the requirement of paragraphs 3(c).

There are other investment funds that are very similar to the funds described above, but are not mutual funds registered under the 1940 Act. Some HCOs may conclude that paragraph 3(c) is limited to only registered mutual funds that allow daily purchases and redemptions by investors and have NAV's that are published in the press each day. Therefore, they believe that nonregistered investment funds are not within the scope of SFAS 124 regardless of the similarities to registered funds. Other HCOs may believe that a broader policy permits each investment to be analyzed to determine whether it represents a pooled investment that has a fair value per share or unit that is determined and published and is the basis for current transactions. In the absence of further guidance, usually either view is acceptable provided that it is applied consistently to all investments and if material, the policy is disclosed in the financial statements. However with respect to the broader policy, it should be limited to those professionally managed investments that (1) pool the capital of investors to invest in stocks (equity securities), bonds (debt securities), options, futures, currencies, or money market securities for current income, capital appreciation, or both consistent with the investment objectives of the fund; (2) have an NAV provided to the investor periodically, but no less frequently than at each month end; and (3) the month-end NAV is the price paid or received by investors purchasing or selling investments at month end. A fund that withholds or holds back a certain percentage of the sale proceeds would generally be inconsistent with having a readily determinable fair value if the withholding/holdback is significant (e.g., greater than 10 percent) or is held for significant periods (e.g., greater than one month). Other terms, such as a notice period that restricts the frequency of transacting fund sales, should be carefully analyzed to determine if they conflict with an assertion that the investment fund has a published fair value that is the basis for current transactions.

4. IF CONSOLIDATION ACCOUNTING, THE EQUITY METHOD OF ACCOUNTING, AND THE ACCOUNTING GUIDANCE IN SFAS 124 DO NOT APPLY TO THE HCO'S INVESTMENT, WHAT ACCOUNTING MODEL SHOULD BE USED?

A. Real estate, oil/gas interests, and other investments not deemed to be "financial instruments."

The definition of "financial instrument" is found in FASB Statement No. 107, *Disclosures about Fair Value of Financial Instruments*. Paragraph 4.02 of the HCO Guide states that investments not deemed to be financial instruments, such as real estate or oil/gas interests, are to be accounted for at amortized cost and are subject to the impairment provisions consistent with FASB Statement No. 144, *Accounting for the Impairment or Disposal of Long-Lived Assets*.

B. Undivided interests

If the HCO's investment legally represents an undivided interest in each underlying asset and is proportionately liable for its share of any liability, then the investor may account for its pro rata share of the assets, liabilities, revenues, and expenses of the investment. However, if control of the investment entity resides with the investors collectively, similar to a limited partnership, then the investment should follow the equity method of accounting. HCOs should refer to the guidance provided in paragraph 11 of SOP 78-9 and EITF Issue No. 00-01, *Investor Balance Sheet and Income Statement Display under the Equity Method for investments in Certain Partnerships and Other Ventures*.

C. Investments included within the scope of SFAS 140

As provided by paragraph 14 of SFAS 140, interest-only strips, retained interests in securitizations, loans, other receivables, or other financial assets within the scope of SFAS 140 that can contractually be prepaid or otherwise settled in such a way that the holder would not recover substantially all of its recorded investment shall be subsequently measured like investments in debt securities classified as available for sale or trading under SFAS 124.

D. Common/commingled/collective trusts

Some pooled investment vehicles are organized as trusts. The trust instrument/trust deed is the legal document under which the trust is formed (similar to articles of incorporation). The trust instrument provides that the beneficial ownership of the trust is divided into interests that are allocated to the beneficiaries. The rights of the beneficial interest holders are defined in the trust deed. The beneficial interest may be structured similar to a separate ownership account in a partnership, on a unitized basis similar to a share in a corporation, or on some other basis. An investment trust may be classified for federal income tax purposes as a partnership, corporation, or trust, depending on its structure.

Investments in non–publicly traded common/commingled/collective trusts that are not within the scope of SFAS 140 as discussed above should follow the hierarchy outlined in this framework. Consistent with the guidance in section 2D above, some clients may adopt a policy to apply the guidance in EITF 03-16 to other organizational forms by analogy. Accordingly, to the extent a noncontrolled trust is considered to have a separate ownership account structure the equity method may be applied, unless the trust investment is so minor that the investor has virtually no influence over the trust's operating and financial policies. Likewise, consistent with the guidance in section 3B above, some clients may adopt a broader policy for applying the mutual fund guidance in SFAS 124. Accordingly, to the extent a trust is not required to apply consolidation accounting or the equity method of accounting and meets the criteria outlined in section 3B, the guidance in SFAS 124 may be applied. Absent meeting one of these levels in the hierarchy, the cost method should be applied as stated in section 4G below.

E. Investments in pools sponsored by other HCOs

Some HCOs may pool their funds for investment purposes. Those investments may be formal arrangements with separate legal structures, such as investment partnerships or investment trusts, or may be structured without the formation of a separate legal entity. In determining the accounting for these investments, it is important that the HCO carefully analyze the nature of the investment structure, which may necessitate the involvement of legal counsel. If the structure of the investment falls within the accounting hierarchy described above, this framework should be applied.

F. Insurance subsidiaries

FASB Statement No. 60, *Accounting and Reporting by Insurance Companies* (SFAS 60), establishes specialized industry accounting and reporting standards for insurance companies. If a not-for-profit HCO conducts insurance activities in a separate subsidiary that are within the scope of SFAS 60, that subsidiary should account for all investments in debt securities and investments in equity securities that have readily determinable fair values in accordance with SFAS 124. For entities that are within the scope of SFAS 60, investments in equity securities that are not addressed by SFAS 115 or SFAS 124 because they do not have "readily determinable fair values" as defined by those Statements shall be nevertheless reported at fair value in accordance with paragraph 46 of SFAS 60.

G. Cost method of accounting

If it is determined that SFAS 124 or any other alternative described above is not appropriate, then the HCO should account for the investment at cost, following the guidance in paragraph 6 of APB 18. Dividends received that are distributed from net accumulated earnings of the investee since the date of acquisition by the investor would be recognized as income. Dividends received in excess of earnings subsequent to the date of investment are considered return of investment and recorded as reductions of cost of the investment. If a series of operating losses of an investee or other factors indicate that a decrease in value of the investment has occurred which is other than temporary then an impairment loss should be recognized and the cost basis of the investment written down to its fair value. Consideration should be given to the requirements of FSP No. FAS 124-1, *The Meaning of "Other-than-Temporary Impairment" and Its Application to Certain Investments.*

(k) Malpractice Contingencies

p. 324. Replace first sentence of second paragraph with the following:

As indicated above, a key determinant of the amount of malpractice losses to be accrued by health care providers is the degree of risk the provider has transferred to an independent third-party insurer versus the risk of loss the organization has retained.

(l) Related Organizations

(ii) Business Combinations.

p. 327. Replace second sentence of first full paragraph with the following:

An acceptable practice for reporting such business combinations is to report the assets, liabilities, and net asset balances of the combined entities as of the beginning of the year and disclose the information that would be required to be disclosed for a pooling-of-interests under APB 16, *Business Combinations.*

CHAPTER SEVENTEEN

Accounting Standards for Other Not-for-Profit Organizations

§ 17.1   ACCOUNTING PRINCIPLES

(b)   Fund Accounting

p. 344. In third line, replace *GAP* with *GAAP*.

(e)   Donated Services

p. 345. In first line, replace *on* with *in*.

CHAPTER EIGHTEEN

Special Accounting Issues for Specific Organizations

§ 18.7 PRIVATE FOUNDATIONS

(b) Distinction between Principal and Income

p. 368. Replace fifth sentence with the following:

In the absence of legal restrictions, these two amounts *should* be combined and reported simply as net assets.

CHAPTER NINETEEN

The Financial Accounting Standards Board and Future Trends in Not-for-Profit Accounting

§ 19.2 TRENDS IN NOT-FOR-PROFIT ACCOUNTING

(b) Reporting Certain Assets at Current Value

p. 381. Modify first sentence in *section 19.2(b)* to read as follows:

Recent years have seen a trend in accounting for all entities (not just not-for-profit organizations) toward more reporting of assets at current fair value (market value when determinable, and best estimates of fair value when market values are not available), rather than just historical cost.

(j) Federal Reporting Requirements

p. 385. Add the following new *subsection (iii):*

(iii) Recent Developments (New). In 2005, the U.S. Senate Finance Committee issued a draft document entitled "Exempt Status Reforms." This document would establish federal Sarbanes-Oxley–type regulations and other rules for not-for-profit organizations. The Senate Finance Committee encouraged the not-for-profit industry to review this draft document and to offer thoughts and comments. The organization leading the industry response is the Independent Sector (www.independentsector.org). Not-for-profit organizations are encouraged to monitor the developments regarding this matter.

p. 385. Add the following new *subsection (k)* **before** *section 19.3:*

(k) State Regulations (New)

In response to a call for additional Sarbanes-Oxley–type regulations for not-for-profit organizations, some states have passed legislation establishing such rules and regulations. Many of the states that have enacted such legislation have it available on their specific state attorney general's web site.

§ 19.3 NEW FASB STATEMENTS OF FINANCIAL ACCOUNTING STANDARDS THAT AFFECT NOT-FOR-PROFIT ORGANIZATIONS

p. 385. Modify first sentence to read as follows:

The FASB has issued many new standards since April 2002:

p. 388. Insert the following at the end of *section 19.3:*

- SFAS 151, *Inventory Costs—An Amendment of ARB No. 43*, Chapter 4, was issued in November 2004. It clarifies the accounting for abnormal amounts of idle facility expense, freight, handling costs, and wasted material (spoilage). It may impact organizations with some inventory, such as a university bookstore. However, it is not likely to have a significant impact on not-for-profit organizations.

- SFAS 152, *Accounting for Real Estate Time-Sharing Transactions*, was issued December 2004. It is not likely to affect not-for-profit organizations.

- SFAS 153, *Exchanges of Nonmonetary Assets*, was issued December 2004. It is not likely to affect not-for-profit organizations.

- SFAS 154, *Accounting Changes and Error Corrections—a Replacement of APB No. 20 and FAS No. 3*, was issued May 2005.

- SFAS 155, *Accounting for Certain Hybrid Financial Instruments*, was issued in February 2006. This Statement amends FASB Statements No. 133, *Accounting for Derivative Instruments and Hedging Activities*, and No. 140, *Accounting for Transfers and Servicing of Financial Assets and Extinguishments of Liabilities*. This Statement resolves issues addressed in Statement 133 Implementation Issue No. D1, "Application of Statement 133 to Beneficial Interests in Securitized Financial Assets."

PwC Observation: If an organization has hybrid financial instruments, the benefit of adopting FAS 155 is simplification—in many instances, valuing the embedded derivative separately from its host contract is more complicated than measuring the entire hybrid instrument at fair value. For example, certain forms of split-interest agreements can have derivatives embedded in the obligation to other beneficiaries. A not-for-profit organization can avoid having to bifurcate (i.e., separately account for) the derivative by electing the fair value option for the hybrid instrument (i.e., by electing to carry the obligation to other beneficiaries at fair value). In this case, fair value measurement could be achieved simply by using a current discount rate in a present value–based calculation of the obligation.

- SFAS 156, *Accounting for Servicing Financial Assets*, was issued March 2006. It is not likely to affect not-for-profit organizations.

- SFAS 157, *Fair Value Measurements*, was issued September 2006. We discuss SFAS 157 and the anticipated impact in our Summary of Emerging Issues for Not-for-Profit Organizations in 2008 in Appendix D in greater detail

- SFAS 158, *Employers' Accounting for Defined Benefit Pension and Other Postretirement Plans—An amendment of FASB Statements No. 87, 88, 106, and 132(R)*, was issued September 2006. We briefly discuss SFAS 158 and the anticipated impact in our Summary of Emerging Issues for Colleges and Universities in 2006, included in Appendix D.

- *SFAS No. 159, *The Fair Value Option for Financial Assets and Financial Liabilities*, which was issued in February 2007, extended the availability of the fair value option to a wide range of financial instruments—both assets and liabilities. An organization may irrevocably elect to apply the fair value option to eligible financial assets and liabilities acquired or issued subsequent to adoption of the standard. The election is also available when a previously recognized asset or liability is subject to a "remeasurement event" as defined in paragraph 8 of FAS 159. FAS 159 generally permits organizations to apply the fair value option on an instrument-by-instrument basis, with some exceptions. The table on the next page provides examples of financial assets and liabilities that are or are not eligible for the fair value measurement election under FAS 159.

Under both FAS 159 and FAS 155, not-for-profit health care organizations report unrealized gains and losses on items for which the fair value option has been elected within the performance indicator or as a part of discontinued operations, as appropriate. For all other not-for-profit organizations, the unrealized gains and losses are reported as changes in net assets or discontinued operations, as appropriate. If the organization reports an intermediate measure of operations, it may report the gains and losses either within or outside that measure.

- SFAS 161, *Disclosures about Derivative Instruments and Hedging Activities*, was issued in March 2008, amends and expands the disclosure requirements in FASB Statement No. 133 (FAS 133), *Accounting for Derivative Instruments and Hedging Activities*, and related literature. Those disclosures had been criticized for not being transparent enough to allow financial statement users to assess a reporting entity's overall risk from derivatives from both a quantitative and qualitative perspective. FAS 161's requirements are aimed at providing users of financial statements with an enhanced understanding of how and why an entity uses derivative instruments; how derivative instruments and related hedged items are accounted for under FAS 133 and its related interpretations; and how derivative instruments affect an entity's financial position, results of operations/changes in net assets, and cash flows. FAS 161 also amends SOP 02-2, *Accounting for Derivative Instruments and Hedging Activities by Not-for-Profit Health Care Organizations, and Clarification of the Performance Indicator*, to require the disclosure of where and in what financial statement captions derivative gains and losses are displayed. FAS 161 focuses only on disclosures; it does not change any of FAS 133's accounting or financial statement presentation guidance.

Among other things, FAS 161 requires that organizations provide disclosure in a tabular format of the Balance Sheet captions in which derivatives are reported, and the fair value amounts of derivative instruments are reported in those captions. Similar disclosures are required for the location and amounts of gains and losses reported in the statement of activities/statement of operations. The latter requires separate categories for derivatives designated and qualifying as fair value hedges, those designated and qualifying as cash flow hedges (for health care organizations), those not designated or not qualifying as hedging instruments, and other categories, if applicable. Within each of the categories, separate line items should further categorize derivatives by purpose (i.e., the item being hedged or the exposure created). For not-for-profit organizations, the disclosure requirements are tailored to FAS 117's not-for-profit reporting model.

- FSP FAS 117-a, *Endowments of Not-for-Profit Organizations: Net Asset Classification of Funds Subject to an Enacted Version of the Uniform Prudent Management of Institutional Funds Act, and Enhanced Disclosures*, was issued in August 2008 and provides guidance concerning: (1) the disclosures that not-for-profit organizations should make with regard to their endowments, and (2) the effect of a state's adoption of the model Uniform Prudent Management of Institutional Funds Act of 2006 (UPMIFA) on the classification of net assets related to donor-restricted endowment funds of not-for-profit organizations within that state.

The exposure draft proposes a number of new disclosures that would be required for endowments of all not-for-profit organizations, not just endowments held in states where UPMIFA has been enacted. These include:

- A description of the governing board's interpretation of the law that underlies the net asset classification of donor-restricted endowment funds

- A description of endowment spending policies

- A description of endowment investment policies, including the organization's return objectives and risk parameters, how those objectives relate to the organization's endowment spending policies, and the strategies employed for achieving those objectives

- An endowment reconciliation by financial statement net asset class that shows cumulative investment returns in the permanently restricted net asset class that relate to the organization's interpretation of relevant law, rather than what is required by explicit donor stipulation

- The composition of an organization's endowment by net asset classification at the end of the period, in total and by type of endowment fund, showing donor-restricted endowment funds separately from board-designated endowment funds

- A reconciliation of the beginning and ending balances of the organization's endowment, in total and by net asset class, including, at a minimum, the following line items:
  - Investment return, separated into investment income and net appreciation or depreciation of investments
  - Contributions
  - Amounts appropriated for expenditure

- ○ Reclassifications
- ○ Other changes
- Disclosure of how much (if any) of additions of investment return to permanently restricted net assets in the current period are the result of the organization's interpretation of relevant law, beyond that required by explicit donor stipulations
- Planned appropriation for expenditures, if known, for the year following the most recent period for which the organization presents financial statements

The FSP provides an illustrative example of such disclosures.

Impact of UPMIFA on Permanently Restricted Net Assets.   UPMIFA is a modernization of the Uniform Management of Institutional Funds Act of 1972 (UMIFA), the model act on which most states have based their laws governing the investment and management of donor-restricted endowment funds. A number of states have already replaced UMIFA with UPMIFA. Among other changes, UPMIFA prescribes new guidelines for expenditure of endowment funds in the absence of explicit donor restrictions. UMIFA allowed only for the spending of the net appreciation on endowment investments

Readers should refer to Appendix D as well as the FASB's web site for the latest discussion of each of these new statements as well as exposure drafts of other statements.

§ 19.4   OTHER FASB PRONOUNCEMENTS AND PROJECTS

p. 390. Insert the following new *subsection (c)* after *subsection (b)*:

(c)   FIN 47 (New)

The FASB published its Interpretation No. 47, *Accounting for Conditional Asset Retirement Obligations—An Interpretation of FASB Statement No. 143*, in March 2005. We briefly discuss FIN 47 and the anticipated impact in our *Summary of Emerging Issues for Not-for-Profit Organizations in 2007*, included in Appendix D.

p. 390. Renumber *subsection (c), EITF Issues 01-8, Determining Whether an Arrangement Is a Lease,* **as subsection** *(d).*

p. 391. Add the following new *subsections (e)* **and** *(f):*

(e)   EITF Issue 05-6, Determining the Amortization Period for Leasehold Improvement (New)

At its June 15–16, 2005, meeting, an EITF Task Force reached a consensus regarding the amortization period for leasehold improvements. We briefly discuss EITF Issue 05-6 in our *Summary of Emerging Issues for Not-for-Profit Organizations in 2007,* included in Appendix D.

(f)   EITF Issue 06-2, Accounting for Sabbatical Leave and Other Similar Benefits Pursuant to FASB Statement No. 43, *Accounting for Compensated Absences* **(New)**

At its March, April, and June 2006 meetings, an EITF Task Force discussed the accounting for sabbatical leave and ultimately reached a consensus. We briefly discuss EITF Issue 06-2 in our *Summary of Emerging Issues for Not-for-Profit Organizations in 2007,* included in Appendix D.

p. 391. Renumber *subsection (d) Pension Plans* **as subsection** *(g).*

(g)   Pension Plans

p. 391. Add the following as the last sentence:

Refer also to the discussion of SFAS No. 158 in section 19.3 above.

PART FOUR

Controlling the Not-for-Profit Organization

CHAPTER TWENTY-FOUR

Effective Internal Accounting Control for Not-for-Profit Organizations

§ 24.1 INTRODUCTION TO INTERNAL ACCOUNTING CONTROL

p. 458. Add new *subsection (f)*:

(f) New Thresholds for Internal Control Weaknesses (New)

In May 2006, the Auditing Standards Board issued Statement of Auditing Standards No. 112, *Communicating Internal Control Related Matters Identified in an Audit*. This Statement, which will be effective for fiscal years ending on or after December 15, 2006:

- Defines the terms *significant deficiency* and *material weakness*, incorporating the definitions already in use for public companies and prescribed by the Public Company Accounting Oversight Board (PCAOB)

- Provides guidance on evaluating the severity of control deficiencies identified in an audit of financial statements
- Requires the auditor to communicate, in writing, to management and those charged with governance (e.g., board of trustees), significant deficiencies and material weaknesses identified in an audit

While this new standard does not change audit procedures, it does change the process for evaluating deficiencies that come to our attention and brings the thresholds for reporting control deficiencies in line with the thresholds required for public organizations. As these revised thresholds effectively lower the bar, it is expected that the reporting of significant deficiencies and material weaknesses will become increasingly common. There is a possibility that items not previously identified as control deficiencies could elevate to a significant deficiency or material weakness. Common areas of weakness include controls in place over the financial statement closing process, information technology (IT) controls over significant systems, segregation of duties, complex spreadsheets, and consideration of the use of third-party service providers.

For entities that receive federal funding, any identified material weaknesses in internal controls would be specified in the Report of Independent Auditors on Internal Control over Financial Reporting and on Compliance and Other Matters Based on an Audit of Financial Statements Performed in Accordance with Government Auditing Standards, which is part of the A-133 report that is filed with the Federal Audit Clearinghouse. Additionally, material weaknesses could negatively impact future debt covenants, as well as public perception of management's ability to oversee the operations of an organization.

§ 24.3 BASIC INTERNAL ACCOUNTING CONTROL SYSTEM

(b) Disbursement of Cash

p. 467. Add the following bullet points:

- Are wire transfers initiated and approved by different individuals? (An approver may be an individual outside of the business office.)

- Is the bank account for incoming wire transfers prohibited (per agreement with the bank) from sending outgoing wire transfers? (This is so that the pertinent information on the account can be distributed to applicable parties without concern of fraudulent outgoing wire transfers.)
- Are wire transfers subject to reviews and controls consistent with writing checks?

(e) Accounts Payable

p. 471. Add the following bullet point:

- Are tax ID numbers and addresses of employees compared to those of accounts payable vendors, in an attempt to identify potentially fraudulent/fictitious businesses?

(g) Fixed Assets

p. 472. Add the following bullet point:

- Is equipment purchased with federal funds easily identifiable to ensure it is not utilized for unallowable activities?

p. 473. Add new *subsection (i):*

(i) Compensation and Expenses (New)

1. Executive Compensation

Executive compensation continues to be a primary focus of the IRS, the media, donors, and others. As evidence of this, the IRS has included a new section in the 2005 Form 990 for organizations to disclose compensation currently paid to former officers and has expanded the disclosure for compensation paid by related organizations.

Leading practices for institutions to consider are:

- Develop a formal process to set executive compensation.
- Obtain and review comparable data—the compensation that other individuals in similar positions in similar organizations receive—to document whether compensation is reasonable.
- Consider all forms of compensation and benefits, including expenses (see below).

- Approve executive compensation at the board level and document the approval in the board minutes. A board member who has a conflict of interest should abstain from the vote. The board may delegate its responsibility to a separate compensation committee, but if it does so, the full board must gain an understanding of the compensation committee decisions, approve the decisions, and document the approval in their meeting minutes. Contemporaneous documentation frequently is overlooked but is essential for an institution to establish a rebuttable presumption of reasonableness in order to reduce the risk of intermediate sanctions.

- Report compensation completely and accurately on Form 990. The audit committee or the external auditors—preferably both—should review the most important disclosures on Form 990.

- Report compensation completely and accurately on the recipient's Form W-2.

Author's observation: Establishing a compensation committee to set compensation levels for senior executives is a best practice.

2. Expense Reporting

Similar to compensation, the IRS and the media are focused on situations where employees are being reimbursed for personal expenditures and these amounts are not reported as compensation. Therefore, it is essential that organizations make certain that their expense-reporting procedures are adequate and are followed by both employees and officers.

Expense reports should be submitted on a timely basis, and they should include adequate documentation in order to satisfy the rules. Receipts must be provided together with the name of the individual(s) involved and the business purpose for the expenditures.

Institutions also should establish appropriate policies regarding the approval and sign-off of expense reports submitted by senior management. For example, the CFO might sign off as to the completeness of the president's expense report and that it is in compliance with institutional policies. Trustees should periodically review the overall level of expenses incurred by the senior management for reasonableness. Such actions protect both the organization and senior management.

Author's Observation: Institutions must establish adequate policies and procedures for reimbursing and documenting business expenses. They also should be aware that some "expenses" may constitute additional compensation. Institutions must identify and appropriately report additional compensation received by key employees through the reimbursement of non-business-related expenses. Additional compensation that is not considered when establishing a rebuttable presumption of reasonableness may result in an automatic excess benefit transaction under intermediate sanctions. Therefore, we recommend that the board consider all forms of compensation, including the reimbursement of personal expenses, when considering whether key employees are receiving reasonable compensation.

§ 24.4 SPECIFIC NONPROFIT INTERNAL ACCOUNTING CONTROLS

(g) Endowments and Investment Income

p. 481. Add the following bullet points:

- Does management have procedures in place to determine the carrying value of hard-to-value investments?

- Are custodian agreements reviewed to determine whether the custodian is permitted to lend out the organization's securities?

CHAPTER TWENTY-FIVE

Independent Audits

*§ 25.2   BENEFITS OF AN INDEPENDENT AUDIT

*p. 489. Insert the following new item:

5.   Open communications between the auditors and those charged with governance

*p. 490. Insert the following new *subsection (e)* before *section 25.3:*

(e)   Open Communications between the Auditors and Those Charged with Governance (New)

Under Statement of Auditing Standards No. 114, *The Auditor's Communication with Those Charged with Governance* (SAS 114), the auditor has certain communication responsibilities with the audit committee, or the group within the client charged with governance.

Matters that should be communicated by the auditors should include:

- The auditor's responsibilities under generally accepted auditing standards.

- The financial statements are presented fairly, in all material respects, in conformity with generally accepted accounting principles.

- The audit does not relieve management or those charged with governance with their responsibilities.

- Audit is to be performed in accordance with generally accepted auditing standards.

- Audit is designed to obtain reasonable, not absolute, assurance about whether the financial statements are free of material misstatement.

- Internal controls are considered in planning the audit, but not for the purpose of opining on the effectiveness of the organization's internal controls over financial reporting.

- An overview of the planned scope and timing of the audit.

- How the auditor will address the significant risk of material misstatement.

- The auditor's approach with regard to internal controls.

- Factors considered in determining materiality.

- Extent of reliance on internal audit (if applicable).

- Significant findings from the audit.

- Auditor's views about the qualitative aspects of the organization's significant accounting practices and accounting policies.

- Significant difficult, if any, encountered during the audit.

- Adjustments recorded by management as a result of the audit.

- Adjustments proposed by the auditors and not recorded by management.

- Disagreements with management, if any.

- Representations being requested from management by the auditors (draft of the management representation letter).

- Management's consultation with other auditors.

- Significant written communications with management.

- Any issues discussed with management prior to the auditors being retained.

§ 25.5   AUDIT COMMITTEES

p. 494. Insert at end of section:

In order to assist audit committees in fulfilling their responsibilities, a subcommittee of the AICPA's Not-for-Profit Expert Panel developed a series of tools that are available free for download at the AICPA's Web site: www.aicpa.org/Audcommctr/toolkitsnpo/homepage.htm.

Administrative Tools

- Audit Committee Charter Matrix
- Financial Expertise
- Sample RFP for CPA Services
- Independence and Related Issues
- Peer Review of CPA Firms
- Evaluating the Auditor's Engagement Letter
- Hiring the Chief Audit Executive
- Hiring External Experts

Audit Process Tools

- Internal Control
- Fraud and the Audit Committee
- Whistleblower Tracking Report
- Conducting an Audit Committee Executive Session
- Issues Report from Management
- Discussions with the Independent Auditors

Performance Evaluation and Other Tools

- Evaluating the Independent Auditors
- Evaluating the Internal Audit Team
- Conducting an Audit Committee Self-Evaluation
- Single Audits—Circular No. A-133
- Unique Transactions and Financial Relationships
- Resources for Audit Committees

CHAPTER TWENTY-SIX

Investments

§ 26.1 VALUING INVESTMENTS

(b) Alternative Investments

p. 513. Add the following paragraph at the end of *subsection (b):*

In July 2005, the American Institute of Certified Public Accountants (AICPA) issued Auditing Interpretations 9328, *Auditing Fair Value Measurements and Disclosures*, and 9332, *Auditing Derivative Instruments, Hedging Activities, and Investments in Securities*. In both of the Interpretations, the AICPA references AU Section 328, paragraph .04, which states:

> Management is responsible for making the fair value measurements and disclosures included in the financial statements. As part of fulfilling its responsibility, management needs to establish an accounting and financial reporting process for determining the fair value measurements and disclosures, select appropriate valuation methods, identify and adequately support any significant assumptions used, prepare the valuation, and ensure that the presentation and disclosure of the fair value measurements are in accordance with GAAP.

This paragraph reiterates that management ultimately has the responsibility to assign a value to *all* of its investments, including the hard-to-value investments. This requirement may cause management to meet with investees and gain an understanding of their processes, judgments, and methodologies.

Due to the increased risk of misstatement inherent with these investments, the Audit Issues Task Force of the Auditing Standards Board established the Alternative Investments Task Force. The Task Force was charged with providing additional guidance to auditors of investor entities as to how the auditor may obtain sufficient appropriate audit evidence in order to conclude that the financial statements are free of material misstatement. As a result, the Alternative Investments Task Force has developed and issued a practice aid for auditors, "Alternative Investments—Audit Considerations." The Task Force believes that this nonauthoritative practice aid will assist auditors in auditing alternative investments. The practice aid includes guidance on:

1. General considerations pertaining to auditing alternative investments

2. Addressing management's financial statement existence assertion

3. Addressing management's financial statement valuation assertion

4. Management representations

5. Disclosure of certain significant risks and uncertainties

6. Reporting

The practice aid also includes the following appendixes:

- Appendix 1: Example Confirmation for Alternative Investments
- Appendix 2: Illustrative Examples of Due Diligence, Ongoing Monitoring, and Financial Reporting Controls

The practice aid can be ordered at the AICPA's Web site (www. aicpa.org).

§ 26.5 PROFESSIONAL INVESTMENT ADVICE

(c) Selecting an Investment Advisor

p. 523. Add the following paragraphs at the end of *subsection (c):*

Management should also consider whether its money managers obtain a "SAS 70 report" (a report issued by the money manager's [or any other outside service provider's] external auditors in accordance with Statement of Auditing Standard No. 70, *Service Organizations*). A Type 2 SAS 70 report will provide the not-for-profit organization with information on the money manager's internal controls and the results of the auditor's testing of those controls. This SAS 70 report will allow the organization to evaluate the money manager at a more detailed level. Additionally, the SAS 70 report will document the "user controls," or those controls/procedures that the service provider is expecting the organization to undertake as part of its internal control structure. A positive SAS 70 report should provide the organization with additional comfort over the information received from the money manager. A negative SAS 70 report, or no SAS 70 report, could cause the organization to reconsider its decision to engage this particular service provider.

It should be noted that there is also a Type 1 SAS 70 report. A Type 1 report only documents the controls in place at the service provider, but the external auditor has not tested these controls; thus no assurance is provided with regard to whether the controls are functioning as designed or not.

*§ 26.7 CONCLUSION

*p. 525. Add the following paragraphs at the end of *section 26.7:*

In October 2008, the FASB issued FSP 157-3, *Determining the Fair Value of a Financial Asset When the Market for That Asset Is Not Active.*

This FASB Staff Position (FSP) clarifies the application of FASB Statement No. 157, *Fair Value Measurements*, in a market that is not active and provides an example to illustrate key considerations in determining the fair value of a financial asset when the market for that financial asset is not active. Statement 157 was issued in September 2006, and is effective for financial assets and financial liabilities for financial statements issued for fiscal years beginning after November 15, 2007, and interim periods within those fiscal years. (Note: FSP 157-2, *Effective Date of FASB Statement No. 157*, amended Statement 157 to delay the effective date of Statement 157 for nonfinancial assets and nonfinancial liabilities, except for items that are recognized or disclosed at fair value in the financial statements on a recurring basis until fiscal years beginning after November 15, 2008, and interim periods within those fiscal years.)

Statement 157 establishes a single definition of fair value and a framework for measuring fair value in generally accepted accounting principles (GAAP) that result in increased consistency and comparability in fair value measurements. Statement 157 also expands disclosures about fair value measurements, thereby improving the quality of information provided to users of financial statements. Statement 157 does not require any new fair value measurements.

This FSP applies to financial assets within the scope of accounting pronouncements that require or permit fair value measurements in accordance with Statement 157.

This FSP clarifies the application of Statement 157 in a market that is not active and provides an example to illustrate key considerations in determining the fair value of a financial asset when the market for that financial asset is not active.

All FASB statements are available at www.fasb.org.

See also the following appendices:

D: Includes further discussion of FAS 157 and FAS 159
E: Brochure on Alternative Investments
G: Fair Value Option considerations under FAS 159

PART FIVE

Principal Federal Tax and Compliance Requirements

CHAPTER TWENTY-SEVEN

E-Business for Not-for-Profit Organizations: How Can Not-for-Profits Manage the Risks to Maximize E-Business Opportunities?

§ 27.5 WHERE ARE WE TODAY?

p. 536. Replace first sentence with the following:

The growth of the Internet has been nothing short of phenomenal. For example, experts estimate that there are over 2.7 billion web pages today; this number is growing at rate of approximately 5 million new pages a day. According to a January 4, 2006, article on the Computer Industry Almanac web site (www.c-i-a.com/), there are 197.8 million Internet users in the United States. China is second with 119.5 million Web surfers. Japan is third, with 86.3 million Internet users. (For more Internet statistics, see Exhibit 27.2.)

§ 27.8   HOW ARE ACADEMIC INSTITUTIONS USING E-BUSINESS?

(c)   E-Learning

p. 558. Replace last sentence in carryover paragraph with the following:

Winning full accreditation, which is the final step in the three-step process, usually takes two to five years, but in the meantime, candidate status should give the university more legitimacy and help its enrollment grow (see www.wgu.edu).

APPENDIX 27 - A

What E-Business Models Exist?

(b) B2B Business Model

p. 561. Replace fourth paragraph with the following:

Recently there has been a lot of focus on the B2B space as new B2B models have emerged. For example, some companies use a third party that creates business-to-business online auctions for buyers who are seeking industrial parts, raw materials, commodities, and other services.

(d) C2B Business Model

p. 562. Replace first paragraph with the following:

There are two primary forms of C2B, which is the customer-to-business model. This first involves consumer demand aggregation. Under this model, consumers who want to buy new televisions, for example, band together to leverage their bulk purchasing power.

CHAPTER TWENTY-EIGHT

Principal Tax Requirements

§ 28.2   CHARITABLE ORGANIZATIONS

(c)   Intermediate Sanctions

p. 570. Insert following second complete paragraph:

In the past, organizations were not required to make Form 990-T, *Exempt Organization Business Income Tax Return*, available for public inspection. However, legislation passed as part of the Pension Protection Act of 2006 requires that organizations make their Form 990-T available to the public upon request. This provision is effective for organizations filing Form 990-T on or after August 17, 2006. The Technical Corrections Act of 2007 (H.R. 4195) expands on the requirement that the organization alone is responsible for making the Form 990-T available for public inspection. The legislation also requires the Secretary of the Treasury (IRS) to make the Form 990-T available to the public. This change will likely result in the Form 990-T being available on the Internet through Guidestar and other sites.

§ 28.3 TAX STATUS OF CHARITABLE ORGANIZATIONS: PUBLIC CHARITY OR PRIVATE FOUNDATION

(a)   Public Charities

p. 572. At the end of fourth paragraph, insert the following sentence:

The Pension Protection Act of 2006 introduced significant new restrictions on the activities of supporting organizations and are summarized in Section 28.12.

*p. 572. Replace last sentence of the second to last paragraph with the following two sentences:

For organizations filing a 2007 Form 990 or earlier, Schedule A calculates public support over an aggregate four-year period and the calculations are performed utilizing the cash method of accounting. For organizations filing a 2008 Form 990 or later, Schedule A calculates public support over an aggregate five-year period and the calculations are henceforth performed utilizing the organization's method of accounting (i.e., an accrual basis organization will complete its support schedule utilizing the accrual method of accounting).

*p. 573. Replace second sentence of second to last paragraph of *subsection (a)* with the following two sentences:

For 2007 and earlier years, Schedule A includes a schedule for certain organizations to complete regarding the support they received for the four years prior to the taxable year. For 2008 and later years, Schedule A includes a schedule for certain organizations to complete regarding the support they received in the current year in addition to the four prior years (five years total).

*p. 573. Delete third sentence of last paragraph of *subsection (a)* that currently reads as:

Also, keep in mind that this mechanical test is applied over a rolling four-year period.

(b) Private Foundations

p. 573. Add the following paragraph before *section 28.4*:

The Pension Protection Act of 2006 doubled the excise tax for the following violations of certain private foundation rules: Self-dealing (IRC §4941), Failure to Distribute Income (IRC §4942), Excess Business Holdings (IRC §4943), Jeopardy Investments (IRC §4944), and Taxable Expenditures (IRC §4945). The increased excise tax percentages are effective for taxable years beginning after August 17, 2006.

§ 28.4 OTHER CONCERNS FOR CHARITIES

(a) Unrelated Business Income

(ii) Exceptions and Modifications.

p. 575. Replace last paragraph with the following:

In addition, items that are generally excluded from unrelated business income are passive investment income such as dividends, interest, royalties, rents from real property, and gains on the sale of property. While excluded from unrelated business income, private foundations must still pay an excise tax on these items of passive income. However, rents that are based on a percentage of the net income of the property are considered unrelated and, thus, taxable. Also, income (passive investment income and rent) from assets acquired by incurring debt (debt-financed property) and rent from personal property may be considered unrelated business income in whole or in part.[10]

(viii) Tax Rates on Unrelated Business Income.

p. 578. Insert as second complete paragraph in *subsection (viii)*:

A majority of states also impose a tax on unrelated business income (UBI). Therefore, it is important for tax-exempt organizations to determine whether the state in which they operate imposes a tax on UBI. Organizations should also consider whether the organization engages in activities in other states either directly or through investments in limited partnerships. As a partner invested in a limited partnership, a tax-exempt organization is subject to a tax on its federal UBI that is generated through a partnership investment. The organization may also be subject to state UBI tax obligations.

(c) Lobbying and Political Activity

p. 580. Add the following sentence to the last bullet:

Based on experience gathered from investigations during the 2004 election cycle, the IRS issued a fact sheet (FS-2006-17) that provides examples of the types of activities identified as violations and gives guidance for ongoing compliance.

(d) Charitable Contributions

(i) Contribution Disclosures.

p. 580. Insert as second complete paragraph in *subsection (i)*:

For contributions made after July 25, 2006, the Pension Protection Act of 2006 amended the requirements necessary to claim a charitable contribution deduction for façade easements with respect to property in a registered historic district. The provision disallows a deduction with respect to a structure or land merely because it is located within a historic district, but continues to allow a deduction with respect to buildings. Façade easements must provide that all portions of the building's exterior (not just the front) remain unchanged, in a manner consistent with the historical character of the exterior. Taxpayers will also have to obtain an appraisal of the qualified real property interest to attach to their returns, along with a written agreement between the donors and the donee organization certifying that the donee organization is (a) a qualified public charity with a charitable purpose of environmental or historic preservation or protection and (b) that the donee organization has the resources and the commitment to manage and enforce the easement restrictions. Effective August 17, 2006, the charitable deduction is reduced if a rehabilitation credit has been claimed with respect to the donated property. For contributions made after February 13, 2007, donors claiming a deduction in excess of $10,000 must pay a filing fee of $500 to the IRS.

(ii) Contribution Acknowledgments.

p. 581. Insert as second complete paragraph in *subsection (ii):*

For tax years beginning after August 17, 2006, the Pension Protection Act of 2006 revises the substantiation requirements for charitable deductions of monetary contributions. The revised record-keeping requirements apply to all monetary contributions, regardless of the amount, and require that the donor maintain either a bank record, such as a cancelled check, or a written communication from the charity showing the name of the charity and the date and amount of the contribution.

(iii) Solicitation Disclosures.

p. 581. Insert the following paragraph at the end of *subsection (iii):*

The Pension Protection Act of 2006 amended the requirements for charitable contribution deductions of clothing and household items for contributions made after August 16, 2006. The new law specified that no deduction is allowed for clothing and household items that are not in good used condition or better. Donors who contribute a single item of clothing or a household item worth more than $500 will be required to file a qualified appraisal of the donated property with the donor's return. The Secretary of the Department of Treasury has the authority to deny by regulation a deduction for any item with minimal monetary value.

(e) Corporate Responsibility and Disclosure

p. 585. Replace item 5 with the following:

5. Transactions with significant book-tax differences (Notice 2006-6 removed this item from the list of categories of reportable transactions, and such transactions are no longer required to be disclosed on returns filed with due dates [including extensions] after January 5, 2006.)

p. 585. Insert the following new paragraph before *section 28.5:*

The Tax Increase Prevention and Reconciliation Act (TIPRA) added new IRC §4965 to the code. This section establishes new excise taxes and disclosure rules for virtually every type of exempt organization that enters into a "prohibited tax shelter transaction." Managers of affected tax-exempt organizations can also be subject to these new excise taxes. In Notice 2006-65, the IRS requested comments on these new rules and plans to issue guidance as part of its Implementing Guidelines in 2007. There is considerable uncertainly around these rules and how organizations must comply. This new law is effective for tax years ending after May 17, 2006. Consultation with a tax specialist is recommended.

§ 28.5   PRIVATE FOUNDATIONS

(a)   Excise Tax on Investment Income

p. 585. Insert as second complete paragraph in *subsection (a):*

For tax years beginning after August 17, 2006, the Pension Protection Act of 2006 amended the definition of capital gains included in net investment income as originally defined in the Tax Reform Act of 1969. Generally, capital gains will now include all capital gains and losses of a private foundation, whereas the old definition included only capital gains and losses from the disposition of property used for the production of interest, dividends, rents, and royalties. An exception to the new definition of *capital gains* is gains from the sale of charitable use property used for exempt purposes for at least one year and exchanged for like-kind property following rules similar to those used in §1031 exchanges. Under the rules of §1031, a qualified intermediary must be involved in the exchange to properly defer the recognition of capital gains on such exchanges.

(b)   Distribution of Income

p. 586. After third sentence of first paragraph, insert the following sentence:

Effective for tax years beginning after August 17, 2006, the initial excise tax increases from 15 to 30 percent of the amount that remains undistributed at the end of the year following the current taxable year.

p. 586. Replace second paragraph with the following:

The minimum investment return is 5 percent of the average fair market value of all the foundation's assets that are not used in directly carrying out the organization's exempt purpose. Cash equal to 1.5 percent of the total foundation's assets is deemed to be used in carrying out the exempt purpose (with additional amounts above 1.5 percent allowed based on facts and circumstances) and is deducted for this calculation. This means that if a foundation has marketable securities and cash with a market value of $1 million, it must make minimum qualifying distributions of 5 percent of $985,000 ($1 million less 1.5 percent of $1 million), or $49,250, regardless of its actual income. If, for example, actual investment income were only $30,000, the foundation would still have to make qualifying distributions of $49,250.

p. 588. Replace first paragraph with the following:

Thus, the distributable amount is $48,250. Qualifying distributions were $70,000, which exceeds the distributable amount by $21,750, and the requirement has been met. This excess distribution can be carried over for five years to meet the requirements of a year in which there is a deficiency. Where there is such a carryover, the order of application of the amounts distributed would be (1) current year, (2) carryover from earliest year, (3) carryover from next earliest year, and so forth.

(c) Excess Business Holdings

p. 588. Insert as second complete paragraph in *subsection (c)*:

The Pension Protection Act of 2006 makes the excess business holdings rules applicable to type III supporting organizations (that are not functionally integrated) as defined in IRC §509(a)(3)(B)(iii) and donor advised funds newly defined by the same law in IRC §4966(d)(2).

p. 588. At end of last paragraph in *subsection (c)*, insert the following sentence:

Effective for tax years beginning after August 17, 2006, the initial excise tax increases from 5 percent to 10 percent of the value of the excess holdings.

(d) Prohibited Transactions

(iii) Prohibited Expenditures.

p. 589. Insert after the third sentence in *subsection (iii):*

Due to tax code amendments in the Pension Protection Act of 2006, foundations must now also exercise expenditure responsibility (or control) over grants made to any type III supporting organization that is not functionally integrated, even though such an organization is recognized as a public charity by the IRS.

§ 28.8   REGISTRATION AND REPORTING

(a)   Initial Registration

*p. 596. Replace third paragraph of** *subsection (a)* **with the following paragraph:**

Previously, an organization that anticipated it would meet one of the public support tests was given an advance-determination letter. This determination letter allowed the organization up to 60 months to meet the public support test without being classified as a private foundation. If, at the end of the 60 months, or the advance determination period, the organization failed to meet the support test, it would be characterized as a private foundation retroactive to the date operations began. On September 8, 2008, the IRS issued temporary regulations that eliminated the advance-ruling process and an organization that is reasonably expected to meet its public support tests will initially be classified as a public charity without any retroactive private foundation ramifications if the public support test is not met after its first five years of operations. In addition, an organization that was in its advance-ruling period at the time the September 2008 temporary regulations were issued can treat its original advance-ruling determination letter as its final IRS determination letter.

p. 596. Insert the following as fourth complete paragraph:

Effective August 17, 2006, the Pension Protection Act of 2006 now requires that each organization intending to maintain donor-advised funds must give notice that it intends to do so when submitting Form 1023. Such notice must also describe how the organization will maintain such funds. Section 28.11 of this chapter discusses new legislative provisions affecting donor-advised funds.

(b)   Annual Return—Public Charities

p. 596. Insert after the first paragraph in *subsection (b)***:**

Effective for tax years ending after August 17, 2006, the Pension Protection Act of 2006 requires every supporting organization defined in IRC §509(a)(3) to file an annual return regardless of its size. In addition, the new law requires organizations with gross receipts of normally less that $25,000 to furnish to the Secretary of the Treasury, in electronic form, the legal name of the organization, its mailing address, identification number, the name and address of its principal officer, and evidence of its continuing basis for exemption.

p. 596. Insert after the second paragraph in *subsection (b)***:**

Some large exempt organizations are now required to file Form 990 electronically. For fiscal years ending on or after December 31, 2005, the electronic filing requirement applies to organizations with $100 million or more in total assets ($10 million for fiscal years ending on or after December 31, 2006) if the organization also files at least 250 federal returns in a calendar year. In determining whether the 250-return threshold is met, organizations should count all income, excise, employment tax, and information returns, including all Forms W-2 and 1099.

(c)   Annual Returns for Private Foundation

p. 597. Insert as second complete paragraph in *subsection (c)***:**

Some private foundations are now required to file Form 990-PF electronically. For fiscal years ending on or after December 31, 2006, all private foundations are required to file Form 990-PF electronically regardless of the private foundation's asset size if the private foundation files at least 250 federal returns in a calendar year. In determining whether the 250 returns threshold is met, private foundations should count all income, excise, employment tax, and information returns, including all Forms W-2 and 1099.

(d) Return Inspection

p. 597. Insert after the third sentence of the first paragraph:

With the signing of the Pension Protection Act of 2006, all the public inspection requirements noted above now apply to any Form 990-T filed after August 17, 2006.

The Technical Corrections Act of 2007 (H.R. 4195) expands on the requirement that the organization alone is responsible for making the Form 990-T available for public inspection. The legislation also requires the Secretary of the Treasury (IRS) to make the Form 990-T available to the public. This change will likely result in Form 990-T's being available on the Internet through Guidestar and other sites.

p. 597. Replace the second paragraph with the following:

The final regulations provide that an organization is not required to comply with requests for copies if the organization has made Form 990 widely available. An organization may satisfy the requirement of making its Form 990 "widely available" if the form is posted on a World Wide Web page established and maintained by another entity where similar documents of other tax-exempt organizations are also available (e.g., www.guidestar.org). A Form 990 will be considered "widely available" if the World Wide Web page clearly informs the reader that the document is available and provides instructions for downloading, the document is posted in a format that exactly reproduces the image of the return as it was originally filed (except for information permitted by statute to be withheld), and an individual with access to the Internet can access, download, view, and print the document without special computer hardware or software and without paying a fee. Treas. Reg. §301.6104(d)-2(b)(2)(i).

§ 28.9 FEDERAL INFORMATION AND TAX RETURN FILING REQUIREMENTS

p. 598. Insert at the end of the second paragraph:

While organizations must now make the Form 990-T available to the public upon request, these forms are not presently on the Internet. However, the Technical Corrections Act of 2007 (H.R. 4195), expands on the requirement that the organization alone is responsible for making the Form 990-T available for public inspection. The legislation also requires the secretary of the Treasury (IRS) to make the Form 990-T available to the public. This change will likely result in the Form 990-T being available on the Internet through Guidestar and other sites.

p. 598. Insert as third complete paragraph:

Some large exempt organizations and private foundations are now required to file Form 990 and Form 990-PF electronically. For fiscal years ending on or after December 31, 2005, the electronic filing requirement applies to Form 990 filers with $100 million or more in total assets ($10 million for fiscal years ending on or after December 31, 2006) if the organization also files at least 250 federal returns in a calendar year. For fiscal years ending on or after December 31, 2006, all private foundations are required to file Form 990-PF electronically regardless of the private foundation's asset size if the private foundation files at least 250 federal returns in a calendar year. In determining whether the 250-return threshold is met, organizations should count all income, excise, employment tax, and information returns, including all Forms W-2 and 1099.

(a) Form 990: Return of Organization Exempt from Income Tax

(i) Who Must File.

p. 598. Replace the fourth bullet with the following bullet:

- Organizations with average annual gross receipts normally $25,000 or less (except all private foundations and supporting organizations no matter how small)

(ii) Filing a Complete Form 990.

p. 599. Replace penultimate paragraph with the following paragraph:

Both the 2005 and 2006 Form 990 and Schedule A include significant changes from prior years Form 990. Some of the changes were legislated as part of the Pension Protection Act of 2006. Most of the changes are designed to provide greater transparency. A detailed listing of Form 990 changes for both the 2005 and 2006 Form 990 has been included in Appendix D: Summary of Emerging Issues for Not-for-Profit Organizations in 2007 (New), Section VI, Tax Issues.

The IRS is currently in the process of completely redesigning the Form 990. The new design will consist of a "core" form for all Form 990 filers to complete, along with numerous other schedules required to be completed if applicable to an organization (e.g., hospitals will be required to complete Schedule H). The redesigned Form 990 is expected to be finalized by the IRS in time for the 2008 tax year to be filed by organizations beginning in 2009. IRS progress and updates related to the redesigned Form 990 can be found by visiting the IRS Web site Charities & Non-Profits page at www.irs.gov/charities.

p. 599. Before last paragraph, insert new paragraph:

The Pension Protection Act of 2006 requires that Form 990 be changed to include several new reporting requirements related to donor-advised funds. For tax years beginning after August 17, 2006, an organization's Form 990 must now include: (1) the total number of donor-advised funds it is managing; (2) the aggregate total assets held in its donor-advised funds; and (3) the aggregate contributions made to and distributions from its donor-advised funds. In light of these new reporting requirements, organizations sponsoring donor-advised funds should track and maintain their records to ensure complete Form 990s can be filed in future years.

(iii) Form 990, Heading.

p. 600. Insert at the end of the *"Gross Receipts"* bullet:

Each supporting organization must complete the rest of the return regardless of the size of its gross receipts. In addition, other public charities below the $25,000 gross receipts threshold must now file a Form 990-N, *Electronic Notice (e-Postcard) for Tax-Exempt Organizations Not Required To File Form 990 or 990-EZ* for tax periods beginning after December 31, 2006. An organization filing Form 990-N is required to provide the legal name of the organization, any other names the organization uses, its mailing address, Web site address (if applicable), identification number, the name and address of the principal officer, it's annual tax period, and a statement indicating its annual gross receipts are still normally $25,000 or less, and indicate if the organization is going out of business. Form 990-N can only be filed electronically. In lieu of filing Form 990-N, an organization can file Form 990 or 990-EZ provided it completes the entire return. An organization that does not meet its annual filing requirement for three consecutive years will have its tax-exempt status revoked by the IRS.

(v) Statement of Functional Expense.

p. 603. Insert the end of the *"Grants and Allocations"* **bullet:**

The revised Form 990 for 2005 requires organizations to disclose whether they make foreign grants.

p. 603. Insert at the end of the *"Compensation of officers, directors, etc."* **bullet:**

The revised Form 990 for 2005 requires that line 25 include compensation paid to former officers, directors, and key employees. The reporting organization must also include a schedule that provides the compensation paid to current and former officers, directors, and key employees by person and by functional expense category (program services, management and general, fundraising).

(vi) Statement of Program Service Accomplishments.

p. 603. Replace the *"Program service accomplishments"* **bullet with the following:**

- **Program service accomplishments**—are related to the activities carried out by the organization that form the basis for the organization's exempt status. Tax-exempt organizations are under scrutiny by donors, the media, the IRS, unions, and others. Health care organizations in particular have been under close scrutiny in the area of charity care and community benefit. It is more important than ever that organizations utilize Form 990 to provide the public with information regarding the charitable activities of the organization. For health care organizations, it is recommended that the organization's community benefit statement be incorporated within Form 990.

(ix) List of Officers, Directors, Trustees, and Key Employees.

p. 604. Insert at the end of the *"Compensation, contributions to employee benefit plans, and expense allowances"* **bullet:**

Form 990 and Schedule A for 2005 have been revised and require the reporting organization to disclose additional information in a variety of areas. Some of the main changes follow. Increased transparency is required in the area of compensation and related-party transactions. For example, compensation paid by the reporting organization to former officers, directors, and key employees must be disclosed. As well, organizations are required to disclose five additional services providers. The organization must also disclose any family/business relationships among the organization's top five highest-paid employees; the organization's top ten service providers; and the organization's officers, directors, and key employees. In addition, the threshold for reporting compensation paid to the officers, directors, and key employees by related organizations was reduced from $100,000 to $50,000. In the past it was required that reporting organizations report loans that they make to their officers, directors, and key employees. This requirement has been expanded to nonkey employees and vendors as well as to former officers, directors, and key employees.

(x) Other Information.

p. 605. Insert at the end of the *"Public inspection"* **bullet:**

In the past organizations were not required to make Form 990-T, "Exempt Organization Business Income Tax Return," available for public inspection. However, legislation passed as part of the Pension Protection Act of 2006 requires that organizations make their Form 990-T available to the public upon request. This provision is effective for organizations filing Form 990-T on or after August 17, 2006.

(xii) Information Regarding Taxable Subsidiaries and Disregarded Entities.

p. 606. Replace existing paragraph with the following paragraph:

This section requests information regarding taxable subsidiaries. This part of the form enables the IRS to monitor reporting of taxable income pursuant to §512(b)(13), which was updated by the Pension Protection Act of 2006 to apply to payments received or accrued after December 31, 2005, and before January 1, 2008, and only where the payment is made pursuant to a binding contract (or renewal of one) that was in effect on August 17, 2006. The new code section states that interest, annuities, royalties, and rents will constitute unrelated business income for the portion of payments made by a 50 percent controlled subsidiary to a tax-exempt parent organization that exceeds the fair market value (as determined in accordance with §482). For any tax returns due after August 17, 2006, tax-exempt organizations must report in this section their interest, rent, annuity, or royalty payments and loans or transfers from a controlled entity. This portion of the form will also allow the IRS to evaluate the extent to which organizations have taxable subsidiaries, in the event that Congress wishes to require exempt organizations to aggregate their activities.

(b) Form 990, Schedule A

(ii) Reason for Nonprivate Foundation Status.

p. 607. After the second bullet, insert the following bullet:

- §509(a)(3)—This category of public charity, called a supporting organization, does not meet a public support test. Instead, it achieves its public status by the close relationship it has with the charitable organization or organizations that it supports. Supporting organizations must now disclose whether they qualify as type I, II, or III.

∗p. 607. Replace the second sentence in the third bullet point with the following two sentences:

For 509(a)(1) organizations filing a 2007 or earlier Form 990 Schedule A, cumulative excessive contributions received during the previous four-year period are excluded from the public support calculation. For 509(a)(1) organizations filing a 2008 or later Form 990 Schedule A, cumulative excessive contributions received during the current and four previous years are excluded from the public support calculation.

(d) Form 990-PF, "Return of Private Foundation"

(viii) Statements Regarding Activities.

p. 612. Insert at the end of the "*Public inspection*" bullet:

Each Form 990-T filed after August 17, 2006, must also be disclosed upon request.

(ix) Statements Regarding Activities for Which Form 4720 May Be Required.

p. 612. Insert after the second sentence of the "*Expenditure responsibility*" bullet:

Grants or payments made after August 17, 2006, to a type III supporting organization that is not functionally integrated now require expenditure responsibility on the part of the private foundation.

(e) Form 990-T, "Exempt Organization Business Income Tax Return"

p. 614. Insert as second complete paragraph:

In the past, organizations were not required to make Form 990-T available for public inspection. However, the recently enacted Pension Protection Act of 2006 requires that organizations make their Form 990-T available to the public upon request. The Internal Revenue Service does not have authority to make these forms public. This provision is effective for organizations filing Form 990-T on or after August 17, 2006.

§ 28.10 STATE INFORMATION AND TAX REPORTING ISSUES

p. 615. Insert as last paragraph before *subsection (a):*

A majority of states also impose a tax on unrelated business income (UBI). Therefore, it is important for tax-exempt organizations to determine whether the state in which they operate imposes a tax on UBI.

Organizations should also consider whether the organization engages in activities in other states either directly or through investments in limited partnerships. As a partner invested in a limited partnership, a tax-exempt organization is subject to a tax on its federal UBI that is generated through a partnership investment. The organization may also be subject to state UBI tax obligations.

p. 616. Insert the following new *sections 28.11* and *28.12*:

§ 28.11 DONOR-ADVISED FUNDS (NEW)

As explained in the relevant legislative history, some charitable organizations, including community foundations, establish accounts to which donors may contribute and thereafter provide nonbinding advice or recommendations with regard to distributions from the fund or the investment of assets in the fund. These accounts are popularly referred to as donor-advised funds. In recent years, a number of financial institutions have formed charitable corporations for the purpose of offering donor-advised funds. Significantly, some established charities have begun operating donor-advised funds in addition to their primary activities. The IRS has recognized both of these types of funds as being included within the exemption for §501(c)(3) charitable organizations. Prior to the Pension Protection Act of 2006, the term *donor-advised fund* was not defined in statutes or regulations.

(a) Definition of Donor-Advised Fund

The Pension Protection Act of 2006 added a new code section to the Internal Revenue Code (IRC), which defines donor-advised funds. In general, IRC §4966(d)(2) defines a donor-advised fund as a fund or account:

1. That is separately identified by reference to contributions of a donor or donors
2. That is owned and controlled by a sponsoring organization
3. With respect to which a donor (or any person appointed or designated by such donor) has, or reasonably expects to have, advisory privileges with respect to the distribution or investment

of amounts held in such fund or account, by reason of the donor's status as a donor.

(b) Excise Taxes and Penalties

The IRC currently imposes excise taxes on excess benefit transactions between disqualified persons and charitable organizations (other than private foundations) or social welfare organizations. Additionally, the Code imposes excise taxes on private foundations and their disqualified persons in a variety of situations: self-dealing between a disqualified person and a private foundation; failure to distribute income by private nonoperating foundations; excess business holdings; investments that jeopardize the foundation's charitable purpose; and taxable expenditures.

The Pension Protection Act of 2006 immediately subjects donor advised funds to IRC §4958 [see section 28.2(c)] relating to excess benefit transactions and applies the private foundation IRC §4943 [see section 28.5(c)] relating to excess business holdings to donor-advised funds for taxable years beginning after August 17, 2006. In addition, two new excise tax sections specific to donor-advised funds were added to the Code. They are IRC §4966, relating to taxable distributions, and IRC §4967, relating to prohibited benefits. The excise tax imposed under IRC §4967 is effective for taxable years beginning after August 17, 2006, and will not apply if the tax under IRC §4958 has been imposed.

The new donor-advised fund excise taxes that can be imposed on donors, donor advisors, related persons, sponsoring organizations, and fund managers are substantial. For taxable expenditures made by a donor-advised fund, IRC §4966 imposes a tax equal to 20 percent of the taxable expenditure on the sponsoring organization and a 5 percent tax on any fund manager who agreed to make the distribution knowing that it was a taxable distribution. For prohibited benefits received by a donor, donor advisor, or related person from a donor-advised fund, IRC §4967 imposes a tax equal to 125 percent of the prohibited benefit on the donor, donor advisor, or related person and a 10 percent tax on any fund manager who agreed to make a distribution from a donor-advised fund, knowing that such distribution would confer a prohibited benefit to the donor, donor advisor, or related person.

(c) Return Reporting Requirements

New information return disclosure requirements were enacted with the Pension Protection Act of 2006. For annual returns filed for tax years beginning after August 17, 2006, a sponsoring organization's return must now include: (1) the total number of donor-advised funds it is managing; (2) the aggregate total assets held in its donor-advised funds; and (3) the aggregate contributions made to and distributions made from its donor-advised funds.

In addition, new applications for exempt status submitted on Form 1023 after August 17, 2006, by sponsoring organizations that intend to maintain donor-advised funds must give notice that they intend to do so. Such notice must also describe how the sponsoring organization will maintain such funds.

Given that this disclosure of donor-advised fund information on a sponsoring organization's annual return will be subject to public inspection, each existing sponsoring organization should immediately begin to track and maintain its records so that the required donor-advised fund data and information on future annual returns can be reported.

(d) Substantiation of Sponsoring Organization Control

A donor making an allowable charitable contribution to a donor-advised fund must now obtain contemporaneous written acknowledgment from the sponsoring organization affirmatively stating that the sponsoring organization has exclusive legal control over the contributed assets. Such written acknowledgment is similar to the current acknowledgment requirement from an organization for contributions received of $250 or more—IRC §170(f)(8).

Each sponsoring organization should incorporate this new provision into its current written gift acknowledgment procedures to help it and its donors meet this written substantiation requirement.

§ 28.12 NEW RESTRICTIONS ON SUPPORTING ORGANIZATIONS (NEW)

The Pension Protection Act of 2006 amended the tax code to provide multiple reforms and new restrictions to supporting organizations defined under §509(a)(3). The main changes are as follows.

(a) Restrictions Applicable to All Supporting Organizations

The following rules apply to type I, type II, and type III supporting organizations:

1. *Expanded definition of disqualified person.* Any person who is a disqualified person with respect to any type of supporting organization will now also be a disqualified person with respect to its supported organization(s)—effective August 17, 2006.

2. *No payments to contributors.* Grants, loans, compensation, or similar payments (including reimbursement of expenses) may not be made to a supporting organization's substantial contributors or to members of their family or businesses they control—effective July 25, 2006. If such a payment is made, the entire payment will be considered an automatic excess benefit transaction and taxed accordingly.

3. *No loans to any disqualified person.* Loans are not permitted to any disqualified person, including foundation managers (officers, directors, trustees of the supporting organization)—effective July 25, 2006.

4. *More information required on Form 990.* The Form 990 for each supporting organization must now list all supported organizations and indicate what type of supporting organization (I, II, or III) the filer is. The filer must also certify that it is not controlled directly or indirectly by disqualified persons (other than those who are disqualified solely by being an organization manager)—effective for Forms 990 filed after August 17, 2006.

(b) Restrictions Applicable Only to Types I and II Supporting Organizations

The following rule applies to types I and III supporting organizations: A charity will not be able to qualify as a type I or type III supporting organization if it accepts a gift from a person who directly or indirectly controls one of its supported organizations—effective August 17, 2006.

(c) Restrictions Applicable Only to Type III Supporting Organizations

The new law creates two different versions of type III supporting organizations—those that are "functionally integrated" and those that are not. A functionally integrated type III supporting organization is one "which is not required to make payments to supported organizations due to the activities of the [type III] organization related to performing the functions of, or carrying out the purposes of, such supported organizations." No type III supporting organizations may support a foreign organization. The following rules apply to type III supporting organizations that are not functionally integrated:

1. *Minimum payout.* The secretary of the Treasury is directed to adopt regulations that create a minimum annual charitable distribution (or payout) requirement for type III supporting organizations (other than those that are functionally integrated) to be based on a percentage of either income or assets—effective August 17, 2006.

2. *Excess business holdings.* The IRC §4943 private foundation rules limiting the degree of ownership of any business enterprise are now applied to type III supporting organizations that are not functionally integrated (effective for tax years beginning after August 17, 2006).

On August 3, 2007, the Department of the Treasury issued a Notice of Advance Rule-Making (REG-155929-06) requesting public comment on rules it intends to propose as regulations. This Notice included a description of: (a) criteria for determining whether type III supporting organization is functionally integrated and adding two additional tests that must be met; (b) the payout requirement for nonfunctionally integrated supporting organizations; (3) modified requirements for type III supporting organizations organized as trusts; and (4) requirements regarding the type of information a type III supporting organization must provide to its supported organizations. It is expected that Treasury will publish proposed regulations on these issues in 2009.

CHAPTER TWENTY-NINE

Audits of Federally Funded Programs

§ 29.1 BASIC REQUIREMENTS

(a) Historical Context

p. 618. Add the following as the last paragraph in *subsection (a):*

The Compliance Supplement is typically updated in its entirety on an annual basis.

The OMB did not completely revise the Compliance Supplement in 2008. Refer to the OMB's web site at www.whitehouse.gov/omb/circulars/a133_compliance/08/08toc.html for the 2008 Compliance Supplement. A detailed description of the changes from the prior version of the Compliance Supplement is included in Appendix 5 of the 2008 Compliance Supplement.

§ 29.3 RESPONSIBILITIES OF THE RECEIVING ORGANIZATION

(a) Compliance with Laws, Regulations, and Other Matters

p. 624. Modify the last sentence in the discussion of compliance requirement B, "Allowable Costs/Cost Principles":

Costs must be net of all applicable credits and must be documented in accordance with federal requirements, specifically in accordance with OMB Circulars A-21, *Cost Principles for Educational Institutions;* A-87, *Cost Principles for State, Local, and Indian Tribal Governments;* A-110, *Uniform Administrative Requirements for Grants and Other Agreements with Institutions of Higher Education, Hospitals, and Other Non-Profit Organizations;* and A-122, *Cost Principles for Non-Profit Organizations,* as applicable.

p. 625. Modify the last sentence in the discussion of compliance requirement I, "Procurement and Suspension and Debarment":

A listing of these companies can be found on the Excluded Parties List System, which can be accessed on the Internet at www.epls.gov.

§ 29.4 WHAT TO EXPECT FROM THE AUDIT

(a) How Is It Different from a Financial Statement Audit?

p. 628. Modify the last paragraph at the end of *subsection (a)* to read as follows:

In 2003, the Government Accountability Office (GAO) issued several revisions to the Government Auditing Standards (GAS—the "Yellow Book") to strengthen and streamline these auditing standards and provide for consistent application of GAS to the various types of audits such as financial, performance, and attestation. The 2003 revisions include significantly expanded standards as they relate to performance of audit and nonaudit services.

In 2007, the GAO further revised the Yellow Book to reflect the changing audit environment in which greater transparency and accountability are expected from auditors and organizations. The 2007 revisions, which are part of the GAO's overall objective, "supporting the Congress and the nation in facing the challenges of a rapidly changing world while addressing the nation's large and growing long-term fiscal imbalance," were comprehensive. Changes include the following:

- Clarified language to distinguish between auditor requirements and guidance/explanatory material.

- Heightened emphasis on ethical principles, devoting an entire chapter to such principles.

- Clarified and streamlined the discussion of nonaudit services and added guidance on required actions if an independence impairment is identified after issuance of an audit report.

- Stressed the role of professional judgment and emphasized the role of competence in performing an audit and reporting the findings and conclusions.

- Incorporated the revised continuing professional education (CPE) requirements, issued by GAO in April 2005, and clarified the CPE requirement includes internal specialists who perform as a member of the audit team.

- Discusses clarifications and changes related to an audit organization's quality control.

- Defined those charged with governance consistent with SAS No. 114, *The Auditor's Communication with Those Charged with Governance*.

- Clarified reporting requirements for internal control deficiencies, fraud, illegal acts, violations of provisions of contracts or grant agreements, and abuse.

- Adopted recent developments in auditing standards, including SAS No. 103, *Audit Documentation*, and SAS No. 112, *Communication of Internal Control Related Matters Noted in an Audit*. The adoption of SAS 112 replaces the terms *reportable condition* and *material weakness* with the terms *significant deficiency* and *material weakness* as those terms are defined in SAS 112.

- Added requirements for reporting on the restatement of previously issued financial statements.

- Expanded discussion of the use of "matter of emphasis" paragraphs in auditor reports to encourage communication of significant concerns, uncertainties, or other unusual or catastrophic events that could have a significant impact on the financial condition or operations of a government entity or program for financial audits.

- Expanded and updated performance auditing standards.

- Added an appendix to provide supplemental guidance to assist auditors in the implementation of generally accepted government auditing standards (GAGAS) to assist auditors in their work.

Visit the GAO Web site for up-to-date information concerning GAS at www.gao.gov.

(c) What Does an Organization Do If the Auditor Finds Something?

p. 630. Add at the end of *subsection (c):*

Organizations receiving federal funds should be cognizant of Statement of Auditing Standards No. 112, *Communicating Internal Control Related Matters Identified in an Audit,* which is discussed in Chapter 24. Although SAS 112 does not address federal award audits directly, the new process of evaluating deficiencies in accordance with the Standard is expected to be applied to these audits as well. This is expected to have the effect of "lowering the bar" with regard to which deficiencies are deemed to be either significant deficiencies or material weaknesses, which would be appropriate for the auditor to include in the *Report of Independent Auditors on Internal Control over Financial Reporting and on Compliance and Other Matters Based on an Audit of Financial Statements Performed in Accordance with Government Audit Standards.*

Deficiencies that are noted in this report could cast management in a negative light and could also lead funding sources to question costs.

As noted above, the GAO issued a revised "Yellow Book" that includes the same definitions for significant deficiencies and material weaknesses as are in the SAS. In addition, the OMB issued a Federal Register Notice in June 2007, which replaces references in OMB Circular A-133 to "reportable condition" and "material weakness" with the terms *significant deficiency* and *material weakness* as those terms are defined in SAS 112 and the Yellow Book.

*p. 630. Add new *subsection (d)* before *section 29.5*:

(d) Filing the Data Collection Form (New)

On August 22, 2008, the Federal Audit Clearinghouse (FAC) implemented a new submission process for Data Collection Forms (DCFs) and related Single Audit reporting packages via the new Internet Data Entry System (IDES). The DCF itself was edited to include minor changes, which are detailed below. The most significant change is that the submission process is now fully electronic, which will require additional coordination between engagement leaders and our clients.

The new submission process is effective for fiscal periods ending in 2008 or later and the IDES system will be used to accomplish the following tasks:

- Enter a Form SF-SAC data online.
- Check Form SF-SAC data for errors using the "Check Data" feature.
- Upload a PDF copy of the Single Audit reporting package.
- Certify Form SF-SAC electronically using a signature code provided by the IDES.
- Submit complete certified Form SF-SAC and Single Audit reporting package to the Federal Audit Clearinghouse electronically.

(i) New Online Submission Process. The most significant change incorporated into the DCF submission process is the requirement that the DCF and Single Audit reporting packages be submitted online. The FAC will no longer accept any paper submissions. The new submission process requires the DCF be submitted online using the IDES. Further, after the DCF passes all edits, an electronic PDF containing the reporting package must be attached.

To use the system, both the client and the auditor will need to utilize their email accounts to obtain certification codes and will also need the ability to upload a PDF file to the IDES. In order to complete the upload, cookies[3.1] must be enabled to allow for proper data transfer between the computer and the IDES. Instructions on how to enable cookies are provided in the detailed IDES instructions.

The process for submission of the DCF and Single Audit reporting packages for fiscal periods ending on or after January 1, 2008, are as follows:

Step	Client Responsibility	Auditor Responsibility
1. Create an online report ID and password using the IDES Introductory Page at the FAC web site: http://harvester.census.gov/fac/collect/ddeindex.html or link to the site from the FAC home page: http://harvester.census.gov/fac.	Client should start this process and communicate report ID and password to PwC once created.	N/A
2. As part of the form creation process e-mail addresses will need to be entered for the auditor and auditee certifying officials. These	Client should start this process.	The auditor should communicate the certifying audit partner to the client.

---

*3.1. Cookies are parcels of text sent by a *server* to a *web client* (usually a *browser*) and then sent back unchanged by the client each time it accesses that server. Cookies are used for *authenticating*, session tracking, and maintaining specific information about users.

Step	Client Responsibility	Auditor Responsibility
officials should include the audit partner on the engagement and the client contact who typically signs the DCF. Additional e-mails can be entered if other users should be notified of actions taken on this particular submission. These e-mails will be used in Step 6.		
3. Complete the DCF—this part of the process is unchanged.	Client completes Part I (except Item 7) and typically lists the federal awards expended in Part III.	Auditor completes Part I, Item 7; Part II; and Part III (except client typically lists the federal awards expended). Please note, however, that in some instances the client completes the full DCF and the auditors review it, which is still acceptable.
4. Check all inputs using the Check Data feature, as done previously.	This can be completed by either the auditor or the client.	This can be completed by either the auditor or the client.
5. Complete component checklist: Locate and open the Single Audit reporting package to be uploaded and find the page numbers as they appear in the PDF version that correspond to the various components in the checklist.	This can be completed by either the auditor or the client.	This can be completed by either the auditor or the client.
6. Upload the Single Audit reporting package.	N/A	The auditor should upload the final published A-133 report to ensure the final version is appropriately attached. This version

Step	Client Responsibility	Auditor Responsibility
		must be in a PDF format that can be opened, read, and edited.[3.2,3.3]
7. Certify the submission. The SF-SAC form will need to be certified by both the client and the auditor. This process replaces the manual signatures completed previously.	• Click the "Certify Form SF-SAC" button from the Main Menu. • Click the "Send Emails" button. The system will send an e-mail to the certifying officials containing instructions to certify the form. • The clients' certifying official will need to log into the submission using the Report ID and password. • They will click the "Certify Form SF-SAC" button from the Main Menu. • The client will click the "Auditee Certification" button. • Client will review the Form SF-SAC and the reporting package for accuracy. • Client will review their respective Certification Statements. • The client will enter their name and title.	• The certifying audit partner will need to log into the submission using the Report ID and password. • They will click the "Certify Form SF-SAC" button from the Main Menu. • The certifying audit partner will click the "Auditor Certification" button. • The certifying audit partner will review the Form SF-SAC and the reporting package for accuracy. • The certifying audit partner will review Certification Statements. • The certifying audit partner will enter their name and title.

---

*3.2. The only purpose of editing would be for the FAC to attach a revised version of the report to the original if a revised report were to be issued in the future for any type of correction to the original report. At the request of the AICPA GAQC executive committee, the Clearinghouse is looking into an alternative to needing an editable PDF file. Further alerts on this topic are expected in late 2008 or early 2009.

*3.3. Please note that since only one PDF can be uploaded, the clients' Corrective Action Plan should be included with the A-133 report. This is practice is common (and preferred), but those who send in separate responses will need to include their Corrective Action Plan with the Single Audit reporting package.

Step	Client Responsibility	Auditor Responsibility
	• Client will enter a unique signature code provided in the e-mail sent to them. • If the auditee agrees to the certification statement, then he/she should click the "Agree to Auditee Certification Statement" button to complete their certification of the Form SF-SAC.	• The certifying audit partner will enter a unique signature code provided in the e-mail sent to them. • If the certifying audit partner agrees to the certification statement, then he/she should click the "Agree to Auditor Certification Statement" button to complete their certification of the Form SF-SAC.
8. If information presented is not correct and either the auditee or the auditor does not certify the information, please see the instructions to the right. Once changes have been made, the certification process will need to be run again. 9. Click "Submit." After both the auditor and auditee certifying officials have certified the Form SFSAC, the checklist will show that both the auditor and auditee certifying officials have certified the Form SF-SAC. An e-mail will be mailed to all representative e-mail addresses as confirmation of the submission.	If the auditee does not agree to the certification statement, then he/she should click the "Reject Auditee Certification Statement" button to dispute the contents of the Form SF-SAC or the reporting package and contact the auditor to discuss making changes. Either party can perform this step.	If the auditor does not agree to the certification statement, then he/she should click the "Reject Auditor Certification Statement" button to dispute the contents of the Form SF-SAC or the reporting package and contact the auditee to discuss making changes. Either party can perform this step.

For additional step-by-step details, please see the link to the full instructions in the "Additional Information" section below. If the form cannot be completed in one session, you may exit the online form and reenter at another time. In order to revisit the online form, you must use your report ID and password.

(ii) Other Items to Note.

- *Passwords.* Passwords to access the DCF are much more complex than previously required and must contain at least 12 non-blank characters, which include:
  - English uppercase characters (A ... Z)
  - English lowercase characters (a ... z)
  - Base 10 digits (0 ... 9)
  - Non-alphanumeric special characters (!, $, #, %)
  - Six of the characters must only occur once in the password
- *Special characters.* A useful method in creating a password to meet these criteria is to insert the special character(s) in place of the letters they resemble. The following examples were provided by the FAC for guidance:
  - MYcompany2%08
  - $anDiegoCharger$#1
  - myFir$tName08
- *Submissions for years ending in 2007 or prior.* The previous version of the DCF will be used for audit periods ending in 2004, 2005, 2006, and 2007 and can be accessed on the FAC web site by clicking on the DCF options link. The final form must be printed, signed, and mailed with the Single Audit reporting package in hardcopy format, as completed previously.
- *Revisions of previous submissions.* Please refer to the links related to the IDE Instruction Booklet and 2008 Single Audit Submission Questions and Answers attached below for additional details.

The electronic submission is new and while relatively straightforward and self-explanatory, still has the potential to be challenging from a coordination standpoint, especially during the first year of use.

(iii) Changes to the DCF Form. The 2008–2010 version of the DCF remains largely unchanged. Two items of particular note are as follows:

1. *Change in terminology.* The term *reportable condition* has been changed to *significant deficiency* in Part II, Items 3 and 4, and Part III, Items 4 and 5 to be consistent with changes made in 2007 to OMB Circular A-133, *Audits of States, Local Governments, and Non-Profit Organizations.*

2. *Secondary auditor information may be entered.* The primary auditor may choose to enter contact information for secondary audit organizations used in conducting the audit work. For instance, for some organizations DCAA performs some of the R&D cluster compliance work. It is recommended that, if applicable, secondary auditor information be entered in order to document the division of responsibility between the lead auditor and the secondary auditor.

(iv) Additional Information.

- Federal Audit Clearinghouse web site: **http://harvester.census .gov/fac/index.html?submit = Return+to+FAC+Home+Page**
- Internet Data Entry System: **http://harvester.census.gov/fac/ collect/ddeindex.html**
- IDE Instruction Booklet: **http://harvester.census.gov/fac/ collect08/main_instruct.pdf**
- 2008 Single Audit Submission Questions and Answers: **http:// harvester.census.gov/fac/2008SAQA.htm**

Accounting and Disclosure Guide for Not-for-Profit Organizations

C. Assets

p. 722. Replace item *C 30* with the following:

30.   Have the provisions of SFAS 144 (Impairment) been complied with?

p. 722. Add new item *C 30A:*

30A.   Have conditional asset retirement obligations under FIN 47 been recorded and disclosed?

D. Liabilities and Net Assets

p. 723. Replace item *D 31(d)* with the following:

31.   Are the following disclosed?

    d.   Employee benefits (SFAS 87, 106, 112—but also consider SFAS 132(R) and 158)

p. 723. Replace item *D 34* with the following:

34.   Are compensated absences, including sabbatical leave, properly accounted for (SFAS 143 and EITF 06- 02)?

*APPENDIX D

Summary of Emerging Accounting, Tax, and Regulatory Issues for Not-for-Profit Organizations in 2008 (New)

Each year, PricewaterhouseCoopers develops a *Summary of Emerging Issues for Not-for-Profit Organizations* for our audit clients and their audit committees. The *Summary* includes a discussion of the accounting, financial reporting, tax, and regulatory compliance issues that we believe are likely to affect our not-for-profit clients. The 2008 *Summary* that follows in Appendix D starts with an update on emerging issues for organizations that follow FASB pronouncements. We then have some discussion of the Uniform Prudent Management of Institutional Funds Act, referred to as UPMIFA, as well as an update to American Institute of Certified Public Accountants (AICPA), Governmental Accounting Standards Board (GASB), and emerging regulatory compliance and tax issues.

Of course, it is the nature of "emerging" issues to keep evolving, and so the status of many of the issues discussed in our 2008 *Summary* has changed. The 2008 *Summary* was current as of early April 2008.

In the first half of 2009, we plan to publish our 2009 *Summary of Emerging Issues for Not-for-Profit Organizations*. Interested readers will find our 2009 Summary on our web site at www.pwc.com this spring. Because the 2008 emerging issues also will continue to evolve, this

Summary includes web site addresses so that interested readers can follow the evolution of the emerging issues until we publish our 2009 *Summary*.

EXECUTIVE SUMMARY

PricewaterhouseCoopers is pleased to bring you this year's edition of our *Summary of Emerging Issues*. The accounting, financial reporting, tax, and regulatory compliance issues described in this summary have been specifically tailored to concentrate on areas of interest to not-for-profit organizations and governmental business-type activities. Once again, we have divided the summary into six areas of relevance: FASB, GASB, AICPA, Other Issues, Regulatory, and Tax.

In the past year, there have been a number of FASB developments affecting not-for-profit organizations, and we expect the coming year to be particularly challenging as organizations begin to adopt two new fair value standards, FASB Statement No. 157, *Fair Value Measurements*, and FASB Statement No. 159, *The Fair Value Option for Financial Assets and Financial Liabilities.* In addition, organizations will continue to face challenges as they apply the "Day 2" accounting and measurement date provisions under FASB Statement No. 158, *Employers' Accounting for Defined Benefit Pension and Other Postretirement Plans.* The FASB is also working to have a proposed FSP related to the Uniform Prudent Management of Institutional Funds Act of 2006 (UPMIFA) finalized and effective for June 30, 2008, year-ends, which, by all appearances, will increase the required disclosures for all endowments, not just those in states affected by UPMIFA.

A major development expected mid-year 2008 for governmental enterprises will be the issuance of the GASB's final standard on derivatives, which will require all governmental organizations to report derivatives at fair value in the Balance Sheet. This comes at a time when governments are also wrestling with implementing the provisions of GASB Statement No. 45, *Accounting and Financial Reporting by Employers for Postemployment Benefits Other Than Pensions.* Additionally, those organizations must deal with new standards on accounting for intangible assets and valuation of certain endowment investments.

The topics included in the "Other Issues" section of this year's summary include the implications of the credit crunch for both the municipal bond market and for investment portfolios of not-for-profit and governmental entities. The credit crunch has been felt throughout the economy, and, in particular, we are seeing its ripple effects on the municipal market. Also discussed are the implications of International Financial Reporting Standards (IFRS) for U.S. standard setting, the proposed new Electronic Municipal Market Access (EMMA) disclosure system for municipal bond issuers, and FASB's project to codify and simplify U.S. generally accepted accounting principles (GAAP).

With respect to regulatory compliance issues, certain issues such as effort reporting, conflict of interest, and export regulations continue to be considered by federal agencies as needing further attention. In addition, new areas with heightened concern such as student loan preferred lender lists and prohibited inducements have surfaced in the past year. These issues and more, as well as updates to the regulatory audit literature, such as the OMB Compliance Supplement and an AICPA interpretation of SAS 112 related to internal controls over compliance with federal award compliance areas are further described in the Regulatory Issues section of this summary.

With respect to tax issues in 2008, the Internal Revenue Service (IRS) released the redesigned 2008 Form 990, *Return of Organization Exempt from Income Tax*, one of the largest projects undertaken by the IRS with respect to exempt organization initiatives in recent history. The redesign is the first comprehensive overhaul of the Form 990 in 30 years. Organizations will begin using the redesigned form for years beginning in 2008, and fiscal year taxpayers will use the new form for years ending in 2009.

The IRS continues to focus on tax-exempt bonds. In 2007 the IRS issued a post-issuance compliance questionnaire to approximately 200 exempt organizations. The questionnaire focused on compliance with record retention rules, private use limitations and arbitrage rebate requirements. The IRS is analyzing responses to these questionnaires and may issue the questionnaire to a wider universe of organizations in 2008 or decide on additional taxpayer assistance and/or enforcement initiatives that should be implemented.

With the upcoming presidential election, it is difficult to predict with certainty the level of emphasis that Congress will place on issues affecting the not-for-profit community. Higher education endowments and the practices of not-for-profit hospitals continue to be areas of focus.

Contributors to this year's *Summary of Emerging Issues* have included John A. Mattie, Paul Hanley, Ralph DeAcetis, Kaye Ferriter, Martha Garner, Tom Gaudrault, Gwen Spencer, Michael George, Steve Luber, Dave Merriam, Shannon Smith, Jocelyn Bishop, Erin Couture, and Jeff Thomas.

Note that we have excerpted some text in this summary from the FASB's and GASB's web sites as well as from other internal sources. Also, because the issues in this Summary are emerging, their status is subject to frequent changes. The latest status of these issues can be found on the following web sites:

- AICPA (www.aicpa.org/)
- FASB (www.fasb.org/)
- GAO (www.gao.gov)
- GASB (www.gasb.org/)
- IRS (www.irs.gov). In particular, see the section for "Charities & Non-Profits."
- OMB (www.whitehouse.gov/omb)

If you have questions about any of the issues in this summary, contact your PricewaterhouseCoopers' engagement team.

TABLE OF CONTENTS

I. FASB PRONOUNCEMENTS AND ACTIVITIES

The following section highlights FASB pronouncements and activities that are already effective (or will be effective in the near future), along with our observations as to how they will impact not-for-profit organizations. We also include several recent Emerging Issues Task Force (EITF) issues and exposure drafts that may impact those organizations.

Pronouncements, Staff Positions, and Interpretations

FASB Statement No. 161 (FAS 161), *Disclosures about Derivative Instruments and Hedging Activities.* FAS 161, which was issued in March 2008, amends and expands the disclosure requirements in FASB Statement No. 133 (FAS 133), *Accounting for Derivative Instruments and Hedging Activities* and related literature. Those disclosures had been criticized for not being transparent enough to allow financial statement users to assess a reporting entity's overall risk from derivatives from both a quantitative and qualitative perspective. FAS 161's requirements are aimed at providing users of financial statements with an enhanced understanding of how and why an entity uses derivative instruments; how derivative instruments and related hedged items are accounted for under FAS 133 and its related interpretations; and how derivative instruments affect an entity's financial position, results of operations/changes in net assets, and cash flows. FAS 161 also amends SOP 02-2, *Accounting for Derivative Instruments and Hedging Activities by Not-for-Profit Health Care Organizations, and Clarification of the Performance Indicator,* to require the disclosure of where and in what financial statement captions derivative gains and losses are displayed. FAS 161 focuses only on disclosures; it does not change any of FAS 133's accounting or financial statement presentation guidance.

Among other things, FAS 161 requires that organizations provide disclosure in a tabular format of the Balance Sheet captions in which derivatives are reported and the fair value amounts of derivative instruments reported in those captions. Similar disclosures are required for the location and amounts of gains and losses reported in the statement of activities/statement of operations. The latter requires separate categories for derivatives designated and qualifying as fair value hedges, those designated and qualifying as cash flow hedges (for health care organizations), those not designated or not qualifying as hedging instruments, and other categories, if applicable. Within each of the categories, separate line items should further categorize derivatives by purpose (i.e., the item being hedged or the exposure created). For not-for-profit organizations, the disclosure requirements are tailored to FAS 117's not-for-profit reporting model.

Simplified examples of certain of the tabular disclosures are provided in the tables for a hypothetical not-for-profit organization whose only derivatives are interest rate swaps tied to debt. Table D.1. illustrates the Balance Sheet tabular disclosure requirements. With respect to the tabular disclosures of gains and losses reported in the statement of activities/statement of operations, Table D.2 illustrates the disclosures for non-hedging derivatives. (For a not-for-profit health care organization, the disclosure should indicate the amount of gain (loss) recognized in the performance indicator, rather than in changes in net assets.) The disclosure must also provide information about derivatives that are designated as fair value hedges and, for a not-for-profit health care organization, for derivatives designated as cash flow hedges. Table D.3 illustrates the tabular cash flow hedging disclosures for a not-for-profit health care organization. Not-for-profit organizations also are required to indicate which class or classes of net assets (unrestricted, temporarily restricted, or permanently restricted) are affected.

Because derivative agreements may have contingency features which give the counterparty a right to terminate the instrument at fair value or demand additional collateral from the organization upon occurrence of a specified triggering event such as a credit downgrade, the standard requires quantitative disclosure about the potential cash outflows that would be required upon the occurrence of certain credit-related events. This is to improve disclosure of the potential impact such features could have on an organization's liquidity. Disclosures related to the volume of derivatives activity must be provided. Additionally, the qualitative disclosures currently encouraged in paragraph 44 of FAS 133 have been clarified to focus on an entity's market risks and strategies to manage those risks.

FAS 161 is effective for fiscal periods beginning after November 15, 2008, and should be applied on a prospective basis (i.e., it does not require comparative information for periods presented prior to the adoption date), with early application encouraged. The disclosures are required for both interim and annual periods.

TABLE D.1

Fair Values of Derivative Instruments

As of December 31	Derivatives Reported as Assets				Derivatives Reported as Liabilities			
	2009		**2008**		**2009**		**2008**	
	Bal. Sheet Caption	*Fair Value*	*Bal. Sheet Caption*	*Fair Value*	*Bal. Sheet Caption*	*Fair Value*	*Bal. Sheet Caption*	*Fair Value*
Interest rate swaps designated as hedging instruments under FAS 133	Other Assets	XX,XXX	Other Assets	XX,XXX	Other Liab.	XX,XXX	Other Liab.	XX,XXX
Interest rate swaps not designated as hedging instruments under FAS 133	Other Assets	XX,XXX		XX,XXX	Other Liab.	XX,XXX		XX,XXX
Total Derivatives		XX,XXX		XX,XXX		XX,XXX		XX,XXX

TABLE D.2

Derivatives not designated as hedging instruments under FAS 133:		
Classification of derivative gain (loss) in Statement of Activities	Amount of gain (loss) recognized in change in unrestricted net assets	
	2009	*2008*
Interest rate swaps: Nonoperating revenue	XX,XXX	XX,XXX

PwC Observation: Recent market events involving bond insurer and issuer downgrades, swap counterparty downgrades, and swap terminations (see the section entitled "Credit Market Events—Municipal Bond Market") highlight the importance of the new disclosures, given the prevalent use of interest rate swaps by not-for-profit organizations in connection with variable-rate debt issuances. In particular, the importance of the new disclosures related to contingent feature provisions (e.g., involuntary terminations due to counterparty credit downgrades) are highlighted in light of the significant impact such features can have on an organization's liquidity.

FASB Statement No. 159 (FAS 159), *The Fair Value Option for Financial Assets and Financial Liabilities.*

FASB STATEMENT NO. 155 (FAS 155), *ACCOUNTING FOR CERTAIN HYBRID FINANCIAL INSTRUMENTS*

Prior to FASB's issuance of FAS 155 and 159, only a limited range of financial assets and liabilities could be measured at fair value in financial statements. Now, those two FASB statements provide organizations with the option to measure many of their financial assets and liabilities at fair value, if desired. This "fair value option" represents a significant step in the evolution of financial reporting because it considerably expands an organization's ability to select the measurement attribute it uses for certain assets and liabilities, and, in many cases, offers an opportunity to simplify the accounting for these assets and liabilities.

TABLE D.3

Derivatives in FAS 133 Cash Flow Hedging Relationships:

Classification of derivative gain (loss) in Statement of Operations	Amount of gain (loss) recognized in the PI (ineffective portion)		Classification of gain (loss) reclassified from below to above PI	Amount of gain (loss) reclassified from below to above the PI (effective portion)		Amount of gain (loss) recognized outside the PI (effective portion)	
	2009	2008		2009	2008	2009	2008
Interest rate swaps: Non-operating revenue	XX,XXX	XX,XXX	Interest income (expense)	XX,XXX	XX,XXX	XX,,XXX	XX,XXX

Issued in 2006, FAS 155 was a narrow-scope standard that made the fair value option available for certain hybrid financial instruments containing an embedded derivative that would otherwise require bifurcation. FAS 155 allows an entity to irrevocably elect to initially and subsequently measure the hybrid financial instrument in its entirety at fair value, in lieu of requiring bifurcation of the embedded derivative.

PwC Observation: If an organization has hybrid financial instruments, the benefit of adopting FAS 155 is simplification—in many instances, valuing the embedded derivative separately from its host contract is more complicated than measuring the entire hybrid instrument at fair value. For example, certain forms of split-interest agreements can have derivatives embedded in the obligation to other beneficiaries. A not-for-profit organization can avoid having to bifurcate (i.e., separately account for) the derivative by electing the fair value option for the hybrid instrument (i.e., by electing to carry the obligation to other beneficiaries at fair value). In this case, fair value measurement could be achieved simply by using a current discount rate in a present value-based calculation of the obligation.

FAS 155 is effective for fiscal years beginning after September 15, 2006; thus, organizations with June 30 fiscal year-ends that did not early adopt FAS 155 still have the ability to elect the fair value option on an instrument-by-instrument basis for hybrid financial instruments that had been bifurcated prior to adoption of the Statement. The effect of adoption should be reported as a cumulative-effect adjustment to the opening balance of the appropriate net asset classes. For all other organizations, the FAS 155 fair value option can be elected only for existing hybrid financial instruments subject to a remeasurement event (as defined in FAS 155) and for new hybrid financial instruments acquired or issued.

FAS 159, which was issued in February 2007, extended the availability of the fair value option to a wide range of financial instruments—both assets and liabilities. An organization may irrevocably elect to apply the fair value option to eligible financial assets and liabilities acquired or issued subsequent to adoption of the standard. The election is also available when a previously recognized asset or liability is subject to a "remeasurement event" as defined in paragraph 8 of FAS 159. FAS 159 generally permits organizations to apply the fair value

TABLE D.4

Assets and Liabilities Eligible/Ineligible for the Fair Value Option

Eligible	Not Eligible
• Debt and equity securities accounted for in accordance with FAS 124*	• Investments in consolidated subsidiaries
• Investments accounted for under the equity method	• Employer benefit–related obligations and assets
• Investments carried at cost	• Financial assets and financial liabilities recognized pursuant to leases
• Multiyear promises to give	
• Split interest agreements without embedded derivatives	
• Beneficial interests in trusts	
• Debt	
• Interest rate swaps*	

*Because these assets and liabilities are already measured at fair value, adoption of the fair value option would only impact income statement geography for health care organizations.

option on an instrument-by-instrument basis, with some exceptions. Table D.4 provides examples of financial assets and liabilities that are or are not eligible for the fair value measurement election under FAS 159.

Under both FAS 159 and FAS 155, not-for-profit health care organizations report unrealized gains and losses on items for which the fair value option has been elected within the performance indicator or as a part of discontinued operations, as appropriate. For all other not-for-profit organizations, the unrealized gains and losses are reported as changes in net assets or discontinued operations, as appropriate. If the organization reports an intermediate measure of operations, it may report the gains and losses either within or outside that measure.

PwC Observation: The fair value option affords organizations an opportunity to simplify their accounting in certain circumstances. For example:

- Currently, not-for-profit organizations initially record multiyear promises receivable at fair value and subsequently amortize them using the same discount rate used in the initial fair value calculation. The same is true for obligations to beneficiaries reported under certain types of split-interest agreements. In those situations, the need to track and use an array of historical discount rates complicates the recordkeeping required for subsequent accounting and reporting. Electing the fair value option would allow an organization to abandon the myriad of historical discount rates and simply use the current discount rate in performing present-value-based calculations for all designated instruments.

- For not-for-profit health care organizations, election of the fair value option on marketable equity securities accounted for under FASB Statement No. 124 (FAS 124), *Accounting for Certain Investments Held by Not-for-Profit Organizations*, may simplify record keeping and result in more symmetrical accounting for gains and losses. According to the audit and accounting guide "Health Care Organizations" (AAG-HCO), recognized gains and losses (including other-than-temporary impairment losses) are included in the performance indicator, while unrealized gains and losses are excluded. If a health care organization has significant unrealized losses deemed to be other-than-temporarily impaired, such losses are required to be reclassified above the performance indicator, while all unrealized gains remain below the performance indicator. Election of the fair value option would eliminate this mismatch, as all gains and losses—realized and unrealized—for those instruments would be reported above the performance indicator. Investments designated under FAS 159, in effect, will be accounted for like FAS 115/124 "trading" securities.

- Electing the fair value option for interest rate swaps and related indebtedness may allow organizations to achieve hedge-like offset accounting without having to apply the complex hedge accounting provisions of FASB Statement No. 133 (FAS 133), *Accounting for Derivative Instruments and Hedging Activities.*

Before making a fair value election for any instrument, however, organizations should weigh the advantages of simplification against the potential for increased volatility in their changes in net assets or performance indicator. Additionally, organizations should recognize that such elections are irrevocable and must continue to be applied until the designated instrument matures or is disposed of in some manner, or until a revaluation event occurs.

FAS 159 is applicable for fiscal years beginning after November 15, 2007. The transition provisions allow organizations to irrevocably elect the fair value option on an instrument-by-instrument basis for assets and liabilities held as of the date of adoption. The effect of adoption should be reported as a cumulative-effect adjustment to the opening balance of the appropriate net asset classes. If the fair value option is not elected for all eligible instruments within a group of similar instruments, an organization must disclose the reasons for its partial election, and disclose the amounts to which it applied the fair value option and the amounts to which it did not apply the fair value option within that group. Additional transition-period disclosures also are required to enable financial statement users to understand the effects of an organization's adoption of FAS 159.

PwC Observation: Since not-for-profit organizations will have only one chance to apply the FAS 159 fair value option for existing financial assets or liabilities at the date of adoption, they should carefully consider their elections.

During 2008, FASB plans to consider the extension of the fair value option to a wider range of financial instruments.

FASB Statement No. 157 (FAS 157), *Fair Value Measurements.* Issued in September 2006, FAS 157 addresses how organizations should measure fair value when generally accepted accounting principles require use of fair value measurement for recognition or disclosure purposes. Previously, different FASB standards contained various definitions of fair value. FAS 157 replaces these various definitions with a common definition of fair value to be used throughout GAAP. FASB believes that the new standard will make the measurement of fair value more consistent and comparable, and will improve disclosures about those measures. Not-for-profit organizations will need to adopt FAS 157 on a prospective basis for financial statements issued for fiscal years beginning after November 15, 2007.

PwC Observation: FAS 157 does not impose fair value measurement on any assets or liabilities; it simply provides the definition of fair value for use in standards where fair value measurement is required.

FAS 157 defines fair value as "the price that would be received to sell an asset or paid to transfer a liability in an orderly transaction between market participants at the measurement date." This definition of fair value retains the exchange-price notion contained (either explicitly or implicitly) in many earlier GAAP definitions of fair value. However, FAS 157 clarifies that the basis for a fair value measure is the price at which a company would sell or otherwise dispose of its assets or pay to settle a liability (i.e., an exit price), not the market price at which a company acquires its assets or assumes a liability (i.e., an entry price). The exit price concept is based on current expectations about the future inflows associated with the asset and the future outflows associated with the liability from the perspective of market participants. Under FAS 157, a fair value measure should reflect all of the assumptions that market participants would use in pricing the asset or liability, including, for example, an adjustment for risk inherent in a particular valuation technique used to measure fair value.

FAS 157 requires disclosures intended to provide information about: (1) the extent to which organizations measure assets and liabilities at fair value, (2) the methods and assumptions used to measure fair value, and (3) the effect of fair value measures on net assets. Further, the disclosure requirements vary depending on whether the asset or liability is measured at fair value on a recurring or nonrecurring basis.

Subsequent to the issuance of FAS 157, FASB indefinitely deferred its application to leases (FAS 13) and deferred the effective date for one year for nonfinancial assets and nonfinancial liabilities that are recognized or disclosed at fair value in the financial statements on a nonrecurring basis. Currently, a proposed FSP has been issued for comment on measuring the fair value of liabilities, which should provide additional perspective on how to apply the FAS 157 framework to liabilities.

PwC Observation: FAS 157 introduces a number of new concepts, such as "exit price," "principal or most advantageous market," "highest and best use," "in-use" and "in-exchange" valuation premises, and the perspectives of "market participants." Organizations will be required to consider these concepts when measuring the fair value of financial assets and liabilities. However, understanding these concepts and applying them in the measurement and reporting of fair value may be a challenge in certain areas.

In order to effectively implement the standard, organizations should prepare an inventory of existing assets and liabilities that may be impacted by FAS 157. A list of potential areas of impact for not-for-profit organizations is highlighted above. In addition, organizations should perform an analysis to determine how fair value is currently measured, compared to how it will need to be measured using the new FAS 157 concepts. This "gap analysis" will help determine what additional information will be needed, what policies need to be documented or added, and what process changes will be required upon and after adoption.

FASB Statement No. 158 (FAS 158), *Employers' Accounting for Defined Benefit Pension and Other Postretirement Plans—an amendment of FASB Statements No. 87, 88, 106 and 132(R).* FAS 158, which was issued in September 2006, has two key provisions. First, it required full recognition of a pension or other postretirement benefit plan's over- or underfunded status on an employer's Balance Sheet.

For not-for-profit organizations, that provision was effective for fiscal years ending after June 15, 2007. Additionally, FAS 158 requires employers that historically used measurement dates prior to their Balance Sheet dates to change their measurement dates to correspond to their Balance Sheet dates, effective for fiscal years ending after December 15, 2008.

Questions have arisen regarding the "Day 2" accounting for amortization of unrecognized gains and losses, prior service costs/credits, and transition assets/obligations, as well as the provisions related to the measurement date change. Those issues are discussed below.

Day 2 "Recycling" of Amortization Expense

FAS 158 required employers to fully recognize a pension plan's over- or underfunded status on the Balance Sheet by recording previously unrecognized gains and losses, unrecognized prior-service costs and credits, and any remaining transition obligation or asset, all with a corresponding offset to unrestricted net assets. FASB did not change how pension benefits are recognized in the statement of activities/statement of operations; accordingly, the amount of net benefit cost included in expenses will not change. Amounts representing actuarial gains and losses, prior service costs/credits and transition assets/obligations will continue to be amortized under existing guidance in FASB Statement No. 87 (FAS 87), *Employers' Accounting for Pensions*, and FASB Statement No. 106 (FAS 106), *Employers' Accounting for Postretirement Benefits Other Than Pensions*, as a component of net periodic benefit cost in the statement of activities/statement of operations. For not-for-profit health care organizations, the recognition or "recycling" of these amounts from net assets into net periodic benefit costs will be reported below the performance indicator. All other not-for-profit organizations report the recognition or "recycling" of the these amounts into net periodic benefit costs, with the contra adjustment or adjustments recorded in the same line item or items within changes in unrestricted net assets (apart from expenses), as was the initial adjustment for the adoption of FAS 158.

Reporting Measurement Date Changes

Under FAS 158, employers are required to measure plan assets and benefit obligations as of the financial statement date, thereby eliminating the provisions in previous guidance that allowed plan assets and obligations to be measured as of an earlier date, provided that date was not more than three months prior to the Balance Sheet date. As a result, employers that have measurement dates prior to their Balance Sheet dates must change their measurement dates to correspond to their Balance Sheet dates. The standard provides employers with two alternatives to transition to a fiscal year-end measurement date:

- **Alternative one** (the "two-measurement" approach) requires an employer to measure plan assets and obligations as of the earlier measurement date, and to use that measurement to compute net benefit expense for the period between that date and the corresponding fiscal year-end, and then perform a second measurement of plan assets and obligations as of the beginning of the fiscal year for which the new measurement date is adopted. For example, an employer with a December 31 year-end that historically had performed its annual measurements on September 30 would perform its first measurement on September 30,

2007, and perform a second measurement on December 31, 2007, to determine pension expense for its 2008 fiscal year. The first measurement would cover the period between September 30, 2007, and December 31, 2007 (referred to as the "transition period"). The net benefit expense for the transition period would be reported as an adjustment to net assets at the beginning of the fiscal year for which the new measurement date is adopted (January 1, 2008, in this example), as would changes in the fair value of plan assets and the benefit obligations (such as for prior service costs and for gains and losses, e.g., due to a change in discount rates at year-end) that occur during the transition period. The second measurement that was performed on December 31, 2007, would also be used to determine net benefit expense to be recorded for fiscal year 2008.

- **Alternative two** (the "one-measurement" or "15-month approach") requires the use of the existing early measurement date to compute net benefit expense for the period between the early measurement date in the prior year and the end of the fiscal year for which the new measurement date is adopted. Continuing with our previous example, this alternative allows the employer to report the net benefit expense for the transition period as an adjustment to either beginning or ending net assets in the year for which the new measurement date is adopted (2008). Changes in the fair value of plan assets and changes in the benefit obligations for prior service costs and gains and losses are recorded below the performance indicator (for not-for-profit health care organizations) or against the same line item or items within changes in unrestricted net assets (apart from expenses) as the initial adjustment for the adoption of FAS 158 for all other not-for-profit organizations.

Any curtailment or settlement gain or loss that occurs during the transition period would need to be recognized in the year ended December 31, 2007.

An employer must select one of the alternative methods of adopting the measurement date provisions of FAS 158 and apply it consistently to all of its benefit plans (i.e., an employer may not select alternative one for some plans and alternative two for others).

PwC Observation: In planning for implementation of this provision of FAS 158, employers will need to consider the timing and scope of the actuarial calculations required, based on the alternative selected. Under alternative one, the employer is required to obtain an additional measurement (i.e., the December 31, 2007, measurement in the example above). Under alternative two, employers will need to ensure that the calculation includes projections covering the period from the original measurement date through the following fiscal year-end (which in our example, would be a 15-month projection covering the period from September 30, 2007, through December 31, 2008).

FASB Interpretation No. 48 (FIN 48), *Accounting for Uncertainty in Income Taxes FSP No. FIN 48-2, Effective Date of FASB Interpretation No. 48 for Certain Nonpublic Enterprises.* Issued in June 2006, FIN 48 prescribes a comprehensive model for how organizations (including not-for-profit organizations) should recognize, measure, present and disclose in financial statements uncertain tax positions that they have taken (or expect to take) on a tax return. FIN 48's provisions are discussed in detail in the Tax Issues section of this Summary document. FIN 48 was effective for fiscal years beginning after December 15, 2006.

FSP FIN 48-2, issued in February 2008, defers by one year FIN 48's effective date for "certain nonpublic organizations" that have not issued a full set of annual financial statements that incorporate the recognition, measurement and disclosure requirements of FIN 48. Nonpublic organizations that issued interim financial information in 2007 that reflected the adoption of FIN 48 would still be eligible for the deferral, as long as they have not yet issued annual financial statements. Organizations eligible for the deferral will not need to adopt FIN 48 in interim financial statements or interim financial information issued in 2008.

PwC Observation: The deferral provided in FSP FIN 48-2 is not available to not-for-profit organizations that meet the definition of a "public enterprise" in FASB Statement No. 109 (FAS 109), *Accounting for Income Taxes.* FAS 109 was amended by FSP FAS 126-1, *Applicability of Certain Disclosures and Interim Reporting Requirements for Obligors for Conduit Debt Securities*, to clarify that not-for-profit organizations which have issued tax-exempt bonds that trade in a public market are *public enterprises*, as that term is defined in FAS 109. Generally, tax-exempt bonds issued in negotiated sales or competitive bids are deemed to trade in a public market; tax-exempt bonds issued in private placements do not. "Public enterprise" nonprofits must still apply FIN 48 in annual financial statements prepared for years ending December 31, 2007, and thereafter.

FASB Exposure Documents

Proposed FASB Staff Position SOP 94-3a and AAG-HCOa, *Omnibus Changes to Consolidation and Equity Method Guidance for Not-for-Profit Organizations.* In September 2007, the FASB issued a proposed FSP to address conflicts in the existing authoritative accounting literature concerning the consolidation and equity method guidance for not-for-profit organizations. The proposed FSP would make several changes to and clarifications of the guidance on consolidation and the equity method of accounting guidance in SOP 94-3, *Reporting of Related Entities by Not-for-Profit Organizations* (SOP 94-3), and the AAG-HCO, as follows:

- Eliminate the "temporary control" exception to consolidation that currently exists for certain relationships between not-for-profit organizations.

- Affirm the continued applicability to not-for-profit organizations of guidance in certain EITF Issues related to consolidation of special-purpose entities (SPEs) that were nullified for organizations within the scope of FIN 46/46R.

    PwC Observation: The proposed FSP clearly indicates that not-for-profit organizations should apply the SPE consolidation guidance in EITF Issues 90-15, 96-21, and 97-1. However, the applicability of Topic D-14, which is referenced in Issue 90-15, is not clear. It also is unclear whether FASB intends for the SPE guidance to apply only to leasing SPEs, or for it to have broader applicability to other types of SPE relationships. The final FSP is likely to provide clarity with respect to those questions.

- Require, for non–health care not-for-profit organizations, consideration of certain existing guidance on the equity method of accounting to "more than minor" interests in for-profit partnerships, limited partnerships (LPs), limited liability companies

(LLCs), or similar organizations, if the not-for-profit organization carries alternative investments at cost.

> **PwC Observation:** Affected not-for-profits that do not wish to use the equity method might consider electing fair value measurement for these investments using the instrument-by-instrument option allowed under FAS 159.

The final FSP is expected to be issued in the first half of 2008. The resulting amendments to SOP 94-3 and AAG-HCO would be effective for fiscal years beginning after June 15, 2008.

Proposed FSP FAS 117-a, *Endowments of Not-for-Profit Organizations: Net Asset Classification of Funds Subject to an Enacted Version of the Uniform Prudent Management of Institutional Funds Act, and Enhanced Disclosures.* In February 2008, the FASB issued a proposed FSP that provides guidance concerning: (1) the disclosures that not-for-profit organizations should make with regard to their endowments, and (2) the effect of a state's adoption of the model Uniform Prudent Management of Institutional Funds Act of 2006 (UPMIFA) on the classification of net assets related to donor-restricted endowment funds of not-for-profit organizations within that state. The key provisions of the proposed FSP are as follows.

EXPANDED DISCLOSURE REQUIREMENTS FOR ALL ENDOWMENTS

The exposure draft proposes a number of new disclosures that would be required for endowments of all not-for-profit organizations, not just endowments held in states where UPMIFA has been enacted. These include:

- A description of the governing board's interpretation of the law that underlies the net asset classification of donor-restricted endowment funds

- A description of endowment spending policies

- A description of endowment investment policies, including the organization's return objectives and risk parameters, how those objectives relate to the organization's endowment spending policies, and the strategies employed for achieving those objectives

- An endowment reconciliation by financial statement net asset class that shows cumulative investment returns in the permanently restricted net asset class that relate to the organization's interpretation of relevant law, rather than what is required by explicit donor stipulation
- The composition of an organization's endowment by net asset classification at the end of the period, in total and by type of endowment fund, showing donor-restricted endowment funds separately from board-designated endowment funds
- A reconciliation of the beginning and ending balances of the organization's endowment, in total and by net asset class, including, at a minimum, the following line items:
  - Investment return, separated into investment income and net appreciation or depreciation of investments
  - Contributions
  - Amounts appropriated for expenditure
  - Reclassifications
  - Other changes
- Disclosure of how much (if any) of additions of investment return to permanently restricted net assets in the current period are the result of the organization's interpretation of relevant law, beyond that required by explicit donor stipulations
- Planned appropriation for expenditures, if known, for the year following the most recent period for which the organization presents financial statements

The proposed FSP provides an illustrative example of such disclosures.

IMPACT OF UPMIFA ON PERMANENTLY RESTRICTED NET ASSETS

UPMIFA is a modernization of the Uniform Management of Institutional Funds Act of 1972 (UMIFA), the model act on which most states have based their laws governing the investment and management of donor-restricted endowment funds. A number of states have already replaced UMIFA with UPMIFA. Among other changes, UPMIFA prescribes new guidelines for expenditure of endowment funds in the absence of explicit donor restrictions. UMIFA allowed only for the spending of the net appreciation on endowment investments in excess of the "historic dollar value" of the underlying gifts. In "underwater" situations (i.e., when the fair value of the fund is temporarily less than historic dollar value), no further spending was permitted. UPMIFA provides more flexibility to organizations for handling "underwater "situations by eliminating the historic dollar value concept. However, elimination of the historic dollar concept raises questions about the potential impact of that change on net asset classifications.

The proposed exposure draft indicates that adoption of UPMIFA does not change an organization's long-term accountability to the donor for a "fund of perpetual duration" (i.e., a permanent endowment). The amount classified as permanently restricted should be the amount that must be retained permanently in accordance with explicit donor stipulations or, in the absence of such stipulations, the amount the governing board determines must be maintained permanently, if any, under that state's version of UPMIFA and any other relevant state law. If the relevant law requires the organization to maintain the purchasing power of an endowment fund, beyond general "prudency standards," and outside the purview of the organization's governing board the amount of permanently restricted net assets should increase accordingly. The amount of permanently restricted net assets should not be reduced by investment losses or by spending in "underwater" situations.

PwC Observation: In substance, the changes brought about by UPMIFA merely provide organizations with short-term spending flexibility to deal with market declines that result in underwater situations. While the amount of assets associated with an endowment fund might fluctuate, the accountability to the donor for a permanent endowment remains unchanged.

The proposed FSP also addresses whether certain specific provisions of UPMIFA require that a temporary time restriction be implied on net appreciation of an endowment. These provisions are section 4(a), which states that "unless stated otherwise in the gift instrument, the assets in an endowment fund are donor-restricted assets until appropriated for expenditure by the institution," and section 4(d), which provides an option for adding a "rebuttable presumption of imprudence" for spending in excess of 7% of the market value of an endowment fund. The proposed FSP states that organizations should apply the guidance in EITF Topic D-49 (Topic D-49), *Classifying Net Appreciation on Investments of a Donor-Restricted Endowment Fund*, in making such determinations. Topic D-49 indicates that not all legal restrictions constitute donor-imposed restrictions for accounting purposes under FASB Statement No. 117 (FAS 117), *Financial Statements of Not-for-Profit Organizations*. Laws that refer to actions that are entirely within the purview of an organization's governing board, such as acting to appropriate funds or exercising prudence in doing so, do not in and of themselves create donor-imposed restrictions. Similarly, laws that provide additional guidance on what constitutes "prudence," rather than establishing absolute ceilings on spending, do not in and of themselves create restrictions. Each organization's governing board must make those determinations based on the specific language in their state's version of UPMIFA and any other relevant guidance.

The proposed FSP would be effective for fiscal years ending after June 15, 2008, with earlier adoption permitted. The cumulative effect of any reclassifications between net asset classes resulting from a state's enactment of UPMIFA would be reported as a separate line item in the statement of activities/statement of operations, outside of any performance indicator or intermediate measure of operations, in the period in which UPMIFA becomes effective.

PwC Observation: Apart from the new disclosure requirements that apply to all organizations with endowments, the proposed FSP may impact net asset accounting depending upon the relevant state UPMIFA law. In light of the short time frame for implementation, not-for-profit organizations should start preparing for the proposed FSP's expanded disclosure requirements as quickly as possible.

Proposed FSP No. FAS 132(R)-a, *Employers' Disclosures about Postretirement Benefit Plan Assets.* In March 2008, the FASB issued a proposed FSP that would enhance and improve employers' disclosures related to postretirement defined benefit plan assets. Additional required disclosures would include:

- The fair value of each major category of plan assets (based on the types of assets held in the plan) as of each annual reporting date for which a Balance Sheet is presented

- The nature and amount of concentrations of risk within or across categories of plan assets

PwC Observation: Although FAS 132(R) already requires certain disclosures regarding major categories of plan assets, FASB believed those disclosures were not specific enough to allow financial statement users to determine the types of assets held as investments and the related concentrations of risk that may arise from a lack of diversification.

- Disclosures about fair value measurements similar to those required by FAS 157

PwC Observation: This provision is included because the disclosure requirements in FAS 157 do not apply to an employer's reporting of postretirement benefits. Such disclosures would provide useful information about the valuation techniques and inputs used for fair value measurements of plan assets, the level within the fair value hierarchy the assets fall, and a reconciliation of the beginning and ending balances of fair value of assets measured using significant unobservable inputs (level 3).

The proposed FSP also includes a technical amendment to Statement 132(R) that would require nonpublic entities to disclose net periodic benefit cost for each period presented (which was inadvertently eliminated from Statement 132(R) by the issuance of FAS 158). That proposed amendment would be effective upon issuance. The amendments related to disclosures about plan assets would be applied on a prospective basis for fiscal years ending after December 15, 2008. Earlier application would not be permitted.

Proposed Financial Accounting Standard, *Not-for-Profit Organizations: Mergers and Acquisitions.* This proposed standard would provide guidance on the accounting and reporting for mergers and acquisitions of not-for-profit organizations. The scope includes combinations of two or more not-for-profit organizations, as well as transactions in which a not-for-profit organization acquires a for-profit organization. (An acquisition of a not-for-profit organization by a for-profit company is within the scope of FASB Statement No. 141R (FAS 141R), *Business Combinations.*)

FASB employed a "differences-based" approach to this project, in that it assumed that the general framework for business combinations set forth in FAS 141R generally would apply; any departures would need to be justified by specific differences in the nature of not-for-profit combination transactions.

PwC Observation: The key difference identified between not-for-profit combinations and business combinations is that a business combination is presumed to be a bargained exchange—a transaction in which each party sacrifices and receives commensurate value—whereas not-for-profit combinations often are motivated by reasons that consider mission in addition to financial considerations. Many not-for-profit mergers do not involve any exchange of consideration other than the assumption of the acquiree's liabilities. Thus, unlike business combinations, there may be some transactions with no exchange price paid to provide evidence of the acquired not-for-profit organization's fair value. Also, if consideration is involved, it may not represent fair value of the acquiree. Consequently, the Board determined that because not-for-profit organizations are not routinely bought and sold in bargained exchange transactions, there generally is no readily available evidence of the "enterprise" fair value of an acquired not-for-profit organization.

FASB issued an exposure draft of the proposed standard in October 2006. Key provisions include:

- A combination is defined as any event that results in initial inclusion of a not-for-profit or business organization in a not-for-profit parent's consolidated financial statements. Circumstances requiring consolidation are described in SOP 94-3 and Chapter 11 of AAG-HCO. Thus, a change in control that would require consolidation under SOP 94-3/Chapter 11 would be a combination transaction.

- Most not-for-profit combinations will be accounted for under the "acquisition" (i.e., purchase) method. However, see "Recent Developments" section.

- Identification of the acquirer will require consideration of all facts and circumstances surrounding a combination, in particular, the ability of one organization to dominate the process of selecting a voting majority of the combined organization's governing board.

- In measuring an acquisition, the acquirer considers: (a) the fair values of identifiable assets acquired (excluding some exceptions such as unrecognized collections and conditional promises to give), (b) the fair values of liabilities assumed, and (c) the fair value of consideration transferred, if any.

PwC Observation: Unlike FAS 141R, the exposure draft does not require the acquiree's fair value to be determined based on an "enterprise value" for the acquired organization as a whole. Rather, the acquiree is valued based on the sum of the fair values of individual assets acquired and liabilities assumed, plus consideration (if any). A primary reason for this difference was due to anticipated difficulties in applying the "market participant" concepts of FAS 157 in estimating enterprise values in such transactions.

- If the fair value of identifiable assets acquired is greater than the fair value of liabilities assumed and consideration transferred (if any), the acquiring organization would recognize **contribution income**. There is no concept of "bargain purchase."
- If the fair value of identifiable assets acquired is less than the fair value of liabilities assumed and consideration transferred (if any), the acquiring organization would recognize **goodwill**.

PwC Observation: This provision of the exposure draft proved to be quite controversial. Many commenters, including PwC, indicated that if the acquisition was charitably motivated (e.g., a financially sound organization takes over a failing organization in order to preserve the acquiree's mission), no tangible or intangible benefit has, in fact, been acquired. Instead, the acquired net deficit should be reflected in the statement of activities/statement of operations as a contribution made. However, we anticipate that goodwill would rarely be recognized by most larger not-for-profits, given that the revaluation to fair value of the acquiree's long-lived assets (i.e., buildings, property and equipment) could result in significant increases to the asset side of the equation.

- The exposure draft tailors the guidance in FAS 160, *Noncontrolling Interests in Consolidated Financial Statements*, to the not-for-profit reporting model to provide guidance for the reporting of nonprofits' minority interests (now referred to as "noncontrolling interests") in for-profit subsidiaries. Noncontrolling interests would be reported in the Balance Sheet as a separate component of the appropriate net asset class.

- Any "inherent contribution" resulting from a combination would be reported in the statement of activities as a line item separate from other contributions. Not-for-profit health care organizations would report the inherent contribution below the performance indicator. Consistent with the requirements of FASB Statement No. 116 (FAS 116), *Accounting for Contributions Received and Contributions Made*, and FAS 117, the contribution would be reported as an increase in permanently restricted net assets, temporarily restricted net assets and/or unrestricted net assets.

- The disclosure requirements of FAS 141R generally would be required, modified as necessary to accommodate the FAS 117 financial reporting model. Certain disclosures unique to not-for-profits would be required for certain acquisitions of collections.

RECENT DEVELOPMENTS

The exposure draft required that an acquirer be designated for every transaction, similar to the requirement in FAS 141R. Based on comments received during the exposure period, in September 2007 FASB reconsidered that decision and determined that in situations where both of the combining organizations cede control to a new economic entity (as opposed to one organization obtaining control over the others), the assets and liabilities of the combining organizations should be brought into the new entity at their carryover bases (i.e., pooling-type accounting).

FASB plans to issue a limited revised exposure draft to solicit comments on this significant change in the first half of 2008. The comment period is expected to be 60 days.

PwC Observation: We expect that a relatively high hurdle will be established in order for transactions to qualify for use of carryover-basis accounting. Governance that is equally shared is a key indicator pointing to a "true merger," but typically it is not solely determinative. The guidance in this area is likely to be in the form of a principles-based standard, rather than prescriptive criteria. One FASB member observed that if feedback obtained from the comment letter process shows an appetite for more detailed guidance, the Board should reconsider its decision to allow special accounting for these transactions. Clearly, FASB has no appetite for re-creating APB 16–like pooling criteria.

The proposed statement would apply prospectively to mergers and acquisitions for which the acquisition date is on or after the beginning of the first annual period beginning on or after the effective date, which is expected to be approximately six months after issuance of the final standard. Earlier application would be encouraged.

The Board's remaining deliberations will focus primarily on the applicability of the changes made during the redeliberations leading to the issuance of FAS 141R and FAS 160 (both issued in December 2007) and on certain issues related to how to apply the acquisition method. The latter would include, for example, whether donor-related intangible assets should be required to be recognized apart from goodwill. FASB hopes to issue the final standard in 2008. Until that time, not-for-profit organizations should continue to apply the guidance in APB 16, *Business Combinations*, when accounting for business combinations.

Proposed Financial Accounting Standard, *Not-for-Profit Organizations: Goodwill and Other Intangible Assets Acquired in a Merger or Acquisition.* This proposed standard provides "Day 2" accounting and reporting guidance for goodwill and other intangible assets recognized in a not-for-profit merger or acquisition. Currently, the effective date of FASB Statement No. 142 (FAS 142), *Goodwill and Other Intangible Assets*, with respect to intangible assets acquired in a combination transaction was deferred for not-for-profits pending completion of this project. As a result, the guidance in APB 17, Intangible Assets, as amended remains in effect for those intangibles, including continued amortization of goodwill. Not-for-profit organizations must also apply all subsequent amendments of APB 17, including those made by standards that have been superseded by FAS 141R and FAS 142.

PwC Observation: FAS 142 is already applicable for intangible assets of not-for-profit organizations other than those acquired in business combinations (e.g., donated intangibles). In addition, the deferred effective date of FAS 142 does not apply to intangible assets of for-profit subsidiaries of nonprofits.

Like the mergers and acquisitions project, the overall approach to this project is that any departures from the general framework for business combinations set forth in FAS 141R/142 would need to be justified by specific differences in the nature of not-for-profit transactions.

FASB issued an exposure draft of the proposed standard in October 2006. Key provisions include:

- Goodwill and certain intangible assets that have indefinite useful lives would no longer be amortized.

- Intangible assets that have finite useful lives would continue to be amortized over their useful lives, but without the constraint of an arbitrary ceiling of 40 years.

- At the date of acquisition, the assets acquired and liabilities assumed (including goodwill, if any) should be assigned to reporting units as presently described in FAS 142 (using "operating segment" concepts from FAS 131, *Disclosures About Segments of an Enterprise and Related Information*). The acquirer must also identify each reporting unit as being either primarily supported by revenues from providing goods and services or alternatively, by revenues from contributions and investment income.

PwC Observation: Because not-for-profit organizations were explicitly excluded from the scope of FAS 131, financial statement preparers may not be familiar with its complex requirements. Further, we believe that few not-for-profit organizations (with the possible exception of some larger hospital systems) regularly review their financial information on the basis of operating segments. Therefore, we expect that the exercise of assigning goodwill to reporting units using FAS 131 concepts (which have proved difficult for for-profit organizations to apply in practice) will prove challenging for many not-for-profits.

- Specific guidance is provided for testing goodwill for impairment:

- If a reporting unit is primarily supported by revenues generated by providing goods and services, goodwill of that reporting unit would be tested for impairment in accordance with the existing requirements of FAS 142.

- If the reporting unit is primarily supported by contributions or investment income, the FAS 142 model is not used. Instead, goodwill is evaluated for impairment based on a "trigger-based" approach. Goodwill must be written off in its entirety upon the occurrence of certain triggering events identified as of the acquisition date.

- The disclosures required by FAS 142 generally would be required, modified appropriately for the not-for-profit financial reporting model. Additionally, certain unique disclosures would be required regarding the triggering events that would result in a write-off of goodwill, if the trigger-based write-off method is applicable.

- Transition adjustments:

  - Preexisting acquired intangibles that do not meet the new recognition criteria for intangible assets must be reclassified to goodwill.

  - Any intangibles that meet the new recognition criteria that are reported as part of preexisting goodwill must be reclassified and accounted for separately (if certain information about those intangibles is available).

  - Any preexisting unamortized credit relating to negative goodwill must be written off and recognized as the effect of a change in accounting principle.

The proposed effective date would be approximately six months after issuance of a final standard and would apply to fiscal years beginning on or after that date, with earlier application encouraged.

During the first quarter of 2008, the Board will continue its deliberations of the exposure draft, focusing especially on goodwill and intangible assets. FASB expects to issue a final standard in 2008.

FASB Projects

Proposed Amendment of FAS 133, *Accounting for Hedging Activities.* The objective of this project is to simplify accounting for hedging activities under FAS 133 and to make the accounting model and associated disclosures easier to understand for users of financial statements. FASB completed its initial deliberations on this project in December 2007, and an exposure draft is expected to be released in early 2008.

The proposed standard would replace FAS 133's current hedging requirements with a simpler "fair value approach." The fair value approach focuses on individually measuring the change in fair value of the derivative and the change in fair value of the hedged item (or for forecasted transactions, the hypothetical derivative). The simplified approach would eliminate the shortcut method and critical terms matching, and would replace the current quantitative approach to assessing hedge effectiveness with a more qualitative approach.

The financial reporting requirements would remain the same under the new approach. For fair value hedges, the derivative and the hedged item would continue to be measured at fair value with changes in value recognized in the performance indicator (for health care not-for-profits) or changes in net assets (for other not-for-profits). For not-for-profit health care organizations, derivatives associated with cash flow hedges would continue to be measured at fair value, with the effective portion of the gain or loss reported below the performance indicator and the ineffective portion reported above the performance indicator.

The expected effective date would be for fiscal years ending after November 15, 2008; earlier application would be prohibited. Transition would involve prospective application for fair value hedges and limited retrospective application (through a cumulative catch-up) for cash flow hedges.

PwC Observation: The fair value approach to hedging bears a similarity to the fair value option under FAS 159, though it will presumably apply to a broader range of financial instruments.

Proposed Amendments to FAS No. 144 (FAS 144), *FSP Projects.*

"MEASURING ASSETS HELD FOR SALE"

Currently, inconsistency exists in practice with respect to accounting for assets held for sale as part of a business combination under FASB Statement No. 144 (FAS 144), *Accounting for the Impairment or Disposal of Long-Lived Assets*. In order to reconcile the differences, this project would amend FAS 144 to require assets classified as "held for sale" to be measured at fair value, rather than at fair value less cost to sell.

PwC Observation: This project was initiated in January 2008. A change in measurement from "fair value less cost to sell" to "fair value" most likely would not have a significant impact on not-for-profit organizations.

"REPORTING DISCONTINUED OPERATIONS"

This proposed FSP develops a converged definition of a discontinued operation with the International Accounting Standards Board (IASB). The FASB and IASB (collectively, the "Boards") tentatively agreed to a revised definition of "discontinued operation" and to requiring additional disclosures when reporting a component of an entity that was or will be disposed of. Currently, FAS 144's criteria for reporting a component as a discontinued operation are that the operations and cash flows of a component has been (or will be) eliminated from the ongoing operations of the entity, and that the entity will not have any significant continuing involvement in the operations of the component after the disposal transaction.

Instead, under the proposed definition, a disposal of a component should be reported as discontinued only if that component is an operating segment as defined in FAS 131. In recognition of the fact that a disposal of a component that does not represent an operating segment may be a significant event to an entity, the entity would be required to disclose in the notes to the financial statements disaggregated information about discontinued components, as well as disaggregated information about discontinued operations.

An exposure draft is expected to be issued in early 2008.

PwC Observation: The Board believes that a discontinued operation should include only a disposal that reflects a strategic shift in an entity's business strategy, and that the disposal of an operating segment would generally be such an event. The segment reporting concepts under FAS 131 can be difficult to apply in practice. Since not-for-profit organizations are explicitly excluded from the scope of FAS 131, many preparers will be unfamiliar with its requirements. However, the Board also has proposed using segment reporting concepts as part of the standards project on not-for-profit goodwill and intangible assets, as noted previously. Any additional guidance related to use of FAS 131 by not-for-profits derived from that project will be helpful in applying its provisions in this proposed FSP.

EITF Issues

EITF 07-1, *Accounting for Collaborative Arrangements.* EITF 07-1 addresses the appropriate accounting for "collaborative arrangements"—that is, for joint-venture-like collaborations between two or more entities that do not involve the creation of a separate legal entity. An arrangement is within the scope of EITF 07-1 if the parties to the arrangement actively participate in the arrangement and are exposed to its risks and rewards.

Prior to the EITF undertaking this project, many not-for-profit organizations relied on a health care-specific AICPA Technical Practice Aid (TPA) 6400.33, *Accounting for a Joint Operating Arrangement*, for guidance in accounting for collaborative arrangements or joint operating arrangements (JOA) that were not conducted in a separate legal entity. The TPA considered such arrangements to be "virtual joint ventures" and, accordingly, encouraged organizations to account for their respective interests using the equity method of accounting.

The EITF reached a consensus that accounting for arrangements that do not involve the creation of a separate legal entity as a "virtual joint venture" using equity-method accounting is not appropriate. Instead, revenues generated and costs incurred by the participants should be reported in the appropriate line items in each participant's statement of operations/statement of activities, pursuant to EITF Issue 99-19, *Reporting Revenue Gross as a Principal versus Net as an Agent*. A line item such as "collaboration revenue" or "collaboration expense" would be used to report "sharing" payments made between the venture participants. The consensus also nullifies TPA 6400.33.

EITF 07-1 is effective for periods beginning after December 15, 2008, and requires retrospective application for arrangements in place as of the effective date.

PwC Observation: EITF 07-1 will impact not-for-profit organizations that have joint operating arrangements/collaborative arrangement that are not conducted in a separate legal entity, but are accounted for by the equity method. Because EITF 07-1 provides a year or more of lead time prior to adoption (depending on an organization's fiscal year-end), affected organizations have time to reconsider the rationale underlying the existing structure and the feasibility of restructuring it into a separate legal entity. If such arrangements are not restructured, organizations should begin to think about implementation issues associated with retroactively applying the EITF 07-1 accounting model, such as obtaining necessary current and historical financial data to present the arrangement on a gross basis for all comparative periods.

EITF 06-10, *Accounting for Deferred Compensation and Postretirement Benefit Aspects of Collateral Assignment Split-Dollar Life Insurance Arrangements.*

EITF 06-4, *Accounting for Deferred Compensation and Postretirement Benefit Aspects of Endorsement Split-Dollar Life Insurance Arrangements*

Many not-for-profit organizations purchase life insurance on key employees. In recent years, the accounting for the compensatory aspect of these arrangements has been subject to varying interpretations. Accordingly, these two EITF Issues focus on the accounting for arrangements in which an employer has agreed to share a portion of the value of the insurance policy with the employee. These arrangements are referred to as "split-dollar" arrangements. Two types of split-dollar life insurance policies exist: *collateral assignment* policies and *endorsement* policies. Generally, the difference lies in the ownership and control of the life insurance policy. In an endorsement arrangement, the employer owns and controls the policy, whereas in a collateral assignment arrangement, the employee owns and controls the policy.

The EITF concluded that the purchase of a split-dollar life insurance policy does not constitute a "settlement" of a postretirement benefit obligation as defined in FASB Statement No. 106 (FAS 106), *Employers' Accounting for Postretirement Benefits Other Than Pensions*. Thus, an employer should recognize a liability for the postretirement benefit in accordance with FAS 106 or APB 12, *Omnibus Opinion—1967*. If in substance a postretirement benefit plan exists, FAS 106 should be followed. If the arrangement is, in substance, an individual deferred compensation contract, APB 12 would be applied. The accounting should be based on the terms of the substantive agreement with the employee. For example, if the employer has agreed to maintain a life insurance policy during the employee's retirement, the estimated cost of maintaining the policy during that period should be accrued. Alternatively, if the employer has effectively agreed to provide the employee with a death benefit, the employer should accrue a liability for the actuarial present value of the future death benefit as of the employee's expected retirement date. All available evidence should be considered in determining the substance of the arrangement.

For collateral assignment arrangements (i.e., those where the insurance contract is owned by the employee), the above guidance applies only if the life insurance arrangement is determined to provide a postretirement benefit. If the employer did not agree to maintain the life insurance policy postretirement or provide the employee with a death benefit based on the substantive arrangement, or the entity otherwise concludes that the arrangement does not provide a postretirement benefit, no obligation should be recorded.

PwC Observation: Determining whether the substantive arrangement provides a postretirement benefit may require significant judgment. A detailed understanding of the insurance contract, the substantive arrangement and the mutual understanding of the parties will be required.

The accounting for the related insurance asset is also addressed. For endorsement arrangements (i.e., those where the insurance contract is owned by the employer), EITF 06-4 states that the asset should be determined pursuant to the guidance in FASB Technical Bulletin 85-4 (FTB 85-4), *Accounting for Purchases of Life Insurance* (see related discussion of EITF 06-5 in this section). For collateral arrangements (i.e., those in which the policy is owned by the employee), EITF 06-10 states that the employer should recognize and measure the asset based on the nature and substance of the collateral assignment arrangement. In assessing the nature and substance, the employer should assess what future cash flows the employer is entitled to, if any, as well as the employee's obligation and ability to repay the employer. For example, a collateral assignment arrangement may provide that the employer is required to receive payment from the employee (or estate) of the premiums paid by the employer with interest. Alternatively, the arrangement might provide that the employee or estate must pay the cash surrender value of the life insurance contract upon the employee's death.

These consensuses are effective for fiscal years beginning after December 15, 2007, with earlier application permitted. Entities should recognize the effects of applying the consensuses as a change in accounting principle through either a cumulative-effect adjustment to net assets as of the beginning of the year of adoption or retrospective application to all prior periods.

PwC Observation: As with any postretirement benefit arrangement, understanding the nature of the benefit promise between the employer and the employee is paramount. In order to determine the proper basis for the benefit accruals, organizations will need to consider all forms of communication with the employees related to these arrangements, not simply the formal plan documents or signed employee acknowledgments.

EITF 06-9, *Reporting a Change in (or the Elimination of) a Previously Existing Difference between the Fiscal Year-End of a Parent Company and that of a Consolidated Entity or between the Reporting Period of an Investor and that of an Equity Method Investee.* Accounting Research Bulletin No. 51 (ARB 51), *Consolidated Financial Statements,* allows a difference of up to three months between the fiscal year-ends of a parent and its subsidiary. ARB 51 and APB 18 allow a similar three-month lag for an investor's reporting of its interest in an equity method investee. This EITF considers the manner of reporting a change to (or elimination of) the lag period arising from a change in year-end of a subsidiary or equity method investee. Historically, some have viewed such changes as a change in accounting principle, while others believe it is not a change in accounting principle and that a direct adjustment to net assets is acceptable.

The EITF reached a consensus that a change in (or elimination of) a lag period is a change in accounting principle that is reported in accordance with the provisions of FASB Statement No. 154 (FAS 154), *Accounting Changes and Error Corrections.* That is, financial statements of all prior periods presented would be retrospectively adjusted and the results of operations and other comprehensive income (or changes in net assets, if the subsidiary is not-for-profit) for the "lag period" immediately preceding the beginning of the earliest period presented would be reported as an adjustment to beginning net assets. In doing so, the EITF also acknowledged that FAS 154 provides an exception to retrospective application when it is impracticable. This consensus should be applied prospectively for changes occurring in fiscal years beginning after November 29, 2006.

PwC Observation: Paragraph 11 of FAS 154 provides guidance on determining whether retrospective application of an accounting change is "impracticable." Depending on whether a subsidiary or equity method investee performs any procedures as of the parent's year-end, circumstances may exist in which it is impracticable to retrospectively adjust the financial statements for all prior periods. For example, if a calendar year-end parent historically used a September 30 Balance Sheet and results of operations to consolidate a subsidiary, and that subsidiary did not perform a "hard close" as of December 31, it may be difficult to determine the appropriate December 31 balances, in prior years, of various accounting estimates (e.g., allowances for doubtful accounts). In such circumstances, retrospective application may be impracticable.

EITF 06-5, *Accounting for Purchases of Life Insurance—Determining the "Amount that Could be Realized" in Accordance with FASB Technical Bulletin No. 85-4.* This EITF clarifies existing guidance in FTB 85-4, *Accounting for Purchases of Life Insurance,* relative to the amount that should be recorded as an asset when an employer carries life insurance policies on employees.

Life insurance policies on individual employees may be purchased for a variety of purposes, including funding the cost of providing employee benefits and protecting against the loss of "key persons." Typically, these policies are issued as: (1) multiple individual policies with a separate, group-level rider agreement; (2) multiple individual policies with a contractual stipulation in each individual policy referencing the other policies as a group; or (3) a group life policy that has multiple certificates. Such policies generally provide for the accumulation of a cash surrender value. In addition, the contractual terms may make additional amounts potentially available to the owner of the policy. Charges are imposed upon surrender of a policy; however, those charges may vary depending on whether policies are surrendered as a group, rather than on an individual basis.

FTB 85-4, which addresses how an employer should account for purchased life insurance, states that "the amount that could be realized under the insurance contract as of the [Balance Sheet] date should be reported as an asset." Diversity exists in the calculation of the *amount that could be realized* under the insurance contract. Some employers consider only the cash surrender value in determining this amount, while others include additional amounts available to them under the contractual terms of the policy. The EITF reached consensus on a number of issues clarifying this guidance, including:

- A policyholder should consider the cash surrender value and any additional amounts provided under the contractual terms of the policy that are realizable at the Balance Sheet date in determining the *amount that could be realized*. Any amounts that are not immediately payable to the policyholder in cash should be discounted to present value.

- In determining the *amount that could be realized*, the policyholder should assume that policies will be surrendered on an individual-by-individual (or certificate-by-certificate) basis, rather than as a group. (If the policy terms allow only for the surrender of all policies or certificates as a group, then the policyholder should determine the amount that could be realized on a group basis.)

PwC Observation: Many arrangements provide for a greater surrender charge when policies are surrendered individually versus surrendering the entire group policy. Thus, the EITF's decision to make the determination on an individual policy basis could result in a reduction in the value of the life insurance asset reported by some organizations. However, the EITF also acknowledged that if the contractual provisions of a group policy permit recovery of prior individual surrender charges when the final policy in the group is surrendered, the determination should assume the surrender of that final individual policy, which may result in recognition of cash surrender value that is similar to a group surrender value.

- Contractual restrictions on a company's ability to surrender a policy do not affect the amount that should be reported under FTB 85-4 but, if significant, should be disclosed.

This EITF is effective for fiscal years beginning after December 15, 2006. Organizations should recognize the effects of applying the consensus through either a cumulative-effect adjustment to net assets as of the beginning of the year of adoption, or through retrospective application to all prior periods.

EITF Issue No. 06-2 (EITF 06-2), *Accounting for Sabbatical Leave and Other Similar Benefits Pursuant to FASB Statement No. 43.* Organizations may provide employees with a benefit in the form of a compensated absence known as a "sabbatical leave," whereby an employee is entitled to paid time off after being employed for a specified period of time. FASB Statement No. 43 (FAS 43), *Accounting for Compensated Absences*, provides guidance on accounting for sabbatical leave programs. Paragraph 6 of FAS 43 states in part that: "An employer shall accrue a liability for employees' compensation for future absences if all of the following conditions are met: a) the employer's obligation relating to employees' rights to receive compensation for future absences is attributable to employees' services already rendered, b) the obligation relates to rights that vest or accumulate, c) payment of the compensation is probable, and d) the amount can be reasonably estimated." Because sabbatical benefits typically do not vest or increase with additional years of service, questions have been raised with respect to whether employee rights to compensated absences under such programs "accumulate" and thus, meet condition 6(b) of FAS 43. The EITF reached a consensus that sabbaticals within the scope of 06-2 do "accumulate" and thus, require accrual over the minimum service period if all other conditions in paragraph 6 are met. EITF 06-2 is effective for fiscal years beginning after December 15, 2006. The effect of adoption should be reported as a cumulative-effect adjustment to the opening balance of the appropriate net asset classes or through retrospective application.

The scope of EITF 06-2 is limited to sabbaticals or similar benefit arrangements where the employee is not required to perform any direct or indirect services for or on behalf of the organization during the compensated absence. Therefore, arrangements under which employees are required to engage in any form of research or public service to enhance the reputation of or otherwise benefit the employer (regardless of the time commitment involved) are outside the scope of EITF 06-2. (Payments made to employees under those types of arrangements represent current compensation, not a compensated absence).

PwC Observation: Organizations that historically have not accrued sabbaticals based on a view that such benefits do not "vest or accumulate" will now need to accrue such benefits over the minimum service period, or else modify the terms of their sabbatical leave and similar benefit programs going forward. For example, if an employee is required to perform a direct or indirect service for the employer while on sabbatical, the sabbatical program would be outside the scope of EITF 06-2 and thus, no accrual would need to be made during the minimum service period.

II. AICPA PRONOUNCEMENTS AND ACTIVITIES

In this section, we highlight certain activities of the American Institute of Certified Public Accountants (AICPA), including overhaul projects for the Health Care Organizations and Not-for-Profit Organizations audit and accounting guides, and key provisions of Statement on Auditing Standards (SAS) No. 114, *The Auditors Communication with Those Charged with Governance.*

AcSEC

AICPA Audit and Accounting Guide Revision Projects. The AICPA's Accounting Standards Executive Committee (AcSEC) is the senior technical committee of the AICPA for financial reporting. AcSEC's mission is to determine the AICPA's technical policies regarding financial reporting standards and to be the AICPA's spokesbody on those matters.

Currently, AcSEC has projects underway to overhaul the AICPA Audit and Accounting Guides, *Health Care Organizations* and *Not-for-*

Profit Organizations. These guides were originally issued in 1996, in conjunction with the effective dates of FAS 116 and 117. Over the ensuing 12 years, many new accounting and auditing issues have emerged, giving rise to the need for comprehensive revision of these guides.

HEALTH CARE ORGANIZATIONS GUIDE

In 2004, an AcSEC task force began work on this guide overhaul project. To date, substantial progress has been made toward developing the new guide. All information related to financial statement display (which is scattered throughout various chapters of the current guide) has been gathered into one chapter on "Basic Financial Statements." The existing cash and investments guidance is being expanded to address accounting for alternative investments and for interests in investment pools sponsored by other not-for-profits. New chapters on "Derivatives" and "Tax-Exempt Debt" are being added, which will include information about interest rate swaps and Securities and Exchange Commission (SEC) oversight of the municipal bond market. Information related to contributions and relationships with foundations (which currently is scattered throughout various chapters) is being gathered into one chapter. The current guidance on managed care accounting will be significantly expanded, and current guidance on CCRC revenue recognition will be clarified. All information specific to governmental (i.e., GASB) hospitals will be housed in a single chapter and expanded.

Because AcSEC can no longer issue authoritative standards, any conclusions reached during the project that conflict with existing category (b) GAAP in the current guide will require action by FASB (e.g., issuance of an FSP) to change the existing guidance. Currently, areas identified where FASB will be required to take action include modifying revenue recognition guidance related to self-pay patients to more closely reflect the requirements of Staff Accounting Bulletin No. 104 (SAB 104), *Revenue Recognition*, modifying the required charity care disclosures, presentation and measurement of insured and self-insured malpractice liabilities and other risk exposures, and changes to managed care accounting, among others.

AcSEC hopes to expose the proposed new guide for public comment later in 2008.

NOT-FOR-PROFIT ORGANIZATIONS GUIDE

Work began on this guide overhaul project in 2005. The initial phase has focused on identifying technical issues where guidance may be needed, and discussing those issues with AcSEC. To date, issues discussed with AcSEC include:

- Accounting for special events held after year-end
- Ambiguous donor stipulations
- Correction of errors in net asset classes
- Contributions of nonfinancial assets such as media time
- Naming opportunities
- Promises to give funded after death
- Display of contributions made
- Remainder interests and noncash assets
- Contributed use of facilities
- Extending the requirement for reporting a statement of functional expenses
- Reporting program information in a statement of functional expenses
- Reporting not-for-profit interests in other entities
- Treatment of Department of Housing and Urban Development (HUD) capital advances
- Need for a performance indicator/measure of operations
- Display of investment expenses
- Incorporation of existing TPAs into guide

During 2008, the Task Force plans to continue its discussions with AcSEC related to specific issues identified. No timetable for a possible exposure draft of a revised guide has yet been identified.

PwC Observation: During the guide overhaul projects, the current guides will continue to be updated for conforming changes on a more-or-less annual basis.

Technical Practice Aids (TPAs). During 2007, the AICPA staff issued the following nonauthoritative TPAs that discuss not-for-profit organizations' reporting of fundraising expense:

- TPA 6140.20, NPOs Reporting No Fundraising Expenses
- TPA 6140.21, Should an NPO Report Amounts Charged to the NPO by a Professional Fundraiser Gross, as Fundraising Expenses, or Net, as a Reduction of Contributions
- TPA 6140.22, In Circumstances in Which the Reporting NPO Undertakes a Transaction in Which Another NPO (Fundraising NPO) Raises Contributions on Behalf of the Reporting NPO, and the Reporting NPO Compensates the Fundraising NPO for Raising Those Contributions (Compensation Including, but Not Limited to, an Administrative Fee), Should the Reporting NPO Report the Fundraising NPO's Compensation Gross, as Fundraising Expenses, or Net, as a Reduction of Contributions?

The TPAs indicate that it would be unusual for a not-for-profit organization to report contributions but have minimal or no fundraising expense. In circumstances in which a professional fundraiser charges a not-for-profit organization for soliciting contributions on its behalf, the amounts charged by the professional fundraiser should be reported gross (as fundraising expense), not netted against the related contribution revenue. Similarly, if a not-for-profit organization compensates a not-for-profit acting as an agent or intermediary to raise contributions on its behalf, that compensation should be reported by the reporting organization as fundraising expense. This would include, but is not limited to, situations in which the fundraiser withholds an administrative fee from contributions solicited on behalf of the reporting organization.

The TPAs can be downloaded from the AICPA's web site at http://aicpa.org/download/acctstd/TIS6100_21_22.pdf.

Auditing Standards Board

SAS No. 114, *The Auditor's Communication with Those Charged with Governance.* This SAS, issued in December 2006, superseded SAS No. 61, *Communications with Audit Committees,* and requires certain matters to be formally communicated (and documented) to parties charged with governance, regardless of the size of the entity. Matters to be communicated include:

- An overview of the planned scope and timing of the audit
- Representations that the auditor is requesting from management
- Evaluation of the adequacy of the two-way communication between the auditor and those charged with governance

Particular attention should be paid to situations where those charged with governance also manage the organization. SAS 114 is effective for audits of fiscal years beginning on or after December 15, 2006.

PwC Observation: In the post-Sarbanes-Oxley environment, one area of focus is the auditor's communications with the audit committee. SAS 114 is generally consistent with SAS 61, but it includes additional matters to be communicated and it focuses more attention on the communication process. Organizations should work with their auditors to ensure that the appropriate communications are being made with those charged with governance.

III. GASB PRONOUNCEMENTS AND ACTIVITIES

In this section, we highlight recent GASB pronouncements that are particularly relevant for governmental business-type activities, along with GASB's proposed standard on derivatives that will be issued later this year.

Pronouncements and Technical Bulletins

GASB Statement No. 52 (GASB 52), *Land and Other Real Estate Held as Investments by Endowments.* Many governmental enterprises hold land and other real estate as part of their endowment portfolios. In November 2007, GASB 52 was issued, which requires assets held by permanent and term endowments to be reported at fair value. As a result, the reporting of real estate investments held by public-sector endowments will be consistent with the reporting of similar investments held by private-sector endowments that report "other investments" at fair value.

PwC Observation: GASB 52's scope extends only to investments held by permanent and term endowments. Land and other real estate investments held by "funds functioning as endowments" (i.e., quasi-endowments) will continue to be reported at historical cost. This was because activities of quasi-endowments present additional reporting issues and considerations that were deemed to be beyond the scope of this statement.

To help users of financial statements better evaluate an endowment's investment decisions and performance, GASB 52 requires governments to report the changes in fair value as investment income. It also requires them to disclose the methods and significant assumptions employed to determine fair value, and to provide other information that they currently present for other investments reported at fair value. While the statement does not provide specific guidance on fair value measurement techniques, the Basis for Conclusions notes that the estimation of fair value depends on the unique facts and circumstances of the specific land or other real estate, and that methods and significant assumptions should consider cost-benefit constraints.

GASB 52 is effective for financial statements for periods beginning after June 15, 2008. Earlier implementation is encouraged.

PwC Observation: By carrying land and other real estate investments at fair value, governmental enterprises will now be more comparable to each other and to their private-sector counterparts, as well as to governmental pension plans, other postemployment benefit (OPEB) plans, external investment pools, and Internal Revenue Code Section 457 deferred compensation plans that already report land and real estate investments at fair value. Generally, reporting such investments at fair value provides more decision-useful information about their composition, current value and recent changes in value.

GASB Statement No. 51 (GASB 51), *Accounting and Financial Reporting for Intangible Assets.* GASB issued Statement 51 in July 2007 to provide users of financial statements with more complete and comparable/consistent information about intangible assets. According to GASB 51, an intangible asset lacks physical substance, is nonfinancial in nature and has an initial useful life extending beyond a single reporting period. Intangible assets within the scope of GASB 51 include easements, computer software, water rights, timber rights, patents, and trademarks, among others.

PwC Observation: Goodwill is explicitly excluded from the scope of GASB 51. The Board concluded that the issues that would need to be deliberated in developing accounting and financial reporting requirements for goodwill extended beyond issues related to identifiable intangible assets.

GASB 51 deems all intangible assets to be "capital assets" (except for those explicitly excluded from its scope, such as goodwill and capital leases) and extends to them all existing authoritative guidance related to accounting and financial reporting for capital assets (e.g., recognition, measurement, depreciation/amortization, impairment, presentation, and disclosure).

PwC Observation: Among other matters, this will require intangible assets other than goodwill to be included in an entity's roll-forward disclosure of capital assets by major classes.

The provisions of GASB 51 are similar (but not identical) to those of FASB Statement No. 142, *Goodwill and Other Intangible Assets*. An intangible asset should be recognized only if it is considered "identifiable," meaning that the asset either: (1) is capable of being separated or divided and sold, transferred, licensed, rented or exchanged, either individually or together with a related contract, asset or liability; or (2) arises from contractual or other legal rights, regardless of whether those rights are transferable or separable from the entity or from other rights and obligations. GASB 51 establishes a "specified-conditions" approach to recognizing intangible assets that are internally generated (e.g., patents and copyrights, internally generated software).

GASB 51 also establishes specific guidance for the amortization of intangible assets, including determining the useful life of intangibles that are limited by legal or contractual provisions. If no factors exist that indicate a limitation on the useful life of an intangible asset, the asset has an indefinite useful life. Indefinite-lived intangibles should not be amortized unless their useful life is subsequently determined to be finite due to a change in circumstances. Like other capital assets, intangible assets within the scope of GASB 51 would be evaluated for impairment in accordance with the provisions of GASB Statement No. 42 (as amended by Statement No. 51).

GASB 51 is effective for financial statements for periods beginning after June 15, 2009, with earlier application encouraged. With certain exceptions (noted in paragraphs 21–23), the standard should be applied retroactively by restating financial statements for all prior periods presented. If restatement is not practical, the cumulative effect of the change should be reported as a restatement of beginning net assets for the earliest period restated.

PwC Observation: Until GASB 51 becomes effective, governmental enterprises that follow paragraph 7 of GASB Statement No. 20 will continue to account for intangible assets in accordance with FAS 142, with impairment of goodwill and indefinite-lived intangibles assessed in accordance with FAS 142 and impairment of finite-lived intangibles assessed in accordance with FAS 144, *Accounting for the Impairment or Disposal of Long-Lived Assets.* Other governmental enterprises continue to account for intangible assets in accordance with APB Opinion No. 17, *Intangible Assets,* until they adopt the new standard.

Because GASB 51's scope excludes goodwill, goodwill will continue to be accounted for in accordance with FAS 142 (for entities that apply paragraph 7 of GASB Statement No. 20) and APB Opinion No. 17 (for all other entities) subsequent to the adoption of GASB 51.

GASB Statement No. 50 (GASB 50), *Pension Disclosures.* GASB 50, issued in May 2007, amends GASB Statements No. 25, *Financial Reporting for Defined Benefit Pension Plans and Note Disclosures for Defined Contribution Plans,* and No. 27, *Accounting for Pensions by State and Local Governmental Employers,* to require governmental enterprises to provide enhanced disclosures and required supplementary information about their pension plans, similar to those required for other postemployment benefits by Statements No. 43, *Financial Reporting for Postemployment Benefit Plans Other Than Pension Plans,* and No. 45, *Accounting and Financial Reporting by Employers for Postemployment Benefits Other than Pensions.*

GASB 50 is intended to improve the transparency of pension information reported by governmental plans and employers by requiring:

- Disclosure of the current funded status of the plan as of the most recent actuarial valuation date in the notes to the financial statements of pension plans and certain employer governments, in addition to the funded status data currently presented as required supplementary information (RSI).

- For governments that use the aggregate actuarial cost method for determining the annual required contribution (ARC), note disclosure of the funded status of the plan, along with inclusion in RSI of a multiyear schedule of funding progress using the entry age actuarial cost method as a surrogate method.

- Additional note disclosures about actuarial methods and assumptions used in the valuations underlying information reported about the annual required contribution and funded status of the pension plan.

- Disclosure by governments participating in cost-sharing pension plans of how the contractually required contribution rate is determined.

- Presentation by cost-sharing employers of the required schedule of funding progress if the plan does not issue a GAAP-compliant report that includes RSI or if the plan is not included in a publicly available financial report of another entity.

The requirements of GASB 50 generally are effective for periods beginning after June 15, 2007, with early implementation encouraged. However, the requirements regarding presentation of funded status information calculated using a surrogate actuarial method are effective for financial statements that present information resulting from the plan's first actuarial valuation date on or after June 15, 2007.

PwC Observation: GASB 50 is likely to impact most governmental employers. Additional information will need to be obtained from actuaries in order to comply with these additional disclosure requirements. We recommend that clients meet with their actuaries to determine the information needed and to discuss the content and timing of when it will be received.

GASB Statement No. 49 (GASB 49), *Accounting and Financial Reporting for Pollution Remediation Obligations.* The GASB issued Statement 49 in November 2006. The standard provides guidance on the accounting and reporting of obligations and costs related to existing pollution remediation, such as obligations to clean up spills of hazardous wastes or to remove contamination (e.g., asbestos). Pollution prevention or control is not within the scope of GASB 49.

PwC Observation: This Statement is expected to have a significant impact on governmental organizations that have environmental contaminations, such as asbestos, on their properties. Originally, the GASB's goal was to comprehensively examine environmental liabilities that related to past, current and future activities, but ultimately they narrowed the scope to focus on the issues they believed most needed guidance, namely existing pollution remediation obligations, including contamination. In the future, the GASB may address other environmental issues, such as pollution prevention obligations and asset retirement obligations.

GASB 49 does not require governments to search for pollution remediation obligations, but instead sets forth triggers that would signal that a government should determine if it has to estimate and report a remediation liability. Those five circumstances (called "obligating events") are when a government:

- Is compelled to take remediation action because pollution creates an imminent endangerment to public health or welfare or the environment, leaving the government little or no discretion to avoid remediation action

- Is in violation of a pollution prevention-related permit or license, such as a Resource Conservation and Recovery Act (RCRA) permit or similar permits under state law

- Is named, or evidence indicates that it will be named, by a regulator as a responsible party or potentially responsible party (PRP) for remediation, or as a government responsible for sharing costs

- Is named, or evidence indicates that it will be named, in a lawsuit to compel the government to participate in remediation

- Has legally obligated itself to commence or is already commencing cleanup activities or monitoring or operation and maintenance of the remediation effort. If these activities are voluntarily commenced and none of the other obligating events have occurred relative to the entire site, the amount recognized should be based on the portion of the remediation project that the government has initiated and is legally required to complete.

GASB 49 requires liabilities, expenses, and expenditures to be estimated using an "expected cash flows" measurement technique. In addition, it requires disclosures about pollution clean-up efforts in the notes to the financial statements. The requirements of this Statement are effective for financial statements for periods beginning after December 15, 2007.

PwC Observation: Some overlap exists between the scopes of GASB 49 and FASB Statement No. 143, *Accounting for Asset Retirement Obligations.* In applying FAS 143, governmental enterprises that follow paragraph 7 of GASB Statement No. 20 must be careful to apply only those portions that do not conflict with requirements of GASB 49 or other GASB standards. Thus, they would not apply FAS 143's provisions concerning asbestos removal. They also would not apply any provisions related to "conditional" obligations, unless those obligations are likely to occur as discussed in NCGA Statement No. 4, *Accounting and Financial Reporting Principles for Claims and Judgments and Compensated Absences.*

An interpretation of FAS 143, FASB Interpretation No. 47, *Accounting for Conditional Asset Retirement Obligations,* clarifies that the term "conditional asset retirement obligation" refers to a legal obligation to perform an asset retirement activity in which the timing and (or) method of settlement are conditional on a future event that may or may not be within the control of the organization. According to the GASB 20 page on GASB's web site (www.gasb.org/st20guide.html), FIN 47 conflicts with the requirements of NCGAS 4 and FASB Statement No. 5 and, therefore, should not be applied by governmental organizations.

GASB Statement No. 48 (GASB 48), *Sales and Pledges of Receivables and Future Revenues and Intra-Entity Transfers of Assets and Future Revenues.* Governments sometimes exchange an interest in future cash flows for immediate cash payments. Issued in September 2006, GASB 48 establishes that such transactions should be reported as a collateralized borrowing unless certain criteria are met that indicates that a sale has taken place. In general, if the government retains control over the receivables or future revenues, then the transaction would be a collateralized borrowing. However, if the government relinquishes control, then: (1) transactions involving receivables would be reported as "sales," and (2) transactions involving future revenue would be reported as "deferred revenue," which would be amortized based on several criteria.

In addition, GASB 48 stipulates that governments should not revalue assets that are transferred between financial reporting entity components. Therefore, any assets (or future revenues) sold or donated within the same financial reporting entity should continue to be reported at their current carrying value when those assets or future revenues are transferred.

GASB 48 requires certain additional financial statement disclosures pertaining to future revenues that have been pledged or sold. The notes to the financial statements should identify the revenues that are pledged, the purposes for which they are pledged, the duration of the commitment, and some measure of the relationships of the pledged portion to the total revenue and of the actual revenues to the amount pledged. (However, an exemption from those disclosures is provided for legally separate entities that report as stand-alone business-type activities whose operations are financed primarily by a single major revenue source.)

The requirements of this Statement are effective for financial statements for periods beginning after December 15, 2006.

PwC Observation: The provisions pertaining to valuation of transfers between financial reporting entity components creates an exception to GASB 34's general rule that transactions between a primary government and its discretely presented component units ("intra-entity transactions") should be reported as if they were transactions with external parties.

GASB Statement No. 45 (GASB 45), *Accounting and Financial Reporting by Employers for Postemployment Benefits Other Than Pensions.* Issued in June 2004, GASB 45 establishes standards for the measurement, recognition and display of OPEB expense and related liabilities (assets), note disclosures, and, if applicable, required supplementary information (RSI) in the financial reports of state and local governmental employers.

GASB 45 improves the relevance and usefulness of financial reporting by: (1) requiring systematic, accrual-basis measurement and recognition of OPEB cost (expense) over a period that approximates employees' years of service, and (2) providing information about actuarial accrued liabilities associated with OPEB and whether and to what extent progress is being made in funding the plan.

GASB 45 requires employers that participate in single-employer or agent multiple-employer defined-benefit OPEB plans (sole and agent employers) to measure and disclose an amount for annual OPEB cost on the accrual basis of accounting. Annual OPEB cost is equal to the employer's annual required contribution (ARC) to the plan, with certain adjustments if the employer has a net OPEB obligation for past under or over contributions.

The ARC is defined as the employer's required contributions for the year, calculated in accordance with certain parameters, and including: (1) the normal cost for the year, and (2) a component for amortization of the total unfunded actuarial accrued liabilities (or funding excess) of the plan over a period not to exceed 30 years. The parameters include requirements for the frequency and timing of actuarial valuations, as well as for the actuarial methods and assumptions that are acceptable for financial reporting. If the methods and assumptions used in determining a plan's funding requirements meet the parameters, the same methods and assumptions are required for financial reporting by both a plan and its participating employers. However, if a plan's method of financing does not meet the parameters (e.g., the plan is financed on a pay-as-you-go basis), the parameters nevertheless apply for financial reporting purposes.

For financial reporting purposes, an actuarial valuation is required at least biennially for OPEB plans with a total membership (including employees in active service, terminated employees who have accumulated benefits but are not yet receiving them, and retired employees and beneficiaries currently receiving benefits) of 200 or more, or at least triennially for plans with a total membership of fewer than 200. The projection of benefits should include all benefits covered by the current substantive plan (the plan as understood by the employer and plan members) at the time of each valuation and should take into consideration the pattern of sharing of benefit costs between the employer and plan members to that point, as well as certain legal or contractual caps on benefits to be provided. The parameters require that the selection of actuarial assumptions, including the health care cost trend rate for postemployment health care plans, be guided by applicable actuarial standards.

A sole employer in a plan with fewer than 100 total plan members (including employees in active service, terminated employees who have accumulated benefits but are not yet receiving them, and retirees and beneficiaries currently receiving benefits) has the option to apply a simplified alternative measurement method instead of obtaining actuarial valuations. The option also is available to an agent employer with fewer than 100 plan members, in circumstances in which the employer's use of the alternative measurement method would not conflict with a requirement that the agent multiple-employer plan obtain an actuarial valuation for plan reporting purposes.

Employers participating in cost-sharing multiple-employer plans that are administered as trusts or equivalent arrangements are required to recognize OPEB expense for their contractually required contributions to the plan on the accrual basis. Required disclosures include identification of the way that the contractually required contribution rate is determined (e.g., by statute or contract or on an actuarially determined basis). Employers participating in a cost-sharing plan are required to present as RSI schedules of funding progress and employer contributions for the plan as a whole if a plan financial report, prepared in accordance with GASB Statement 43, is not issued and made publicly available and the plan is not included in the financial report of a public employee retirement system or another entity.

PwC Observation: GASB 45 is likely to impact almost all governmental enterprises, and based on the facts and circumstances, amounts of liabilities and their impact on net assets could be material. It is important for institutions to understand the reporting guidance and engage technical experts early to prepare the necessary actuarial valuations. For institutions that participate in pooled arrangements (e.g., with a state system), it is important to understand the accounting and reporting requirements applicable to employers participating in cost-sharing multiple-employer plans. In instances where a public college or university participates in pooled arrangements, the public college or university should consider verifying with the state's comptroller the terms of the plans and whether there is a requirement or expectation to "push down" the accounting from the state to the public college or university.

Employers that participate in defined-contribution OPEB plans are required to recognize OPEB expense for their required contributions to the plan and a liability for unpaid required contributions on the accrual basis. GASB 45 also includes guidance for employers that finance OPEB as insured benefits and for special funding situations.

The requirements of GASB 45 are effective in three phases based on a government's total annual revenues in the first fiscal year ending after June 15, 1999. Governments with annual revenues of $100 million or more (i.e., phase 1 governments) are required to implement GASB 45 in periods beginning after December 15, 2006. For phase 2 governments (i.e., those with total annual revenues of $10 million or more but less than $100 million), the statement is effective for periods beginning after December 15, 2007, and for phase 3 governments (total annual revenues of less than $10 million), the statement will be effective for periods beginning after December 31, 2008. Earlier application is encouraged. Component units should implement these requirements no later than the same year as their primary government.

Simultaneously with the implementation of GASB 45, governmental enterprises should implement the provisions of GASB Statement No. 47, *Accounting for Termination Benefits*, for any termination benefits provided through a defined-benefit OPEB plan, and should also implement the provisions of Technical Bulletins 2006-1 and 2004-2 pertaining to federal subsidies for Medicare Part D prescription drug coverage and the timing of reporting of expenses related to contractually required contributions, respectively.

PwC Observation: Some governmental organizations account for their OPEB liabilities in accordance with FASB Statement No. 106 (FAS 106). Once GASB 45 becomes effective, FAS 106 should no longer be applied. When transitioning to GASB 45, those organizations should consider the guidance in question 8.69.3 of GASB's Comprehensive Implementation Guide for assistance in determining whether their "qualifying" trusts under FAS 106 will meet the requirements for a qualifying "trust or equivalent arrangement" under GASB 45.

Because GASB 45 generally provides for prospective implementation, those organizations should also reverse any OPEB liabilities previously recognized under FAS 106.

Concept Statement No. 4, Elements of Financial Statements. GASB's Concepts Statements are intended to provide a conceptual framework of interrelated objectives and fundamental concepts that can be used as a basis for establishing consistent financial reporting standards. Concepts Statements do not themselves represent specific standards that must be applied in the preparation of financial statements; rather, they provide the GASB with the basic conceptual foundation for considering the merits of alternative approaches to financial reporting and help the Board develop well-reasoned financial reporting standards. They also help preparers, auditors. and users better understand the fundamental concepts underlying financial reporting standards.

GASB's newest concepts statement, issued in June 2006, establishes definitions for the seven elements of financial statements of state and local governments. Elements of financial statements are the fundamental components of financial statements. The elements of a statement of financial position are defined as follows:

- *Assets* are resources with present service capacity that the government presently controls.
- *Liabilities* are present obligations to sacrifice resources that the government has little or no discretion to avoid.
- A *deferred outflow* of resources is a consumption of net assets by the government that is applicable to a future reporting period.
- A *deferred inflow* of resources is an acquisition of net assets by the government that is applicable to a future reporting period.
- *Net position* is the residual of all other elements presented in a statement of financial position.

The elements of the resource flows statements are defined as follows:

- An *outflow* of resources is a consumption of net assets by the government that is applicable to the reporting period.
- An *inflow* of resources is an acquisition of net assets by the government that is applicable to the reporting period.

These definitions are primarily based on the inherent characteristics of each element. Central to most of these definitions is a resource, which in the governmental context is an item that can be drawn on to provide services to the citizenry.

PwC Observation: Prior to completing its work on Concepts Statement 4, GASB had relied on the financial statement elements defined in FASB Concepts Statement No. 6: assets, liabilities, equity/net assets, revenues, expenses, gains, losses, comprehensive income, investments by owners, and distributions to owners. GASB's elements framework adds two new Balance Sheet elements that do not appear in the FASB framework—"deferred outflows" and "deferred inflows." The Concepts Statement 4 project was closely linked to GASB's derivatives project—in fact, GASB issued Concepts Statement 4 just three days prior to issuing the derivatives exposure draft. This was because the two new Balance Sheet elements defined earlier are an essential component of GASB's proposed model for reporting hedging derivatives.

GASB Technical Bulletin No. 2006-1 (GTB 06-1), *Accounting and Financial Reporting by Employers for Payments from the Federal Government Pursuant to the Retiree Drug Subsidy Provisions of Medicare Part D.* Medicare Part D is a federal program that provides prescription drug benefits to eligible Medicare recipients. Employers that provide postretirement prescription drug coverage benefits may receive federal subsidy payments related to Medicare Part D prescription drug coverage. This GASB technical bulletin, issued in June 2006, clarifies how state and local governments or plans should report those federal subsidy payments. In general:

- Governmental employers should report these payments as voluntary nonexchange revenue; they should not be netted against costs.

- If the subsidy payment is made directly to a government's OPEB plan, the government should report the subsidy as an "on-behalf payment for fringe benefits," in accordance with GASB Statement No. 24, *Accounting and Financial Reporting for Certain Grants and Other Financial Assistance.* Plans should report the payments separately from the contributions they receive from the government.

The technical bulletin further clarifies that the accounting and reporting for OPEB is not affected by the Medicare Part D payment.

Therefore, the calculation of the long-term obligation related to OPEB, the annual OPEB cost and a government's annual required contribution for OPEB would not be reduced by the federal payments that are expected in the future.

TB 2006-1 was effective upon issuance. However, the provisions that relate to the measurement, recognition or required supplementary information requirements of GASB 43 should be applied simultaneously with the implementation of GASB 43 or GASB 45.

PwC Observation: GASB's reporting requirements for these payments differ from the FASB guidance applied by private-sector entities. Private-sector organizations net the subsidy payments against the related other postemployment benefit costs and liabilities, as required by FSP No. FAS 106-2.

GASB Technical Bulletin No. 2004-2 (GTB 04-2), *Recognition of Pension and Other Postemployment Benefit (OPEB) Expenditures/Expense and Liabilities by Cost-Sharing Employers.*   Issued in December 2004, GTB 04-2 clarifies the requirements in GASB 27, *Accounting for Pensions by State and Local Governmental Employers*, and GASB 45 regarding accounting for employers' contractually required contributions to cost-sharing pension and OPEB plans. Per GTB 04-2, expense related to contractually required contributions are recognized in the period they are due "for," rather than the period they are due "in." For example, pension or OPEB expenditures that are "for" (i.e., related to) December's payroll should be recorded in December, even if they are not due until February 1. This point was not clear in GASB 27 and 45, and was causing confusion.

The provisions of GTB 04-2 are already in effect for pension transactions. For OPEB transactions, the technical bulletin should be applied simultaneously with the implementation of GASB 45.

PwC Observation: Note that GTB 04-2 relates to both GASB 45 and GASB 27.

GASB Exposure Drafts

Proposed GASB Statement, *Accounting and Financial Reporting for Derivative Instruments.*   GASB issued an exposure draft of its proposed derivatives standard, along with an accompanying "plain-language supplement," in June 2007. The exposure draft proposes that, generally, derivatives should be reported at fair value on the statement of net assets. Hedge accounting would be required if an effective hedge is present, and there would be multiple methods allowed for evaluating hedge effectiveness. If a derivative effectively hedges (i.e., significantly reduces) an identified risk of losing cash flows or fair values, then its annual fair value changes would be reported as Balance Sheet deferrals until the derivative ends or ceases to be effective. At that time, the accumulated changes, if any, would be reported as investment income or loss.

PwC Observation: GASB's Concepts Statement No. 4 (discussed previously) incorporates two new elements of financial statement— deferred inflows and deferred outflows—to accommodate this aspect of the proposed GASB derivatives accounting model.

The annual change in the fair value of nonhedging derivatives would be reported immediately as investment income or loss. Additional information would be required to be disclosed in the notes to the financial statements, including identification of the risks to which derivatives expose the organization.

The proposed GASB standard uses the same basic definition of a derivative as is used in FASB Statement No. 133, *Accounting for Derivative Instruments and Hedging Activities* (as amended) and, like FAS 133, it requires derivatives to be displayed at fair value on the Balance Sheet. However, it differs from FAS 133 in several significant respects. The proposed standard would mandate that governments assess all potential hedging relationships for effectiveness (that is, hedge accounting would be mandatory, not elective as it is under FAS 133). The effective portion of hedges would be reported in special Balance Sheet accounts (deferred inflows and deferred outflows), rather than in the statement of revenues, expenses, and changes in net assets. The proposed standard identifies the SIFMA (formerly the BMA) swap index and the AAA general obligation bonds index as benchmark interest rates for hedges of tax-exempt debt; FAS 133's benchmarks are the London Interbank Offered Rate (LIBOR) and the interest rates on direct treasury obligations.

PwC Observation: The proposed standard identifies LIBOR as a benchmark interest rate for hedges of taxable debt, but not as a benchmark rate for hedges of tax-exempt debt.

The comment period ended on October 26, 2007 and a public hearing was held on November 1, 2007. The Board anticipates issuing this proposed standard in final form in June 2008. An implementation guide is expected to be available shortly thereafter. The proposed effective date would be for periods beginning after June 15, 2009, with earlier application encouraged.

Until a final GASB derivatives standard is issued and effective, governmental organizations that apply paragraph 7 of GASB 20 will continue to apply FAS 133 and related statements that interpret it, to the extent they do not contradict or conflict with the provisions of existing GASB pronouncements. Governmental organizations that do not apply paragraph 7 continue to apply the guidance in FAS 52, *Foreign Currency Translation*, FAS 80, *Accounting for Futures Contracts*, and GASB Technical Bulletin 2003-1, *Disclosure Requirements for Derivatives Not Reported at Fair Value on the Statement of Net Assets*.

PwC Observation: In our comment letter on the proposed standard, PwC expressed concern that mandating hedge accounting would make implementation of the standard overly complex and unduly burdensome for a number of governmental organizations, particularly smaller organizations. In its redeliberations to date, the Board still supports mandatory hedge accounting.

Other GASB Guidance and Projects

Comprehensive Implementation Guide Update. In September 2007, GASB's 2007–2008 Comprehensive Implementation Guide was released. The guide was updated to incorporate the impact of pronouncements issued since June 2006 and to address additional issues that came to the attention of the GASB staff in the intervening period.

PwC Observation: The Comprehensive Implementation Guide can be ordered through the GASB on their web site at www.gasb.org.

IV. OTHER ISSUES

In this section, we provide a summary of four issues of general interest: the implications of International Financial Reporting Standards (IFRS) for financial reporting in the United States, the economic credit crunch, the Municipal Securities Rulemaking Board's proposed new Electronic Data Gathering, Analysis, & Retrieval (EDGAR)-like system for municipal bond disclosure documents (EMMA), and the implications of the new FASB Codification now being tested.

International Financial Reporting Standards (IFRS)

In November 2007, the SEC unanimously approved amendments to its rules and forms that will eliminate the requirement for foreign private issuers (FPIs) using IFRS as issued by the International Accounting Standards Board (IASB) to reconcile their financial statements to U.S. GAAP. This decision signals the SEC's acknowledgment of the globalization of the capital markets, the quality of the IFRS accounting and reporting framework, and the progress achieved through the convergence efforts of the IASB and the FASB. It also increases the importance of IFRS in the United States.

PwC Observation: A growing dialogue has developed in recent years about the future of financial reporting—and in particular the relevance and complexity of today's reporting model. At the 2006 AICPA National Conference on Current SEC and PCAOB Developments, the discussion regarding IFRS focused on **whether** the United States should move to IFRS. This year, the conversation was directed at **when** U.S. public companies would be permitted (if not required) to report using IFRS, how the change should take place, and what companion regulatory and behavioral changes were needed to precede such a change. PwC and the other large accounting firms are engaged in discussions with stakeholders around the world on a number of issues critical to the long-term strength and stability of the capital markets, including financial reporting. These discussions have indicated overwhelming support for IFRS as a single set of high-quality accounting standards that can be used around the world.

As IFRS gains momentum in the United States, it raises questions about the future of financial reporting for nongovernmental entities, including not-for-profit organizations—namely, should all authoritative guidance for public, private, and not-for-profit organizations ultimately emanate from the global standard setter? Other countries are facing similar questions, and in some cases have reached a decision. Canada, for example, has decided to pursue separate standard setting for these three types of reporting entities. Other countries have adopted a single strategy for all types of reporting entities.

PwC Observation: At this point, there are a number of unanswered questions related to not-for-profit organizations. Is there a consistent universal definition in accounting literature of a not-for-profit? What types of entities are included in or excluded from that definition? (For example, the U.S. not-for-profit sector includes many not-for-profit health care organizations; in some other countries, health care resides entirely within the governmental sector). If there are numerous differences, does it make sense to try to craft "one-size-fits-all" rules?

Credit Market Events

Investment Valuations. The current capital market environment has become extremely challenging as it relates to valuation of certain investments tied to subprime mortgages. While not-for-profit and governmental entities may not have directly invested in structured finance vehicles involving subprime mortgages as heavily as some other sectors of the economy, they may have invested indirectly through hedge funds or funds with significant concentrations in that area—for example, collateralized debt obligation (CDO) funds, mortgage funds, enhanced or structured debt funds, or other high-yield funds. Additionally, their pension funds or employee benefit plans may have invested directly in subprime residential mortgage-backed securities, subprime CDOs, and similar investments, given the high investment ratings some of these investments enjoyed until recently.

PwC Observation: Not-for-profit and governmental organizations should evaluate their investment portfolios, including alternative investments, endowment funds, pension funds, and employee benefit plans, and consider whether recent events could have caused these investments to sharply devalue or become illiquid. Valuation of these investments may be challenging due to market uncertainty and concerns regarding liquidity, and may require the use of a specialist. Information about events occurring subsequent to the Balance Sheet date may need to be considered to determine whether those events were confirmation of facts and circumstances that existed at the Balance Sheet date and, thus, require adjustment of recorded financial statement amounts. Consideration should also be given to whether additional disclosures under SOP 94-6, *Disclosures of Risk and Uncertainties,* may be required. Disclosure pursuant to SOP 94-6 is required if both (1) known information available prior to issuance of financial statements indicates that it is reasonably possible that an estimate will change in the near term due to one or more confirming events, and (2) the effect of the change would be material.

Tax-Exempt Debt. The capital market environment for not-for-profit organizations and governmental entities that have issued tax-exempt debt has become more challenging in light of the impact of subprime loan exposure on bond insurers. Of the seven companies that provide AAA-rated bond insurance—MBIA, AMBAC, FSA, FGIC, XLCA, Assured Guaranty, and CIFG—the majority have been under review for possible downgrades or have already received a downgrade from a major ratings agency. Roughly half of the $2.5 to $3 trillion of municipal securities currently outstanding is insured. Concerns over the weakening credit of AAA bond insurers is driving up municipal bond yields (which translates into higher borrowing costs) and creating market pressures on institutional investors (such as money market funds) to divest their holdings in insured municipal bonds. Bond insurance facilitates liquidity in the municipal market because investors will bid on insured bonds without having particular knowledge of the underlying credit of the issuer. When the value of the insurance is called into question, liquidity suffers.

Many not-for-profits and governments issue insured variable-rate bonds, typically in the form of auction-rate securities (ARSs) or variable-rate demand obligations or notes (VRDOs, VRDNs). Some key considerations for these securities are as follows:

- **ARS**—These securities typically have maturities of 30–40 years. They are characterized by an interest rate that periodically resets (typically every 7, 14, 28, or 35 days) through a Dutch auction process involving parties who want to sell the securities and parties who want to buy them. Because most ARSs are insured, insurer downgrades (actual or potential) may have a negative impact on marketability of the bonds and cause investors to demand higher interest rates. As a result, organizations that have issued ARSs are exposed to risk for substantially higher interest rate resets in future auctions, as well as the potential for sellers to outnumber buyers in future auctions (resulting in a failed auction). If an auction fails, the interest rate resets to a maximum rate defined for the issue (typically, a multiple of a reference rate, such as LIBOR, or a fixed percentage). To mitigate these risks, many organizations with outstanding ARSs are evaluating the feasibility of converting those bonds to another form of variable-rate debt (such as VRDOs or VRDNs) or to fixed-rate debt.

- **VRDNs/VRDOs**—Unlike ARSs (which represent long-term debt), these securities are short-term debt because of the "put" or demand feature that gives the bondholder the ability to "put" the bonds back to the issuer's remarketing agent. Under normal market conditions, if a bondholder exercises the put feature, the remarketing agent usually can obtain funds to honor the put by simultaneously reselling the bonds to another investor. If the put bonds cannot be remarketed to another investor, a liquidity facility issued by a financial institution (e.g., standby bond purchase agreement [SBPA], letter of credit [LOC], line of credit) typically provides the backup funding. Under market conditions where supply outweighs demand, the risk of "remarketing failure" increases significantly. Liquidity facilities typically contain financial covenants, some of which may involve rating triggers, which could cause the issuer to be in technical default and result in termination of the facility. The termination of a liquidity facility can have a devastating ripple effect on an organization's financial stability. If the terms of the liquidity facility previously supported Balance Sheet classification of the debt as long-term, termination of the liquidity facility or acceleration of the payment terms could result in reclassification of the debt to current. Such an event could trigger "waterfall" technical defaults of financial liquidity covenants associated with the bond indenture or other borrowing arrangements. If cross-default provisions or springing lockbox arrangements exist, the risk increases.

Increased usage of ARSs and VRDOs has also fueled the growth of the municipal interest rate swap market. Many organizations have chosen to synthetically convert their variable interest rate payments on debt to fixed interest rate payments by entering into floating-to-fixed interest rate swaps. However, organizations with interest rate swaps should be aware that swap values can be highly sensitive to changes in the participants' credit. Rating downgrades of the issuer, the counterparty or their financial guarantors to below levels specified in the swap agreement typically are considered to be termination events. Therefore, an organization participating in swaps is exposed to termination risk arising from a counterparty downgrade, its own downgrade or the downgrade of a guarantor. Regardless of which party's downgrade triggered the termination, if the swap is terminated earlier than expected, and the organization is "out of the money" at the termination date, the organization could be required to make a substantial termination payment (inclusive of the "out of money" payment) to the counterparty to settle the swap. In certain instances, a counterparty might allow the organization to post collateral in lieu of terminating the swap, but this still could have significant implications on liquidity.

PwC Observation: Actions such as the following may help an organization assess and monitor the impact of credit market events:

- Review all existing debt and swap agreements to inventory any references to insurance or counterparty-related downgrade triggers.

- Discuss the financial and legal implications for specific debt and swap structures with parties, such as bond counsel, underwriters and financial advisors.

- If downgrades have occurred, evaluate whether a condition of technical default (as spelled out in the underlying agreements) has occurred. If it has, an organization should develop a remediation plan, determine if any other loan agreements are impacted, and assess the classification of debt and treatment for associated deferred financing fees as well as how to account for amounts incurred to cure the default.

- Develop a contingency plan for mitigating or managing the exposure associated with swaps, particularly those used to hedge ARS. This may include assessing the feasibility of voluntary termination of a swap and its associated implications—for example, is the swap "out of the money" (i.e., in a liability position) and, if so, how much would the organization be required to pay to the counterparty in order to terminate?

- If cash flow hedge accounting is used, evaluate the impact of actual or potential swap counterparty downgrades on hedge effectiveness.

- If subject to SEC Rule 15c2-12 continuing disclosure agreements, discuss with bond counsel the need for filing material events notices with nationally recognized municipal securities information repositories (NRMSIRs).

- Evaluate the adequacy of debt and derivatives disclosures in financial statements.

- If previously issued financial statements are to be included in an OMB Circular A-133 filing or a bond offering, consider the need for a subsequent events footnote.

- If a refunding or mode conversion on existing bonds is executed, consider applicable accounting literature on extinguishment and modifications of debt, and the related implications for deferred financing costs. Relevant literature includes (but is not limited to) EITF 96-19, *Debtor's Accounting for a Modification or Exchange of Debt Instruments;* FAS 140, *Accounting for Transfers of Financial Assets and Extinguishments of Liabilities;* APB 26, *Early Extinguishment of Debt;* FAS 78, *Classification of Obligations that are Callable by the Creditor;* GASB 7, *Advance Refundings that Result in Defeasance of Debt;* GASB 23, *Accounting and Financial Reporting for Refundings of Debt Reported by Proprietary Activities;* and GASBI 1, *Demand Bonds Issued by State and Local Governmental Entities,* as appropriate.

New "Electronic Municipal Market Access" (EMMA) System for Municipal Disclosure Documents

The Municipal Securities Rulemaking Board (MSRB) is working to implement EMMA, a municipal market version of the SEC's EDGAR system that makes annual, quarterly, and material events information of SEC registrant companies publicly available. Subject to SEC approval,

EMMA is expected to be implemented in stages, with the initial stage scheduled to pilot in March 2008 (for official statements and advance refunding documents). Additional stages would follow later in 2008 in which EMMA would expand to become a full-fledged EDGAR-type online public dissemination vehicle. At that point, all official statements, annual and quarterly financial information, and material event notices for all issuers required to make continuing disclosure filings under SEC Rule 15c2-12 would be made available online free of charge. The system would also provide trade pricing information for municipal securities that is similar to the New York Stock Exchange (NYSE) or Nasdaq.

Initially, submissions to EMMA would be voluntary; however, the SEC is expected to eventually mandate its use to replace the current vendor-based system of nationally recognized municipal information repositories (NRMSIRs), as well as Disclosure USA, the "central post office" disclosure facility operated by the Municipal Advisory Council of Texas.

PwC Observation: The establishment of an EMMA warehouse will provide one location for submitting and retrieving data, versus the numerous data portals that currently exist. Municipal market participants should monitor EMMA's progress, given the expectation that it could be in place before the end of 2008. Before MSRB can implement the full-fledged EMMA system (complete with secondary market disclosure documents), the SEC will need to amend Rule 15c2-12 to require secondary market disclosure documents to be filed with the MSRB, rather than with the NRMSIRs. The SEC expects to complete drafting the proposed rule changes during the first quarter of 2008, but it could take an additional six months or so to finalize them and obtain approval from SEC commissioners.

FASB Launches Verification Phase for the FASB Accounting Standards Codification

Private-sector GAAP is a proliferation of thousands of standards established by a variety of standard setters—FASB, the AICPA, and the EITF, among others—over the last 50+ years. As such, the standards lack a consistent and logical structure. Additionally, there has been an explosive increase in the volume of financial reporting guidance over the past 20 years, which has compounded the difficulties encountered by preparers and auditors in applying and interpreting GAAP. In response to concerns that the current structure of GAAP is unwieldy, difficult to understand, and difficult to use, several years ago the FASB launched a project to codify and simplify authoritative private-sector GAAP. In contrast to the current multitiered GAAP hierarchy, this codification was envisioned as integrating all accounting standards within levels A through D of the current GAAP hierarchy (including FASB, AICPA, EITF and related literature) into one central, topically organized, electronically searchable place. The GAAP hierarchy would be eliminated, and all information within the codification would be considered level A (authoritative) GAAP.

In January 2008, the FASB launched the one-year verification (testing) phase of the Codification. During the verification period, constituents are encouraged to use the online Codification Research System free of charge to research accounting issues and provide feedback on whether the Codification content accurately reflects existing GAAP for nongovernmental organizations. Users are advised that the Codification content is not yet approved as authoritative and, therefore, they must verify research results using their existing resources for the currently effective literature. After the one-year public comment period, the FASB will finalize the Codification and it will become the single authoritative source of GAAP for nongovernmental organizations, superseding all of the existing, separate standards.

PwC Observation: The Codification does not change GAAP; instead, it reorganizes the thousands of GAAP pronouncements into roughly 90 accounting topics, and displays all topics using a consistent structure. Like other sectors, not-for-profit organizations are expected to benefit from these efforts to simplify and improve GAAP. Organizations should make use of the one-year verification phase and help "kick the tires." The Codification also has an indirect impact on governmental enterprises because a significant portion of the level A guidance in the governmental GAAP hierarchy consists of FASB standards that have been made applicable to governmental business-type organizations. GASB is exploring various options for preserving that important component of the governmental GAAP hierarchy.

V. REGULATORY ISSUES

This section highlights issues affecting the regulatory environment as well as changes to the professional literature and regulatory standards.

Changes to the Professional Literature and Regulatory Standards

Yellow Book 2007 Revision. In July 2007, the Government Accountability Office (GAO) posted the 2007 revision to "Government Auditing Standards," also known as "GAGAS" or "the Yellow Book," to its web site (www.gao.gov). The 2007 revisions were comprehensive and include:

- Clarification of the use of terms *must, should,* and *may* when describing the auditor's responsibility
- A new chapter on ethics
- Adoption of AICPA Statement on Auditing Standards No. 112, *Communication of Internal Control Related Matters Noted in an Audit* (SAS 112). The new definitions of significant deficiency and material weakness that have been incorporated into the Yellow Book are likely to affect the auditor's risk assessment for major programs under OMB A-133. They also are likely to affect the number and type of control deficiencies reported in Yellow Book audits. The revised Yellow Book incorporates SAS 112 effective for financial statement audits conducted under GAGAS for year-ends after December 15, 2006.
- Additional disclosure requirements related to the restatement of previously issued financial statements (e.g., discussion of the specific internal control deficiencies that contributed to the restatement)
- Expanded discussion of the use of "matter of emphasis" paragraphs in an auditor report (e.g., uncertainties about an institution's financial future)

- Many edits to modernize and incorporate current thinking concerning best auditing practices
- Expanded and updated performance audit standards

The 2007 Yellow Book revisions go into effect for audits of periods beginning after January 1, 2008. Printed revisions of the Yellow Book are available from the Government Printing Office (866-512-1800).

In January 2008, the GAO also issued a guidance document, *Government Auditing Standards: Implementation Tool—Professional Requirements for Use in Implementing Requirements Identified by "Must" and "Should" in the July 2007 Revision of Government Auditing Standards*.

PwC Observation: The changes to the Yellow Book are substantial. They reflect the changing audit environment in which greater transparency and accountability are expected from auditors and institutions. Broadly, the proposed Yellow Book revisions are part of the GAO's overall objective to support "the Congress and the nation in facing the challenges of a rapidly changing world while addressing the nation's large and growing long-term fiscal imbalance."

The guidance document allows the auditor and other interested persons to focus on the most significant requirements contained in the Yellow Book. However, we recommend the guidance document not be used as a substitute for reading the Yellow Book because the Yellow Book contains much explanatory material in addition to the minimum requirements.

New AICPA Auditing Standard and Related Interpretation. As reported in the 2007 edition of this document, the AICPA has replaced its Statement on Auditing Standards No. 60 (SAS 60) with SAS 112. The new SAS incorporates the Public Company Accounting Oversight Board's (PCAOB's) definition of significant deficiency and material weakness from the PCAOB's Auditing Standard No. 2, *An Audit of Internal Control over Financial Reporting Performed in Conjunction with an Audit of Financial Statements*.

This new SAS impacts the audits of not-for-profits as well as other types of organizations that require an audit under the Yellow Book. It also impacts grant audits conducted under various state regulations, because some states follow the federal reporting guidelines. OMB and federal agencies have considered the impact of SAS 112 on OMB

Circular A-133 and specific federal agency program audit regulations and guides, and the use of SAS 112 has been mandated when auditing major federal programs under the provisions of OMB Circular A-133.

The AICPA issued an interpretation of SAS 112 (AU Section 9325) in 2007 that provides definitions of "control deficiency," "significant deficiency" and "material weakness" in a compliance environment.

In its 2007 risk alert titled *"Government Auditing Standards and Circular A-133 Audits,"* the AICPA also issued further guidance concerning the application of SAS 112 to compliance auditing, including examples of control deficiencies that ordinarily might be considered to be significant deficiencies and those that might ordinarily be considered material weaknesses.

PwC Observation: The revised Yellow Book standards that incorporate SAS 112 definitions may result in more internal control-related findings being reported to management and audit committees, including more significant deficiencies or material weaknesses for both the financial statement (Yellow Book reporting) and major program (A-133) reporting.

OMB A-133 Compliance Supplement.   OMB is currently drafting the 2008 Compliance Supplement, which is expected to be issued in the second quarter of 2008. Significant changes anticipated include:

- Various program updates to many individual Catalog of Federal Domestic Assistance (CFDA) sections and the addition of some new program sections in part four
- No significant changes to the 14 compliance requirements in part three
- No significant changes to the research and development cluster in part five; however, there may be added emphasis on certain of the applicable 14 compliance requirements
- Several technical updates made throughout the Student Financial Aid cluster, including changes in the return of funds requirements and potentially the addition of new required compliance procedures concerning preferred student lender lists and the acceptance of prohibited inducements from lenders

PwC Observation: Institutions should review the 2008 Compliance Supplement, when it becomes available, with their auditor to determine the impact of these changes on the scope of their 2008 A-133 audit. The Compliance Supplement will be posted to OMB's web site at www.whitehouse.gov/omb.

Current Regulatory Environment

Department of Health and Human Services (HHS).

(1) TIME AND EFFORT REPORTING

Time and effort reporting continues to be a challenging area, particularly for institutions that receive funding from HHS. In most federal awards, personnel costs, including direct labor charges, fringe benefits and the related indirect costs, represent the largest charges to the government. The HHS Office of Inspector General (OIG) and the Department of Justice are aggressive in bringing charges for noncompliance with labor cost requirements and for overcharging for labor costs on federal awards.

The HHS OIG fiscal 2007 and 2008 work plans, which set the direction for the OIG's audits, include among the areas HHS OIG plans to focus on, including:

- *Effort reporting*: Are the institutions accurately reflecting the portion of researchers' efforts spent on grants sponsored by the National Institutes of Health (NIH)?

- *Administrative and clerical salaries*: Are institutions appropriately charging administrative and clerical salaries to federally sponsored grants and cooperative agreements?

- *Cost transfers*: Are cost transfers supported by documentation that fully explains the reasons for the transfer? Have responsible grantee officials certified the correctness of the new charges?

- *Compensation of graduate students*: Is compensation for graduate student researchers' who receive tuition remission as a component of compensation charged to NIH grants consistent with NIH guidelines? Note that Congress has requested this review.

Regarding effort reporting, the OIG notes in its work plan for fiscal year 2007 (at www.oig.hhs.gov), "... the growing number of settlements under the False Claims Act regarding this issue indicates that some major research universities continue to engage in practices that do not result in an equitable distribution of their employees' activities, resulting in overcharges to NIH grants and a reduction in funds available for other research costs."

PwC Observation: Institutions that receive federal awards from HHS should pay particular attention to these areas of audit focus. When HHS finds that institutions have not complied with effort reporting, multimillion-dollar repayments and fines can be imposed.

Federal recipients should review their time and effort reporting systems—and strengthen them where needed. Some specific areas to address include:

- Timeliness of certification
- Access to a suitable means of verification for the person certifying the effort
- Accountability of time incurred at other related and unrelated entities
- Reconciliation of actual effort to the effort committed via award documents
- Review of central administration policies
- Review of effort report formats for OMB A-21

In addition, symptoms of potential deficiencies in time and effort reporting systems might include:

- Missing or incomplete effort reports
- A high volume of cost transfers
- Multiple documents recording faculty effort
- Incentive pay agreements

In particular, research institutions with the following characteristics should continue to be aware of the potential risks associated with their time and effort reporting systems in the current environment:

- "Collaborative" research agreements with other institutions
- Rapid growth in clinical research

- Recent system implementations
- Closely affiliated faculty practice plans
- Pre- and post-award processes that are outdated and under-staffed
- Closely affiliated hospitals and research institutions

In March 2007, the Council on Governmental Relations published *Policies and Practices: Compensation, Effort Commitments and Certifications*. This document discusses in detail many issues related to effort reporting.

(2) HHS Grants Policy Statement

Recipients of awards from the various operating divisions of the HHS Public Health Service (PHS) look to the PHS Grants Policy Statement, published in 1994, for guidance concerning the administration of those awards. Recipients of awards from other HHS divisions must use numerous other sources to obtain information for those awards.

In October 2006, HHS issued a Grants Policy Statement (GPS), which superseded the PHS Grants Policy Statement. It is intended to make available in a single document the general terms and conditions of HHS discretionary grant and cooperative agreement awards.

GPS is applicable to all HHS discretionary grant programs except NIH awards. The source of information concerning the administration of NIH awards continues to be the NIH Grants Policy Statement, which is dated December 1, 2003. In addition, GPS does not apply to mandatory grant programs or awards to individuals, such as fellowships. Although not completely finished, GPS has been posted to the HHS Health Resources and Services Administration web site (www.hrsa.gov/grants), and the most recent available GPS is dated January 1, 2007. It is effective for all new competing, continuation, and noncompeting continuation HHS and cooperative agreement awards with beginning dates on or after January 1, 2007.

The GPS contains four parts:

I.   HHS Grants Process

II. Terms and Conditions of HHS Grant Awards

III. Points of Contact

IV. Specific information and Terms and Conditions for Awards from HHS Operating Divisions with Requirements that Supplement the Information Contained in Parts I, II, III of GPS

PwC Observation: This is a substantial document that, when completed, will allow for greater consistency in the administration of federal awards from HHS.

National Institutes of Health (NIH).

(1) HHS OIG Review of NIH Oversight of Conflict of Interest Policies and Reporting at Grantee Institutions

The HHS OIG completed its review of the oversight exercised by NIH over the conflict of interest policies and reporting by grantee institutions to NIH. In its January 2008 report (OEI–03–06–00460), the OIG found that NIH needs to improve its oversight and recommended:

1. Increased oversight of grantee institutions to ensure their compliance with federal financial conflict of interest regulations

2. NIH require grantee institutions to provide details regarding the nature of financial conflict of interest and how they are managed, reduced or eliminated

3. Requiring all NIH institutes to forward to the NIH Office of Extramural Research (OER) all financial conflict of interest reports received by grantee institutions and ensuring the OER conflict of interest databases contain information on all conflict of interest reports provided by grantee institutions

PwC Observation: NIH agreed with recommendations (1) and (3) above, but believes recommendation (2) would effectively transfer management of conflict of interest from the grantee institutions to the federal government. We believe the issue remains a top priority of HHS and focus will continue in this area. Institutions should review their conflict-of-interest policies to ensure that they meet current federal regulations and that they are being applied consistently throughout the institution.

(2) NIH Tuition Reimbursement Policy

In August 2006, NIH issued a new policy concerning salary caps used in funding reimbursements for tuition and other costs for graduate students and postdoctorial researchers. This policy change was necessary because reimbursement requests from NIH award recipients continue to outpace the growth in the NIH budget over the last few years.

The policy will be piloted in fiscal 2007 and 2008 and then reevaluated based on progress reports submitted in fiscal 2008 and 2009. NIH stated the policy will be finalized and issued in fiscal 2010.

Details of the new NIH finding provisions can be found in the NIH Notice NOT-OD-06-090, which was released August 4, 2006, at http://grants.nih.gov/grants/guide/.

PwC Observation: Although the changes to reimbursement caps will likely shift more costs to institutions, there are also changes to the rebudgeting rules contained in the NIH Policy Statement that are favorable to institutions.

Department of Education. In September 2007, the Department of Education issued Dear CPA letter CPA-07-03, which amends the January 2000 audit guide *"Audits of Federal Student Financial Assistance Programs at Participating Institutions and Institutional Servicers."* The subjects of this amendment include prohibited inducements paid by lenders and denying student's access to lenders and guarantee agencies of their choice. This amendment became effective for all audits conducted using the January 2000 audit guide with field work starting or in process on October 12, 2007.

This amendment contains mandatory audit procedures that are designed to identify prohibited inducements paid by lenders to schools or individuals at the schools related to the FFEL program and the denial of student access to FFEL lenders and guaranteed agencies of their choice.

PwC Observation: This amendment to the 2000 audit guide is a result of student loan abuses that surfaced in 2007. The criteria for determining what a prohibited inducement is will require auditors to make judgments when reading agreements between schools and lenders.

We recommend that institutions evaluate their internal controls over compliance with this area of the FFEL regulations and be prepared to assist their auditors in completing the new mandatory procedures.

The Department of Education is likely to propose similar mandatory procedures for audits of the student financial aid cluster performed within the provisions of OMB Circular A-133 (see "OMB Compliance Supplement" above). In addition, a Dear CPA letter, CPA–07–2, also issued in September 2007 and later revised and reissued as Dear CPA letter 08-1 in March, 2008, contains similar mandatory procedures for audits of lenders conducted under the Department of Education December 1996 audit guide for lenders and lender servicers participating in the FFEL program.

Office of Management and Budget (OMB).

(1) FEDERAL AWARD REPORTING REQUIREMENTS

OMB Circular A-110 Section 52 requires the submission of a "Financial Status Report (FSR)." Federal awarding agencies establish the frequency of submission, generally not more than quarterly and at least annually. For example, according to the NIH Grants Policy Statement, reports generally should be submitted within 90 days after the close of the annual budget, except for awards under the NIH Streamlined Non-Competing Award Process (SNAP) program, which requires an FSR to be submitted within 90 days of the end of the award or competitive segment.

Federal agencies are concerned with the higher delinquency rates associated with both financial and technical reports because they have resulted in significant delays to award closeouts. This problem is pervasive throughout the research industry and all federal agencies.

For instance, in 2004, HHS, NIH Office of Inspector General (OIG) and the National Science Foundation (NSF) OIG issued reports detailing the late reporting, which is in the double digits. The HHS and NSF OIG reports include similar recommendations to NIH and NSF program management officials:

- Develop automated reminder systems
- Improve ability for electronic submission of documents
- Focus more attention on late reporting

- Consider withholding future funding until the researcher and/or organization is caught up on late reports

PwC Observation: Financial Status Reports may be late for many reasons. For example, reporting deadlines may be too tight, especially for complex awards involving subrecipients. Also, federal agencies sometimes cannot respond in a timely manner to requests from institutions for additional information. However, federal agencies have been known to withhold funding to principal investigators when the delinquency rate is particularly high. Institutions must work with the federal agencies to strike a reasonable balance. The completeness and accuracy of reports should not be sacrificed for better timeliness.

(2) LATE A-133 REPORTS

OMB A-133 audit reports are required to be submitted to the Federal Audit Clearinghouse no later than nine months after the auditee's year-end. An OMB advisory task force has been studying the impact of late A-133 reporting. The task force's preliminary conclusion is that late A-133 reports—even if they are late by one day—should preclude an entity from being designated as a low-risk auditee. Also, obtaining an extension from the cognizant or oversight agency should not preserve low-risk status. Several federal agencies believe nine months is a sufficient amount of time. Federal agencies are concerned about the possibility that the reports are late because of underlying management and internal control problems that may not be reflected in A-133 audit reports.

PwC Observation: Institutions should make every effort to submit their A-133 reports to the Clearinghouse on a timely basis. If your institution has had difficulties in the past, we advise you to contact your auditor and work out a plan to submit the FY'07 report on time. It is expected that OMB will issue its view on this matter by June 30, 2008.

Export Regulations. The U.S. export laws continue to be a compliance concern for colleges and universities that are engaged in the transfers of export-controlled technical data and research, as well as access of export-controlled technical data and research from visiting foreign nationals. In December 2006, the U.S. GAO issued a report to the

House Committee on the Judiciary regarding export controls in which it indicated that its risk assessment of selected universities suggested a lack of clear understanding of export control laws and a failure to mitigate a university's risk accordingly. The government will apply increased scrutiny to university-sponsored programs to assess and decrease potential risks associated with the failure to report and apply for licenses where deemed exports are being transferred along with fundamental research.

The report concluded that both the commerce and state departments should strategically assess vulnerabilities in the conduct and publication of fundamental research in order to address findings that institutions misunderstand their obligations to self-regulate their potential to illegally transfer deemed exports. While the report indicated governmental guidance and support have been minimal, institutions still have an obligation to be self-compliant and implement internal controls, such as strategic contracting, access controls and modifications in the ways in which research is conducted, in order to ensure their research programs do not compromise national security. The report issued recommendations for the commerce and state departments to increase vigilance and scrutiny of institutions conducting research—fundamental or otherwise—in accordance with existing export control regulations.

The deemed export rule states that a transfer of certain controlled source code or technology to a foreign national located in the United States is deemed to be an export to the home country of that individual and is therefore subject to U.S. export controls. To determine if the deemed export rule applies, institutions must establish the reasons for controls (e.g., national security, nuclear proliferation) associated with the technologies/source code and identify if they apply to the home country of the foreign national. If the controls apply to the foreign national's home country, institutions in the United States may be required to secure export licenses from the Commerce or State departments before they can transfer or give access of controlled technical data to the foreign national. Many countries trigger licensing requirements, depending on the degree of control associated with the technical data and the particular country involved. These countries can include so-called "business-friendly" countries throughout the world, as well as embargoed countries, such as Cuba and Iran, that are highly restricted.

Failure to obtain the required licenses can result in substantial civil and criminal penalties, including monetary fines, loss of export privileges, reputation damage, and imprisonment.

PwC Observation: Certain types of research that qualify for the fundamental research and public domain exclusions may be exempt from export controls, including the deemed export rule, if institutions meet the exclusion requirements. However, exemption from export controls requires careful analysis of the project activities and close scrutiny of contract and project terms (e.g., publication restrictions) to avoid disqualifications, as well as diligent compliance with several regulatory requirements.

Other Issues

Federal Funding Accountability and Transparency Act. On September 26, 2006, President Bush signed into law the Federal Funding Accountability and Transparency Act of 2006. This bill requires the OMB to develop a searchable web site that taxpayers can access at no charge that will enable them to determine certain information about the grants, contracts, loans and cooperative agreements their tax dollars are funding. OMB can designate other federal agencies to assist in the development, operation, and support of the web site.

By January 1, 2009, all primary award recipients will be required to submit information on all subawards and subcontracts to federal agencies for inclusion on this new web site. The U.S. Department of Agriculture is piloting a program to determine the best way to implement a cost-effective process to submit subaward and subcontract data. The pilot program is scheduled to end in June 2008.

Regarding the reporting of subawards, award recipients can allocate as indirect costs reasonable costs for the collection and reporting of subaward data.

PwC Observation: Implementation of this Act allows the general public access to detailed information about the federal awards an institution is receiving and the tax dollars being spent on it.

Institutions should follow the developments with the reporting of subaward and subcontract information in order to plan for the effort that will be required to gather and submit subaward and subcontract data to federal agencies.

National Single Audit Sampling Project. The Department of Education and several other federal agencies, including HHS, NSF, Department of Defense (DOD) and HUD, designed a statistically valid approach to performing quality control reviews of single audits. Congress provided several million dollars to fund this effort, called the National Single Audit Sampling Project. The quality control reviews conducted under this project began in early 2005 and were concluded in the first quarter of 2007. A report summarizing the results of this initiative was issued by the President's Council on Integrity and Efficiency (PCIE) to OMB and provided to Congress as well as federal agency officials in June 2007.

The report noted several audit quality issues in varying degrees of significance that the PCIE recommends be addressed by both the accounting profession and federal regulators, including OMB. The recommendations include enhanced training requirements and revisions to the Single Audit Act standards and guidance.

In response to the findings included in this report, the AICPA created several task forces to develop solutions to audit quality issues and act upon the recommendations noted in the report. Similarly, several federal agencies have also formed task forces.

PwC Observation: The AICPA created the Governmental Audit Quality Center to promote and improve the quality of audits conducted under Governmental Auditing Standards (the Yellow Book). Membership in this center is voluntary and requires a CPA firm to adhere to several stringent audit quality practices. Presently, the GAQC member firms audit federal award recipients that account for more than 80% of federal awards to not-for-profit organizations that require a single audit. The GAQC web site (www.aicpa.org/gaqc) includes more information regarding Governmental Audits and Audit Quality.

VI. TAX ISSUES

In this section, we address tax matters impacting tax-exempt organizations, including the IRS's Exempt Organization Implementing Guidelines for fiscal year 2008 and the redesigned Form 990. We also include information regarding items of continuing interest to tax-exempt organizations, including compensation, public disclosure of Form 990-T and international activities.

New Issues

The Redesigned Form 990 for 2008. After receiving substantial input on the proposed 2008 Form 990, which was released to the public earlier in the year, the IRS released the redesigned 2008 Form 990, *Return of Organization Exempt From Income Tax*, on December 20, 2007. According to the IRS, the redesigned Form 990 was based on the three guiding principles of transparency, compliance, and minimizing taxpayer burden. Organizations will begin using the new form for years beginning in 2008, so that fiscal year taxpayers will use the new form for years ending in 2009. The 2008 Form 990, as well as other key information describing the redesign, is available on the IRS's web site, www.irs.gov/eo.

BASIC STRUCTURE OF THE NEW FORM 990

The 2008 Form 990 consists of an 11-page core form that each filing organization must complete. In addition, the Form utilizes 16 schedules designed to require reporting of information only from those organizations that conduct particular activities.

KEY FOCUS AREAS OF THE REDESIGNED FORM

Governance and Management: The new Form 990 asks for the number of voting members of an organization's governing body, as well as the number of voting members who are independent. It also inquires whether an officer, trustee, director, or key employee has a family or business relationship with another such person. The form now asks not only whether an organization has a written conflict of interest policy, but also about the monitoring and enforcement of that policy. It also inquires about the existence of whistle-blower and document-retention policies. While many of the new questions on the Form 990 are not mandated by law, they highlight best practices for tax-exempt organizations.

Compensation: Compensation on the 2008 Form 990 will be reported consistently with the Forms W-2 and 1099 issued during the fiscal year covered by the return. On Form 990, all of the organization's current officers, directors, trustees, and key employees must be disclosed, along with their compensation from the reporting organization and related organizations. Further, disclosure is required for:

- Former officers and key employees receiving more than $100,000 of reportable compensation from the organization and any related organizations
- Former directors and trustees receiving, in their capacity as a former director or trustee, more than $10,000 of reportable compensation from the organization and any related organizations

For certain officers, directors, trustees, key employees, and highest compensated employees, additional detail regarding compensation arrangements must be disclosed on Schedule J. On Schedule J, organizations also will be required to disclose the existence of certain practices, including whether there is a written policy regarding payment or reimbursement of certain expenses; whether the organization reimburses for first-class travel, club dues, or use of a personal residence; and whether compensation is paid or accrued contingent on the revenues or net income of the organization or an affiliate. While these are permissible practices, organizations should consider whether they will want to publicly disclose that they are engaged in these activities.

Hospitals: Particularly in response to congressional pressure, the IRS is requiring hospitals to report on Schedule H additional information focusing on charity care and other community benefits. For hospital systems, each hospital will need to complete its own Schedule H. Schedule H supports the use of the Catholic Health Association community benefit reporting model and requires reporting of a hospital's community benefit (including charity care). The Schedule also asks for a description of a hospital's community needs assessments, how it educates patients on their eligibility for assistance, and its community building activities. The IRS is providing transition relief for the completion of most of this Schedule until the 2009 Form 990.

Tax-Exempt Bonds: The new Schedule K will require additional detail on tax-exempt bonds on an issue-by-issue basis, including reporting on proceeds, private business use, and arbitrage. For example, in connection with private use, organizations will need to disclose, by bond issue, the percentage of financed property used by entities other than a section 501(c)(3) organization or a state or local government, as well as the percentage of financed property used in a private business as a result of an unrelated trade or business activity. This will require organizations to calculate the private business use percentage according to IRS rules and underscores the need to retain relevant documentation supporting its use of bond-financed facilities. The IRS is providing transition relief for the completion of most of this Schedule until the 2009 Form 990.

PwC Observation: Organizations should proactively prepare for the new reporting requirements. Although the 2008 Form 990 will not be filed until 2009 (or even 2010 for many fiscal year organizations), preparation should begin in 2008, including:

- Reviewing the redesigned Form 990 in detail and considering how the changes will impact the organization.

- Reviewing policies and practices in light of new disclosure requirements, recognizing that modification of existing or creation of new policies may be needed.

- Identifying where collection of new data might be required.

- Modifying existing financial and information data systems to accommodate new data collection and reporting requirements.

Tax-Exempt Bonds. As part of its efforts to focus on post-issuance compliance for tax-exempt bonds, in 2007 the IRS issued a postissuance compliance questionnaire to approximately 200 organizations. The questionnaire focused on compliance with record retention rules, private use limitations, and arbitrage rebate requirements. The IRS will analyze the responses to the questionnaire and may issue the questionnaire to a wider array of charities or decide that additional taxpayer assistance and/or enforcement initiatives should be implemented.

The IRS is continuing its audits of approximately 30 health care and housing bonds. These examinations began in August 2006. It is expected that the results of these audits will be published in fiscal year 2008.

Tax-exempt bonds will lose their tax-exempt status if both the private use and private payment limitations are exceeded. Private use occurs when bond-financed property is used in the trade or business of an entity that is not tax exempt. Private payments are revenues generated from private use. For private institutions, the limitation on private use and private payment is 5%. For not-for-profit governmental institutions, the applicable limitation is 10%. The private use/private payment limitations are reduced to the extent that proceeds are used for issuance costs. Up to 2% of bond proceeds may be used to fund issuance costs.

At the time of issuance, bond counsel would have engaged in a detailed review of all of the anticipated uses of and contracts associated with the financed facilities. Institutions need to review any postissuance changes in the use of financed facilities. Agreements should be reviewed to determine whether there will be private use/private payments as a result of the new agreements. "Qualified management contracts" (see Rev. Proc. 97-13) and "qualified research agreements" (see Rev. Procs. 97-14 and 2007-47) will not result in private use. The IRS will work with institutions to resolve violations of these rules where appropriate.

PwC Observation: Institutions should review any changes in the use of bond-financed facilities subsequent to the issuance of tax-exempt debt to determine if there is private use in excess of the allowable limits. Any proposed contracts that involve the use of bond-financed space, including all research agreements with for-profit organizations, should be reviewed for compliance. If not already developed, organizations should develop a tracking mechanism for private use of tax-exempt facilities. Further, institutions should ensure that they have a record retention system in place. As mentioned previously, Schedule K of the redesigned Form 990 will require substantial reporting associated with tax-exempt bonds.

Legislative Update. In the previous Congress, the House and Senate tax-writing committees placed significant emphasis on charity reform and charitable-giving incentives, resulting in the inclusion of various charity provisions in the Pension Protection Act of 2006. Congress remains interested in tax-exempt organization issues, focusing on specific areas where it sees a potential need for reform. Senator Charles Grassley (R-Iowa), the senior Republican on the Senate Finance Committee, has been a driving force behind this year's Congressional scrutiny.

Congress is focused on four major issues with respect to exempt organizations: hospitals and the provision of charity care, unrelated business income tax (UBIT) and hedge fund investing, college and university endowment earnings, and extension of charity and education tax incentives that expired at the end of 2007. It also may revisit charity reforms in the Pension Protection Act to provide clarification or correct drafting errors.

Hospital Charity Care: As mentioned earlier, Congress is examining the practices of tax-exempt hospitals with respect to the provision of charity care and community benefit. Health care represents a significant area of federal tax policy, and legislators want to understand how the benefits afforded to hospitals by their tax-exempt status are helping the public.

An IRS report released last summer raised concerns that a significant number of hospitals provide little charity care. According to the report, many hospitals spend 3% or less of total revenue on free charity care. Senator Grassley is considering legislation intended to make hospitals more accountable and improve transparency. Options under consideration include requiring that hospitals meet a minimum charity care threshold in order to qualify for tax exemption, and imposing sanctions or revoking exempt status for failure to meet such minimum charity care requirements. Senator Grassley's staff presented these options in a discussion draft released in July 2007.

Tax-exempt hospitals should be aware of the Senate Finance Committee's scrutiny of charity care and community benefit reporting. Further, hospitals should plan now for the new reporting requirements on the redesigned 2008 Form 990, Schedule H. In addition to use by the IRS and general public, Congress undoubtedly will use the schedule as a way to collect information about hospitals' operations.

Hedge Fund Investments: Congress is also examining investments by tax-exempt organizations in hedge funds through offshore entities, commonly known as "blocker" corporations. In order to increase their rate of return, hedge funds generally use debt to leverage investments. A tax-exempt organization's ownership of hedge funds through blockers avoids UBIT under current law that otherwise would be due on debt-financed investments. Blockers allow colleges, universities, pension funds and other tax-exempt organizations to take bigger investment risks, and reap bigger returns, without directly incurring tax liabilities. As a result, colleges, universities, and pension funds have invested heavily in hedge funds.

Higher Education Endowments: In light of rising tuition costs, members of Congress have raised concerns regarding the practices of colleges and universities with respect to their endowments. At a September hearing, witnesses appearing before the Senate Finance Committee spoke about high endowment investment returns and what is perceived to be low payout rates by colleges and universities. According to the Congressional Research Service, the average value of university endowments last year increased 15.3%, and schools paid out an average 4.6% of their endowments to help cover such costs as salaries, scholarships, and capital improvements. At the same time, the College Board reports that the average cost of tuition has risen at a rate above the rate of inflation.

Senator Grassley has been the most vocal critic of schools' endowment spending practices. He has endorsed a 5% minimum payout requirement for large college and university endowments, similar to the private foundation minimum distribution requirement. In January 2008, Senator Grassley, along with Senator Max Baucus (D-Montana), wrote to 135 U.S. colleges and universities with endowments of $500 million or more, asking a series of questions about endowment growth and spending on student aid.

Expiring Charity and Education Tax Incentives: A number of charity and education tax incentives expired at the end of 2007. Congress has expressed a willingness to extend many of the expiring provisions, but "paying" for the extenders will prove challenging. Congress has adopted procedural rules that impose restrictions on tax reductions and spending increases, known commonly as the "pay-as-you-go" rule. The pay-as-you-go rule requires any tax cuts to be offset with tax increases or reductions in mandatory (entitlement) spending. It is unknown at this time if Congress will extend these incentives retroactively.

Possible Technical Corrections to the Pension Protection Act: Congress and the Administration are considering possible technical corrections to the charity reforms enacted in the Pension Protection Act of 2006. Provisions under review include the new requirements for supporting organizations, the restrictions on donations of fractional interests of property and the UBIT rules on transfers from controlled organizations to their controlling organization. As mentioned above, a one-year extension of the special rule for transfers between controlling and controlled organizations is included in the Ways and Means tax extender bill.

PwC Observation: With the focus on the upcoming presidential election, it is difficult to predict with certainty the level of emphasis that Congress will place on issues affecting the tax-exempt community. Nevertheless, the current Congress increased its oversight of tax-exempt organizations in general, and it passed several pieces of legislation that contained charity reform provisions and charitable-giving incentives. The emphasis of the previous Congress on oversight and reform should serve as a reminder for organizations to remain alert to future oversight and the potential for legislative changes. Congress, particularly the Senate Finance Committee, remains active in their scrutiny of hospitals and universities.

Applicability of FIN 48 to Tax-Exempt Organizations. The FASB issued FIN 48 in an effort to clarify the accounting for uncertainty in income taxes recognized in an organization's financial statements pursuant to FAS 109, *Accounting for Income Taxes*. As a result of FIN 48, tax-exempt organizations' financial statements will reflect anticipated tax liabilities related to uncertain tax positions that exceed a materiality threshold. Tax positions include determining whether income is unrelated; whether to file Form 990-T; allocating expenses between related and unrelated activities; and classifying an organization, transaction or other position in a tax return as tax-exempt. FIN 48 applies only to income taxes—federal, state, local, and foreign—and therefore other taxes, such as sales and employment taxes, do not need to be considered for purposes of this analysis. Tax-exempt organizations that have outstanding tax-exempt bonds are required to comply with FIN 48 for fiscal years beginning after December 15, 2006.

FIN 48 prescribes a two-step process—recognition and measurement—for evaluating uncertain positions taken, or expected to be taken, that impact current or deferred income or liabilities. These steps are required not only for the current fiscal year, but also for all previous years for which the statute of limitations remains open.

The first step—recognition—is fulfilled by taking an inventory of all tax positions and determining whether it is more likely than not that each position would be sustained upon examination. "More likely than not" is defined as a position having a more than 50% likelihood of success upon audit. If a position cannot meet the more-likely-than-not threshold, a liability may need to be recognized for financial statement purposes.

If a position does not have a more-likely-than-not chance of being sustained upon examination, the second step—measurement—is completed by determining the amount of liability to be recognized in the organization's financial statements.

As a result of this two-step process, there may be: (1) an increased liability for income taxes (including interest and penalties) payable or a reduction in an income tax refund receivable, and/or (2) a reduction in a deferred tax asset or an increase in a deferred tax liability reported on an organization's financial statements. Recognition and measurement of uncertain tax positions should be reassessed each tax year, and conclusions are subject to change based on changing facts and circumstances.

PwC Observation: The requirements of FIN 48, in conjunction with the IRS's current focus on unrelated business income, make it particularly important for tax-exempt organizations to analyze their sources of revenue and determine which sources may result in treatment as unrelated business income. As a preliminary step, organizations should inventory all revenue sources and document the positions they are taking for income tax reporting purposes, including revenue recognition criteria, expense allocation methodology, and allocation and apportionment of state and local taxes. However, FIN 48 clearly requires additional documentation processes and procedures.

It is also important to note that, while an organization's financial statements are not required to be attached to Form 990, the redesigned Form 990 will require disclosure of an organization's FIN 48 footnote from its financial statements. Consequently, the IRS and state taxing authorities, among others, will be able to access information regarding an organization's uncertain tax positions if a FIN 48 disclosure has been made in its financial statements.

IRS Issues Fiscal Year 2008 Exempt Organization Implementing Guidelines. On December 13, 2007, the IRS released its fiscal year 2008 Exempt Organization (EO) Implementing Guidelines that outline the IRS's work plan for the coming year. When releasing the guidelines,

Lois Lerner, IRS Director of EO, noted that the IRS plans to use many "flexible and interdisciplinary" tools to achieve strategic goals of enhancing enforcement of the tax law and improving customer service.

The following are highlights of the guidelines that apply to tax-exempt organizations and their affiliates, which may be found in their entirety at www.irs.gov/pub/irs–tege/fy08_implementing_guidelines.pdf.

1. **Form 990 Redesign:** After reviewing over 3,000 pages of comments from the public regarding the draft redesigned Form 990 and its Schedules, the IRS released its final version of the 2008 Form 990 in December 2007. Instructions for the 2008 Form 990 and the Schedules are anticipated to be released in spring 2008, according to the IRS.

2. **National Research Program (NRP):** NRP is a comprehensive effort by the IRS to measure compliance for different types of taxes and various sets of taxpayers. Currently, the NRP is focused on a compliance study for employment taxes, which will involve all employment tax filers, including exempt organizations.

3. **Research and Compliance Initiative for Colleges and Universities:** The IRS will initiate a research and compliance initiative involving colleges and universities, similar to the hospital project it began last year. The IRS anticipates sending compliance check questionnaires to a cross-section of small, medium, and large colleges and universities. The questionnaires will focus on how colleges and universities report income and expenses on the Form 990, calculate and report losses on the Form 990-T, allocate income and expenses in calculating unrelated business taxable income (including how institutions calculate and report losses on Form 990-T), invest and use their endowments, and determine executive compensation. Based on the results of the questionnaire, the IRS will conduct focused examinations of some of the institutions.

4. **Section 509(a)(3) Supporting Organizations:** The IRS considers supporting organizations a significant area for potential abuse. During 2008, the IRS will begin a review of 500 organizations that are in their third to fifth years of existence to determine

whether they continue to qualify as supporting organizations. The IRS will also conduct compliance checks of 300 supporting organizations that were expected to file Form 990 but did not.

The IRS EO Division, in conjunction with the IRS chief counsel and the Department of Treasury, develops and regularly issues guidance to taxpayers. In fiscal year 2008, the IRS's priority guidance plan includes:

- Various provisions in the Pension Protection Act of 2006, including supporting organizations, donor-advised funds, and e-postcard notification
- Regulations to implement Form 990 revisions
- Regulations governing qualified tuition programs under IRC section 529
- Final regulations on excise taxes on prohibited tax shelter transactions and related disclosure requirements
- Final regulations on revocation standards for organizations that engage in excess benefit transactions
- Additional guidance relating to charitable trusts

In addition to the priority guidance, the IRS intends to work on other projects, including, in particular, its Executive Compensation Compliance project. The IRS will continue its project with 200 compliance checks and 50 additional single-issue examinations, focusing on organizations with loans to officers and trustees. The IRS will also continue executive compensation examinations initiated in the Hospital Compliance project.

Finally, the implementing guidelines state that fiscal year 2008 will continue the IRS' emphasis on education and outreach in the tax-exempt organization community. Consistent with this objective, the IRS will publish guidance through its electronic newsletter, the *EO Update*. Individuals can subscribe to this free service by visiting the IRS's web site at www.irs.gov/charities.

In addition to the fiscal year 2008 EO Implementing Guidelines, the Tax Exempt Bonds (TEB) division of the IRS publishes its own work plan. For fiscal year 2008, TEB will continue to focus on the following projects:

Charitable financing examination project: The charitable financing examination project began in 2006 with 30 focused examinations of charitable financing of health care and housing financings. It is anticipated that the results of this first stage will be published in fiscal year 2008.

Postissuance Compliance Questionnaire: TEB will also focus on analyzing the responses to the postissuance compliance questionnaire distributed to approximately 200 charities in 2007. TEB may issue the questionnaire to a wider array of charities or decide that additional taxpayer assistance and/or enforcement initiatives should be implemented.

PwC Observation: The EO Implementing Guidelines provide an important road map of the IRS's planned activities that will impact tax-exempt organizations. For this reason and also because of other related initiatives, such as FIN 48, it is important for tax-exempt organizations to be familiar with the Implementing Guidelines. The breadth of the fiscal year 2008 Implementing Guidelines makes it clear that the IRS will continue to focus on exempt organizations. The IRS will continue the trend toward paperless processing by applying an electronic filing process similar to that used with the Form 990 to online processing of applications of exemption. Moreover, the IRS will continue to focus on compliance checks and the use of questionnaires to gather data and identify organizations for more in-depth examinations. In light of this additional attention, exempt organizations should continue to be vigilant with their compliance responsibilities.

E-Postcard Filing Requirement for Small Tax-Exempt Organizations. Small tax-exempt organizations, whose gross receipts are normally $25,000 or less, have not had an annual federal filing requirement because they typically were not required to file Form 990 or Form 990-EZ. However, beginning in 2008, these small organizations are required to electronically file Form 990-N, Electronic Notice (e-Postcard) for Tax-Exempt Organizations Not Required to File Form 990 or 990-EZ, on an annual basis. Questions on the Form 990-N are basic, including the name, address and EIN of the organization. Exceptions to this requirement include private foundations that are required to file Form 990-PF, organizations that are included in a group return, and section 509(a)(3) supporting organizations that are required to file Form 990 or Form 990-EZ.

The new filing requirement applies to tax periods beginning after December 31, 2006. Organizations that do not file Form 990-N, Form 990 or Form 990-EZ for three consecutive years but were required to do so will lose their tax-exempt status. The IRS began notifying small tax-exempt organizations of the new filing requirement in July 2007. The e-Postcard filings are maintained by the Urban Institute in partnership with the IRS and can be found at http://epostcard.form990.org/.

PwC Observation: The Form 990-N filing requirement was created as part of the movement to improve transparency within the nonprofit sector. The Form 990-N filing requirement will not directly impact larger tax-exempt organizations. However, they should be aware of the requirement if they have related small organizations that wish to retain their tax-exempt status.

Items of Continuing Interest—Compensation-Related Issues

Executive Compensation and Excess Benefit Transactions. Executive compensation at tax-exempt organizations continues be a focus of Congress, the IRS, the media, donors, and others. The IRS recently announced that compensation questions will be part of all future compliance check questionnaires. In December 2006, the Senate held hearings with respect to the tax status of educational institutions. Then Chair of the Senate Finance Committee, Senator Grassley, indicated concern with the amount of compensation paid to the presidents and other senior officers at educational institutions. Concurrently, the media reported issues involving executive compensation and benefits at a variety of tax-exempt organizations, and has continued to do so.

In 2004, the IRS announced the tax-exempt compensation enforcement project. The goal of this initiative was to identify and halt abuses by tax-exempt institutions that pay excessive compensation and benefits to their officers and other insiders. The IRS released the results of its three-year project in 2007, which included its assessment of over $21 million in intermediate sanction/self-dealing excise taxes, $5 million of which was imposed on public charities, while the rest was on private foundations. The IRS also incorporated an executive compensation component into its hospital compliance questionnaire which was commenced in 2006 and the final report is anticipated in 2008.

In light of these initiatives and the focus on compensation, organizations should implement procedures to establish a rebuttable presumption of reasonableness for the compensation paid to their key employees. The establishment of a rebuttable presumption of reasonableness puts the onus on the IRS to prove that compensation is unreasonable. If contact is initiated, questions will be directed toward establishing whether the organization's procedures met these criteria. Additionally, the redesigned Form 990 asks tax-exempt organizations specifically whether the steps to satisfy a rebuttable presumption of reasonableness have been carried out.

A rebuttable presumption of reasonableness is established if the organization meets the following three requirements:

- The compensation and benefits (especially deferred compensation plans) must be approved by the organization's governing board, which must be comprised persons who do not have a conflict of interest.

- The governing board must rely upon appropriate data (i.e., comparables) in deciding whether to approve the compensation and benefits.

- The governing body must document its actions (usually in the board's minutes).

PwC Observation: Organizations should make sure that their policies and procedures are sufficient to establish a rebuttable presumption of reasonableness as described earlier. Because documentation is essential for establishing a rebuttable presumption of reasonableness and because it has been a primary focus of the IRS, documentation should be an area of focus for tax-exempt organizations. Organizations also should consider other leading practices for executive compensation, such as:

- Establishing a compensation committee
- Developing a formal process to determine executive compensation
- Reporting compensation completely and accurately

Expense Reporting. Similar to compensation, the IRS and the media are focused on situations where employees are being reimbursed for personal expenditures and these amounts are not reported as compensation. Therefore, it is essential that organizations make certain that their expense reporting procedures are adequate and are followed by both employees and officers.

Expense reports should be submitted on a timely basis, and they should include adequate documentation in order to satisfy the rules. Receipts must be provided together with the name of the individuals involved and the business purpose for the expenditures.

Organizations should also establish appropriate policies regarding the approval and sign-off of expense reports submitted by senior management. For example, the chief financial officer might sign off as to the completeness of the president's expense report and that it is in compliance with institutional policies. Trustees should periodically review the overall level of expenses incurred by the senior management for reasonableness. Such actions protect both the organization and senior management.

PwC Observation: Organizations must establish adequate policies and procedures for reimbursing and documenting business expenses. They also should be aware that certain paid or reimbursed "expenses" may constitute additional compensation. The redesigned Form 990 asks tax-exempt organizations to disclose whether they provide reimbursement for certain business expenses, such as first-class travel, and also whether the organization required substantiation of such business expenses prior to reimbursement.

Organizations must identify and appropriately report additional compensation received by key employees through the reimbursement of non-business-related expenses. Additional compensation that is not considered when establishing a rebuttable presumption of reasonableness may result in an automatic excess benefit transaction under Intermediate Sanctions. Therefore, the board should consider all forms of compensation, including the reimbursement of personal expenses, when considering whether their key employees are receiving reasonable compensation.

Cellular Telephones and Other Listed Property. Increasingly, organizations are providing their employees with cellular telephones and other electronic equipment, such as personal digital assistants, to improve employee accessibility when they are not in the office. In addition, over the past few years, cell phone plans have become much more affordable and organizations are now issuing cell phones and other electronic equipment to a broader population of employees. Similar to automobiles, such electronic equipment is considered "listed property."

The Internal Revenue Code and Treasury Regulations explicitly set forth special documentation rules for listed property. The Code and Regulations require employers to follow burdensome documentation rules when reimbursing employees for expenses associated with listed property. For example, an employee must identify the date of the call, the length of the call and the business purpose for the call. The employee must either submit the documentation to his/her employer or retain the documentation and regularly attest to the employer the amount of business/personal use. The IRS has audited a number of institutions on this issue, and, consequently, organizations are actively reviewing their current policies.

Many organizations have chosen to reimburse and/or charge employees for the use of electronic equipment in ways that attempt to approximate a reasonable amount for personal use, but that do not strictly comply with the documentation requirements for listed property. Because of the serious potential consequences of not complying with the listed property rules, if officers and other disqualified individuals are not following the accountable plan rules for their cell phones, an organization should consider including the full value of the cell phones in their income.

PwC Observation: The IRS has posted its cell phone policy on its web site, demonstrating that it takes these rules seriously. Institutions should consider the impact of these rules on their accountable plan policies and the potential exposure to Intermediate Sanctions. It is possible that Congress may enact legislation to exclude cell phones from the listed property designation in the near future. However, no specific legislation has been introduced at this time, and we still expect that the accountable plan rules would apply.

Nonqualified Deferred Compensation Plans of Tax-Exempt Institutions Affected by IRC §409A. Nonqualified plans maintained by tax-exempt employers are typically governed by Section 457(f) of the Code. In this type of plan, amounts owed to an employee are taxed when there is no longer a substantial risk of forfeiture. Under section 457(f), a substantial risk of forfeiture exists when an employee must perform substantial future services in order to receive the compensation.

Section 409A further addresses nonqualified deferred compensation as it applies to employees of both tax-exempt and taxable organizations. It has added an additional level of complexity to nonqualified deferred compensation plans. Generally for tax-exempt organizations, section 409A applies after the first possible vesting date for compensation subject to section 457(f). The rules under section 409A are more restrictive than those of section 457(f). Under section 409A, agreements not to compete and/or a rolling risk of forfeiture will not qualify as a substantial risk of forfeiture. Section 409A applies when the payment of compensation that is earned and vested in one tax year is delayed and paid in a later year. This may occur if organizations and employees agree to extend the vesting date beyond the original date. At this time, the concern is that because a "covenant not to compete" does not qualify as a substantial risk of forfeiture, section 457(f) plans with such a covenant as the only substantial risk of forfeiture may be immediately subject to section 409A.

The consequences of an agreement not conforming to section 409A are severe. All compensation deferred under the plan will immediately become subject to federal income tax, and a 20% penalty on the amount of includible compensation will be added if the failure is not corrected within the statutory and regulatory guidelines. Because of the complex nature of section 409A, transition rules are in place to allow for amendments of agreements that do not meet the new requirements. The IRS has extended the deadline for taxpayer compliance until December 31, 2008.

The only types of programs excluded from the section 409A regime are qualified retirement plans (including section 403(b) plans, section 457(b) plans, simplified employee pension plans [SEPs] and individual retirement accounts [IRAs]), vacation, sick leave, compensatory time, bonus (if the bonus is payable within 2~HF months of year-end), and disability and death benefit programs. Among others, severance programs are not excluded from the definition and, accordingly, are potentially subject to section 409A.

Finally, there are additional operational and documentation requirements for nonqualified deferred compensation plans. Failures in this regard will not accelerate taxation for section 457(f) plans, because taxation is delayed until the substantial risk of forfeiture expires (when amounts would already be subject to tax). However, because a failure to satisfy these additional rules may result in the imposition of penalty taxes in the amount of 20% of the compensation includible, employers should review and amend their plans to ensure compliance.

PwC Observation: While the Treasury Department has provided an additional year of transition relief, organizations should not delay their review of existing deferred compensation plans and the requirements for plan amendments. Employers should take the following actions:

1. *Inventory their plans.* Look at programs denominated as retirement plans, as well as at employment agreements, severance policies, and other cash-based benefit programs. The definition of nonqualified deferred compensation plans is very broad, and is not limited to programs between employers and employees. Thus, programs for directors or trustees and independent contractors would also be covered.

   The identification and redesign of affected plans may involve a significant effort spanning tax, human resources, legal, finance, and other departments. Thus, it is important that the analysis be started as soon as possible to avoid adverse tax consequences to participants.

2. Review deferred compensation plans. Once all deferred compensation plans are identified, they should be reviewed and amended, if appropriate. Revisions to comply with section 409A can be made until the end of 2008. The consequence of failing to amend an affected plan may be current taxation of all amounts deferred for all years (as well as a 20% penalty tax when the amounts are included as compensation to the individual).

Other Items of Continuing Interest

Telephone Tax Refund. In May 2006, the Internal Revenue Service announced that it would stop collection of the long-distance telephone excise tax beginning August 1, 2006. The IRS further announced that it would allow individuals, businesses, and tax-exempt organizations to obtain a refund for long-distance excise taxes billed after February 28, 2003. This refund is available as a one-time payment on the 2006 income tax return (reporting for fiscal year 2007).

Tax-exempt organizations may calculate their refund request using either: (1) the actual amount of the refundable long-distance telephone excise tax paid, or (2) a formula developed by the IRS. The formula method was adopted after the IRS received public input about the burden associated with the actual-amount method. Under the formula method, organizations can figure their refund by comparing their April 2006 and September 2006 phone bills to determine the percentage of their telephone expenses attributable to the long-distance excise tax. Once a method is selected, it must be used for the entire refund period.

The refund is capped at 2% of phone expenses for small businesses (250 or fewer employees) and 1% for large business (more than 250 employees). When determining business size, organizations should use the number of employees for the pay period that included June 12, 2006 (Line 1, Form 941 for the second calendar quarter of 2006). Interest is added to the refund amount.

The telephone excise tax refund can be requested by filing the 2006 Form 990-T, Exempt Organization Business Income Tax Return, and attaching Form 8913, Credit for Federal Telephone Excise Tax Paid. The 2006 Form 990-T includes a new line (44f) on which the taxpayer can claim the refund. The Form 990-T can be utilized to claim the credit regardless of whether the organization has unrelated business income to report.

If an organization files a 2006 Form 990-T to report unrelated business income and claim the telephone excise tax refund, Form 8913 will be subject to public inspection. However, if the Form 990-T is used only to request a refund of the telephone excise tax, the Form 990-T and Form 8913 are not subject to the public inspection requirements.

PwC Observation: Organizations should review their files to determine if they have access to the information necessary to complete the calculation. If an organization would like to calculate its refund using the actual-amount-paid method, it will need to have copies of 41 months of phone bills. Organizations should also determine if they would like to prepare their own refund request or use a paid tax preparer to prepare the calculation.

Public Disclosure of Form 990-T. In 2006, Congress passed a law requiring public disclosure of a section 501(c)(3) organization's Form 990-T. However, while Congress had intended for the Form 990-T to be available to the public in the same manner and to the same extent as Forms 990 and 990-PF, the law was written such that Form 990-T was available only by request from the organization, and not accessible from the IRS. Congress has addressed this omission in the Tax Technical Corrections Act of 2007, signed into law on December 29, 2007. As a result of this change, it is likely that Form 990-T will soon become easily accessible on the internet, similar to the current accessibility of Forms 990 and 990-PF.

PwC Observation: At this time, it is our understanding that the IRS will not require disclosure of additional Forms, such as Forms 8865, 926, 8886, and 5471, that are typically attached to (but not an integral part of) Form 990-T. These additional forms often provide information with regard to alternative investments and/or reportable transactions, but are not needed to support the unrelated business income tax calculation.

International Activities. Increasingly, colleges and universities are engaging in collaborations with institutions in foreign countries. These collaborations may include joint education and/or sponsored research programs as well as consulting arrangements. Some involve the granting of dual degrees within the foreign jurisdiction. Although colleges and universities may be considered tax-exempt institutions for U.S. income tax purposes, they may be subject to taxes and a variety of reporting requirements in foreign jurisdictions.

Various issues may arise as a result of foreign activities. For example, intellectual property may be developed out of these collaborations, which could result in foreign tax implications when the funds are repatriated. If employees work in the foreign jurisdiction for periods ranging from a couple of days to well over a year, they also could be subject to taxation in the foreign jurisdiction. In addition, the hiring of foreign workers in the foreign jurisdiction may have tax reporting consequences.

Institutions should review the specific facts to determine whether their activities result in income tax nexus in the foreign jurisdiction. In addition, tax treaties should be reviewed as they may be applicable. There may also be withholding and other taxes and reporting requirements associated with the activities. If there are tax liabilities associated with the foreign program, it may be possible to negotiate for the foreign collaborator to assume responsibility for any tax liability and for the institution to receive its payment net of tax.

PwC Observation: It is important for institutions to understand the tax and registration requirements related to proposed activities before entering into agreements. Up-front planning is important not only to ensure tax compliance in the foreign jurisdiction, but also for the institution to properly assess the economic results of the project. To control costs and avoid lengthy negotiations, institutions need to develop policies and procedures for compensating employees on international assignments. Schedule F in the redesigned Form 990 requires organizations to report on their international activities.

Supporting Organizations Required to File Form 990. The Pension Protection Act of 2006 (PPA) introduced significant new restrictions on supporting organizations. The overarching purpose of the changes was to reduce the number of abuses by donors creating supporting organizations. A supporting organization, described in section 509(a)(3), is an organization that enjoys tax-exempt status as a public charity because of its close relationship with a limited number of other public charities. A supporting organization provides financial and/or programmatic support to designated public charities that are tax-exempt because of the activities they carry out.

For tax years ending after August 17, 2006, the PPA requires each supporting organization to file Form 990 or Form 990-EZ annually, even if its gross receipts are normally less than $25,000. A supporting organization must demonstrate that it is governed by a variety of individuals who were selected based on their special knowledge or expertise in the field in which the organization is operating, or because they represent the particular community that is served by the supported public charity, rather than just the substantial contributor and his/her family. Additionally, the organization must indicate on Form 990 its type and provide a list of public charities it supports.

PwC Observation: The PPA imposes several restrictions on supporting organizations in addition to the revised filing requirement. If an organization is currently classified as a supporting organization but would be more appropriately classified as another type of public charity, the IRS has issued Announcement 2006-93, which outlines the procedure to allow the organization to change its public charity status.

Electronic Filing. For tax years ending on or after December 31, 2006, tax-exempt organizations with total assets of $10 million or more who file at least 250 returns annually, must file their Forms 990 electronically. In addition, private foundations and charitable trusts, regardless of their asset size, will be required to file Forms 990-PF electronically if they file at least 250 returns annually.

The "at least 250 returns" requirement includes income tax, excise tax, employment tax, and information returns filed during the calendar year. All original returns filed by a tax-exempt organization during the calendar year are counted. Corrected or amended returns are not counted. For example, if a tax-exempt organization has 245 employees, each Form W-2 and quarterly Form 941 is considered a separate return. Therefore, the organization files at least 250 returns (245 Forms W-2, four Forms 941, and Form 990).

If an organization that is subject to the regulations fails to file its Form 990 or Form 990-PF electronically, the organization will be deemed to have failed to file the return. For institutions with gross receipts exceeding $1 million, the penalty for nonfiling is $100 for each day the failure continues, up to a maximum of $50,000 per return. In addition, the person responsible for nonfiling will be charged a penalty of $10 a day, up to a maximum of $5,000, unless he or she shows that not complying was due to reasonable cause.

Institutions will need to file their return using either the services of a professional tax preparer or an IRS-approved e-file software provider. A list of approved e-file software providers can be found on the IRS's web site at www.irs.gov. If an organization chooses to file its own return using an approved e-file software provider, it may be required to file with the IRS for e-file services as a "large taxpayer." As part of the registration process, the organization will have to designate at least two individuals at the organization as the "responsible officials" for e-file purposes. The responsible officials will be required to supply the

IRS with their adjusted gross income from their current or prior year individual tax return for identification purposes. It is recommended that organizations complete the registration at least 45 days before they plan to electronically file their return and register at least two responsible officials.

In addition to the Forms 990 and 990-PF, institutions may also file the extension, Form 8868, for these forms electronically. Institutions that are not required to e-file can continue to file a paper return or file electronically. E-file of amended and final returns became available in 2007. Tax-exempt institutions should check with the appropriate state agency to determine e-file requirements for state returns.

PwC Observation: Institutions that are subject to the e-filing requirement should continue to evaluate whether they will use a tax professional to prepare the electronic return or if they will prepare and file their own return. Organizations that file their own return should make sure they have identified and registered at least two individuals within the organization who will serve as the "responsible officials" for e-file purposes. Additionally, organizations filing their own returns should make sure their software systems are updated on a yearly basis.

403(b) Plans.   A 403(b) tax-sheltered annuity (TSA) plan is a retirement plan offered by schools, hospitals, charities and certain other tax-exempt organizations. An individual 403(b) annuity can be obtained only under an employer's TSA plan. Generally, these annuities are funded by elective deferrals made under salary reduction agreements and nonelective employer contributions.

Effective for 2009 Form 5500 filings, 403(b) plans are subject to annual 5500 reporting and audit requirements similar to 401(k) plans. Large plans (100 or more participants) are required to file audited financial statements. Small plans (fewer than 100 participants) are eligible to use the short Form 5500 and waive the audit requirement. The Employee Retirement Income Security Act of 1974 (ERISA) requires comparative statements of net assets; therefore December 31, 2008, balances are subject to audit.

PwC Observation: 403(b) plans may be large, with many years of operations. Initial audits will need to address the accumulation of the opening participant balances, accuracy of participants transfers between/among 403(b) and other qualified plans at a single employer, and the completeness of participants (both active and deferred vested), among other considerations. Institutions with 403(b) plans should commence focusing on the new requirements.

APPENDIX E

Auditing Alternative Investments

A Practical Guide for Investor Entities, Investee Fund Managers and Auditors

Our perspective

We are pleased to provide you with this publication, entitled *Auditing Alternative Investments, A Practical Guide for Investor Entities, Investee Fund Managers and Auditors*, on an important topic that has been the focus of the various entities that invest in alternative investment funds, as well as to management of the investee funds.

As you are aware, many types of investors have been investing an increasing percentage of their investment portfolios in alternative investments and other non-traditional types of financial instruments. Recently, outside organizations, regulators and the accounting and auditing rule makers, such as the American Institute of Certified Public Accountants ("AICPA"), have begun to scrutinize the inherent risks associated with alternative investments, with a particular focus on the issues associated with due diligence, oversight and transparency.

In 2005, the AICPA issued an auditing interpretation (the "Interpretation") and, in 2006, a practice aid (the "AICPA Practice Aid"), which required auditors and management to respond quickly to new guidance with respect to the existence and valuation assertions associated with alternative investments. The main focus of the new guidance is as follows:

- With respect to existence, the question is: Do the investor entity's alternative investments exist at the financial statement date, and have the related transactions occurred during the period? While confirming the existence of assets that are held by third parties generally provides adequate audit evidence, the Interpretation and AICPA Practice Aid say that, by itself, a confirmation in the aggregate does not constitute adequate audit evidence.

- With respect to valuation, the question is: Are the alternative investments stated in the investor entity's financial statements at fair value? Confirming the value of the alternative investments from an investee fund manager provides one piece of evidence. Based on the guidance in the AICPA Practice Aid, additional audit evidence could be obtained.

More recently, on February 22, 2007, the President's Working Group on Financial Markets (the "PWG") publicly released its "Agreement among PWG and US Agency Principals on Principles and Guidelines regarding Private Pools of Capital" (the "PWG Principles and Guidelines"). These PWG Principles and Guidelines acknowledge the "significant benefits" that "private pools of capital," including hedge funds, bring to the financial markets and the challenges they pose. It encourages all relevant market participants (i.e., investors, creditors, counterparties, fund managers and regulators) to address them. It also acknowledges that "these pools can involve complex, illiquid or opaque investments and investment strategies that are not fully disclosed," and that such risks are "most appropriately borne by investors with the sophistication to identify, analyze and bear these risks." Interestingly, several of the principles and guidelines set forth by the PWG focus on transparency and due diligence, which are two of the main underlying themes addressed in the AICPA Practice Aid and discussed in this paper. For example, the PWG Principles and Guidelines state the following:

- Investors in private pools of capital should obtain accurate and timely historical and ongoing material information necessary to perform due diligence regarding the pool's strategies, terms, conditions and risk management, thereby enabling such investors to make informed investment decisions. (No. 4)

- Managers of private pools of capital should have information, valuation and, risk management systems that meet sound industry practices and enable them to provide accurate information to creditors, counterparties and investors with appropriate frequency, breadth, and detail. (No. 9)

The PWG Principles and Guidelines also acknowledge the balance that is necessary with respect to transparency. For example, No. 7.4 states that the "information that creditors and counterparties should seek to obtain from a private pool includes both quantitative and qualitative indicators of a private pool's net asset value, performance, market and credit risk exposure, and liquidity. The level of detail expected should respect the *legitimate interest of the private pool in protecting its proprietary trading strategies*" [emphasis added]. In No. 9.3, the PWG Principles and Guidelines further state that the "information provided by managers of private pools to their creditors, counterparties and investors should adhere to the sound practices articulated in industry guidelines. Managers of private pools of capital should provide information frequently enough and with sufficient detail that creditors, counterparties and investors stay informed of strategies, and the amount of risk being taken by the pool, and any material changes."

PricewaterhouseCoopers is uniquely positioned to provide leadership in the areas identified as concerns by regulators, the AICPA and others. We maintain a leadership position as auditors for both investee funds and investor entities – serving many of the largest and most complex alternative investment funds, and many of the most well-endowed higher education and not-for-profit organizations across the country. Our leadership position in both industries gives us a unique perspective and ability to converse with investors and investees, and to understand the implications and challenges for each. We have devoted considerable time and energy to studying these important issues, speaking about the new requirements and – most importantly – listening to the concerns of investors, investees and other industry participants. It is from this position of leadership that we have authored the enclosed publication.

The objective of this PricewaterhouseCoopers' publication is to summarize and highlight the AICPA's interpretative guidance on alternative investments. In addition, this publication is designed to address, from a practical perspective, the issues of most importance to officers, senior management, general partners, fund managers, board members and auditors of many diverse entities (e.g., hedge funds, private equity funds, fund-of-funds, colleges, universities and other highly endowed institutions). These issues include:

- What are the internal controls and leading practices that investor entities should consider implementing?

- How should transparency be viewed at the investor and investee level? Can transparency also be viewed broadly to encompass all forms of information and/or access requested by, or provided to, investors by management of investee funds?

- What is the importance of a management-developed risk assessment of the alternative investment portfolio? How does management view the risks compared to how the auditor views the risks?

- What are some practical suggestions for improving an investor entity's documentation of their internal controls?

- What lessons have we learned from the last two years of audits? How can we all be better prepared for the year-end audits of investor entities such as fund-of-funds, colleges, universities and other highly endowed institutions?

We are pleased to provide this publication to you and hope that it will serve as an informative and thought-provoking document that highlights existing guidance and provides a common message to both investors and investees as to how policies, procedures and controls might be enhanced.

Sincerely,

Mark J. Casella, Assurance Partner
National Alternative Investment Funds
Practice Leader

John A. Mattie, Assurance Partner
National Education and Not-for-Profit
Practice Leader

Note: This paper is not intended to drive asset allocation decisions. It is meant to summarize and highlight key issues associated with the AICPA's interpretative guidance on alternative investments.

Contents

1 | Executive summary

Recently, there has been considerable discussion regarding the audit requirements related to investor entities that invest in alternative investments. This discussion resulted from the issuance of the following guidance by the American Institute of Certified Public Accountants ("AICPA"):

- Interpretation No. 1 to AU332 (the "Interpretation"), also referred to as AU9332 (issued July 2005)

- A non-authoritative practice aid entitled *Alternative Investments – Audit Considerations* (the "AICPA Practice Aid") based on input from the AICPA's Alternative Investments Task Force and certain AICPA member firms (issued July 2006)

The Interpretation and the AICPA Practice Aid provide guidance to help auditors address the existence and valuation assertions associated with alternative investments because a readily determinable fair value does not exist and, generally, investee fund managers provide limited investment information. These requirements are currently in effect and will impact the way auditors interact with clients and client investee funds. These requirements will also likely impact the relationships between investor entities and investee funds, as well as affect the nature, timing and extent of information shared between these two parties relating to the investee fund's investment portfolio and the investee fund's valuation policies and procedures.

Alternative investments include private investment funds meeting the definition of an "investment company" under the provisions of the *AICPA Audit and Accounting Guide: Investment Companies*, such as hedge funds, private equity funds, real estate funds, venture capital funds, commodity funds, offshore fund vehicles, and fund-of-funds, as well as bank common/collective trust funds. Collectively, these types of investment funds are referred to in the AICPA Practice Aid and herein as "alternative investments." Alternative

investments may be structured as limited partnerships, limited liability corporations, trusts or corporations.

The Interpretation was issued in July 2005 to help auditors apply the provisions of AU332 to alternative investments. Since the Interpretation clarified existing guidance, it was effective upon issuance. It provided guidance on the confirmation of an investor entity's interest in an investee fund by the investor entity's auditor. The Interpretation was controversial because it stated that simply confirming investments in the aggregate does not constitute adequate audit evidence with respect to the existence assertion. It stated that, in certain circumstances, it would be necessary to confirm the investee fund holdings on a security-by-security basis. Uncertainty existed over concerns whether auditors would be required to disclaim opinions on investor entities because of scope limitations resulting from the likely unwillingness of investee fund managers to confirm all requested information. Additionally, even if investee fund managers provided portfolio listings, it was unclear what investor entities and their auditors would be expected to do, or even could do, with the information.

The AICPA Practice Aid was issued in July 2006 to clarify certain key points from the Interpretation. The AICPA Practice Aid should be of interest to management of investor entities, including, but not limited to, other investment companies (e.g., fund-of-funds or funds that hold alternative investments), colleges and universities, hospitals and pension plans, as well as to management of the investee funds. Some of these entities invest a small percentage of their investment portfolios in alternative investments, while others invest a substantial percentage. In addition, the underlying investment portfolios held by alternative investments can range from marketable securities to complex derivatives and/or illiquid investments.

Key points

The following paragraphs summarize the key points
from the AICPA Practice Aid and the Interpretation.

Management's responsibility

The existence and valuation of an alternative investment is
the responsibility of the investor entity's management.
Management of the investor entity that uses audited
financial statements or other information as support for the
valuation of an alternative investment must be prepared to
take responsibility, in its own right, for the valuation.
Therefore, if management of the investor entity ultimately
determines that it is comfortable with the valuation provided
by the investee fund, management of the investor entity
then takes responsibility for that valuation.

This is particularly reinforced in the AICPA Practice Aid,
which states that "management of the investor entity is
responsible for the valuation of alternative investment
amounts as presented in the investor entity's financial
statements" and that "this responsibility cannot, under any
circumstances, be outsourced or assigned to a party
outside of the investor entity's management." Therefore,
although the investor entity's management may look to the
investee fund manager for the mechanics of the valuation or
to certain third parties to assist with the due diligence and
ongoing monitoring efforts, management of the investor
entity must have sufficient understanding and supporting
information to evaluate and either accept or independently
challenge the investee fund's valuation.

To take such responsibility, management of the investor
entity must have an effective process and related internal
controls in place to ensure a sufficient understanding of
their alternative investments. This includes a sufficient
understanding of:

- The investment strategies and the manner in which they
are employed
- The underlying investment portfolios and the
reasonableness and reliability of the inputs and
methodologies used for their valuation

The nature, timing and extent of management's process will
depend on management's risk assessment of the
alternative investments.

Auditor's responsibility

An important element in determining the nature, timing and
extent of the audit procedures is the auditor's
understanding of the reliability of the process the investor
entity's management uses to determine estimated fair
value.

The auditor's approach is based on an assessment of the
risk of material misstatement of the financial statements. As
stated in AU section 312.11, *Audit Risk and Materiality in
Conducting an Audit* (AICPA Professional Standards, vol. 1),
the auditor's consideration of materiality is a matter of
professional judgment, and materiality judgments involve
both quantitative and qualitative considerations. The risk of
material misstatement includes inherent risk and control
risk. Accordingly, the auditor's risk assessment, after
considering management's process, will determine the
quantity and quality of audit evidence necessary to support
the existence and valuation assertions.

The auditor's risk assessment should consider various
factors, including, but not limited to:

- The materiality of the alternative investments
- The nature and extent of management's process and
related controls associated with the alternative
investments
- The degree of transparency available to the investor entity
to support its valuation process and related conclusions
(including portfolio detail and/or audit reports)
- The nature, complexity and liquidity of the investee funds
and their underlying investments

A subtext to the AICPA Practice Aid is that, because the
investments presented in an investor entity's financial
statements represent the investor entity's assertion, the
auditor should not rely exclusively on information obtained
from the investee fund manager while ignoring the investor
entity's controls, including its monitoring process.

Confirmation process

The AICPA Practice Aid reinforces the Interpretation, which states that simply confirming investments in the aggregate **does not constitute adequate audit evidence** with respect to the existence assertion. The AICPA Practice Aid clarifies that, while confirmation of the holdings of the investee fund on a **security-by-security basis** (or contemporaneous audited financial statements) typically would constitute adequate audit evidence with respect to the existence assertion, the auditor for the investor entity should consider **alternative or additional procedures** directed at the existence of the alternative investments. In addition, Appendix 1 to the AICPA Practice Aid provides an illustrative confirmation for use by auditors.

Despite the guidance included in the AICPA Practice Aid, it is still unclear to many industry participants how the confirmation of the investee fund's holdings on a security-by-security basis adequately addresses the existence assertion. Without information on other assets or liabilities of the investee fund and the investor entity's percentage ownership in the net assets of the investee fund, a security-by-security listing of the underlying investments would not generally provide adequate information for the investor entity or its auditor as to the existence or appropriateness of the recorded value of the alternative investment. Further, without other assurance (which may include management's monitoring controls), the auditor may not have sufficient evidence that the listed investments are genuine.

So, why then is it necessary for the auditor to request confirmation of the investee fund's holdings on a security-by-security basis?

- First, the confirmation request is necessary because confirmation of the investee fund's holdings on a security-by-security basis is required by the Interpretation. In fact, the AICPA Practice Aid reinforces that uncertainty about whether the investee fund manager will provide the requested information does not obviate the auditor's requirement to obtain sufficient appropriate audit evidence – either through confirmation or otherwise. If the confirmation request is not returned to the auditor or the details of the underlying investments are not otherwise provided by the investee fund manager, the auditor should perform alternative procedures. The AICPA Practice Aid is helpful in this respect because it acknowledges that alternative procedures can be performed – the Interpretation was silent on this issue. Even if all the requested information is provided, additional procedures may also be necessary in certain circumstances.

- Second, the confirmation request is necessary because confirmation of the investee fund's holdings on a security-by-security basis, or other adequate information about the investee fund and its investment portfolio, may be helpful or necessary with respect to the existence and valuation assertions. This is because such information should serve to corroborate information the investor entity has represented or directly provided to the auditor with respect to the nature, complexity and liquidity of an investee fund.

Impact to audit report

An auditor cannot audit what management has not done. Therefore, auditors need to evaluate both (i) the adequacy of **management's** process and related documentation to support the amounts in management's financial statements, and (ii) the quantity and quality of audit evidence available to support the **auditor's** opinion on those financial statements. In evaluating the quantity and quality of audit evidence to support specific audit objectives, the auditor should consider factors including, but not limited to:

- The significance of the alternative investments for which neither the underlying security-by-security detail nor audited financial statements was available as of the balance sheet date
- The sufficiency of alternative procedures performed and supporting documentation obtained in situations where the security-by-security detail was not provided to the auditor
- The adequacy of management's process and related internal controls, including those related to the extent of its understanding of the complexity and liquidity of the underlying investment portfolio and related valuation process, and the degree of transparency provided by the investee fund manager

If the auditor concludes that management's valuation procedures are adequate or reasonable and that the underlying documentation supports the valuation, the auditor would generally issue an unqualified audit opinion. In certain circumstances, an auditor might include a so-called "fair value paragraph" (i.e., as an emphasis of matter paragraph) in the audit report because of inherent uncertainty in management's estimated fair value for a significant portion of the investment portfolio. If the auditor concludes that management's valuation procedures are inadequate or unreasonable, or that the underlying documentation does not support the valuation, an auditor could issue a qualified opinion or an adverse opinion. For further discussion of such reporting option, see the *AICPA Audit and Accounting Guide: Investment Companies*, paragraph 11.06.

If an auditor cannot obtain sufficient and appropriate audit evidence to support their audit objectives, the auditor may qualify or disclaim an opinion on the financial statements because of a scope limitation.

Moving forward

With respect to the new guidance in the AICPA Practice Aid, management of both investor entities and investee entities should carefully consider these requirements and evaluate the following:

Degree of transparency

The demands of a growing and more institutional investor base, along with other pressures, have combined to force management of investor entities and investee fund managers to grapple with the issue of transparency. This means that hedge fund managers, in particular, are increasingly being asked to divulge more information on their strategies, portfolios and performance, whereas traditionally they have not been required to provide such information. In addition, private equity fund managers are being asked to provide more transparency around their portfolio company investments at a time when concerns around this information already exist as a result of the recent Freedom of Information Act requests.

The issue of transparency should be considered broadly to incorporate all forms of information and/or access requested by, or provided to, current and potential investors, consultants and others. The focus on the monitoring controls utilized by management of the investor entity is likely to increase their contact with funds, as well as requests for various types of information throughout the year – not just on investor entities' annual reporting dates. As a result, at both the investee and investor levels, portfolio managers, risk management, legal/compliance and finance/accounting personnel need to collectively prepare for and assess these requirements.

Due diligence programs

Management of the investor entity must establish controls over its alternative investments to support the existence and valuation assertions. These controls include:

- Initial due diligence (procedures performed before the initial investment)
- Ongoing monitoring (procedures performed after the initial investment)
- Financial reporting controls (procedures related to the accounting for and reporting of the investment)

The design and effectiveness of these controls are particularly important because they can affect the nature, timing and extent of audit procedures performed by the investor entity's auditor over alternative investments. **In light of the guidance provided in the AICPA Practice Aid, management of investor entities should examine their due diligence programs, related controls and documentation over alternative investments.**

2 | Implications for investor entities

A. Management's procedures and controls

This section addresses an investor entity's procedures and controls over alternative investments and how those procedures and controls can be designed or enhanced to meet the requirements of the audit guidance issued during the past few years.

Directly or through third parties acting on its behalf, management of the investor entity must establish strong procedural controls over the initial due diligence and ongoing monitoring of their alternative investments. These controls may include those listed in Appendix 2 to the AICPA Practice Aid. That list, however, is not intended to be all-inclusive or to be used as a checklist by management or the auditor. Management must design controls appropriate to its organization and the nature and extent of its alternative investments.

To take appropriate responsibility for its portfolio of alternative investments, management of the investor entity must have an effective process and related internal controls in place to ensure a sufficient understanding of their alternative investments. These controls include:

- Initial due diligence (procedures performed before the initial investment)
- Ongoing monitoring (procedures performed after the initial investment)
- Financial reporting controls (procedures related to the accounting for and reporting of the investment)

The design and effectiveness of these controls are particularly important because they can affect the nature, timing and extent of audit procedures performed by the investor entity's auditor over alternative investments. In light of the guidance provided in the AICPA Practice Aid, management of the investor entity should examine its due diligence programs and related controls over alternative investments. In particular, management of the investor entity should evaluate the following, each of which is discussed further below:

1. Design and effectiveness of its due diligence programs
2. Documentation and other evidence available to support its due diligence programs
3. Knowledge, experience and training of the personnel responsible for its due diligence programs and adequacy of related systems
4. Coordination and communication between all parties
5. Financial reporting controls, including valuation

1. Design and effectiveness of due diligence programs

Initial due diligence

It is critical that appropriate controls begin with initial due diligence before choosing to invest in a particular alternative investment. Initial due diligence often incorporates both top-down and bottom-up analysis to evaluate whether a prospective investee fund manager meets the investor entity's risk/return objectives. This would typically involve quantitative and qualitative analysis of a fund manager's investment style and process and an assessment of the effect the investment would have on the investor entity's overall portfolio. Initial due diligence also involves assessing the investee fund manager's personnel, operations, controls, systems, policies and procedures. This is often accomplished through on-site front office and back office reviews, as well as a review of the key legal, tax and compliance issues.

There are a variety of approaches and procedures used by investor entities in their investment decision-making process. Many investor entities have very sophisticated and well-established policies and procedures to identify, select and approve alternative investments, which incorporate quantitative and qualitative analysis, dedicated teams, comprehensive due diligence questionnaires, and formal review and approval processes. Some colleges, universities and other highly endowed institutions rely on third parties to perform pre-investment due diligence, while fund-of-funds typically have their own dedicated personnel. Regardless of which approach is followed, the investor entity is still ultimately responsible for performing sufficient due diligence, making an informed choice, and documenting the

process. The degree to which this process is effectively documented has historically varied depending on the sophistication and resources available to the investor entity. The AICPA Practice Aid reinforces the need for management to **document** their initial due diligence process.

Ongoing monitoring

Due diligence should continue after an investment is made. In addition to an ongoing analysis of investment results and risk/return objectives, post-investment monitoring involves ensuring that the investee fund manager – and the investor entity in its role as a prudent investor and fiduciary – continues to have adequate controls, systems, policies and procedures in place.

An effective ongoing monitoring process requires that the investor entity's management (directly or through agents acting on its behalf) has sufficient information on the underlying investee fund and its investments. The investor entity's management may not be able to obtain full transparency into the underlying investments, including a detailed listing of the underlying investment portfolio held by the alternative investments. This is particularly true for hedge funds, which have historically been reluctant to provide such information, and for certain types of investor entities, where the receipt of such information may fall under the Freedom of Information Act. Nevertheless, management should apply a broader view of transparency to incorporate all forms of information and/or access provided by investee fund managers. Therefore, management must find other information or conduct other activities that will provide valuable information on the alternative investments and the investee fund managers. For example, management of the investor entity can:

- Conduct periodic interviews, including on-site front office reviews, with the investee fund manager to update their understanding of the investee fund's strategy, positions, exposures, key performance drivers, etc.
- Ask about changes in the investee fund manager's detailed valuation policies and procedures, and obtain updated copies or summaries, as applicable. (Note: An excerpt from the investee fund's offering document does **not** constitute adequate valuation policies and procedures for this purpose.)
- Compare the fund's performance to benchmark returns, peer groups and/or historical returns, to the extent applicable, to see if the return is reasonable
- Review periodic investor reports and letters, including performance and risk statistics, summary or detailed portfolio information, and other information related to leverage, exposure levels, large positions, etc.
- Attend the investee fund manager's annual investor conference, if applicable. (Note: This is common for private equity funds.)
- Obtain and review annual audited financial statements and interim (i.e., quarterly or semi-annual) unaudited financial statements, to the extent available. For audited financial statements, note whether the opinion is qualified and, if so, why. Also note whether there was a change of auditors, or a change in valuation policies (or a change in

the amount of "fair valued" investments[1]) or other unusual disclosures associated with related party transactions or otherwise.

- Review SAS 70 reports[2], if available, and ensure that identified user controls are in place.
- Review press reports for significant management, structure, or personnel developments. Inquire about staffing level changes. When key personnel changes occur, consider making background checks, asking for and checking references, and searching the NASD and SEC websites, as applicable.
- Review the Schedule K-1 for each investee fund taxed as a pass-through entity (e.g., limited partnership, limited liability company), as applicable, to determine if it has resulted in any tax considerations.
- Review information on the investee fund's and investee fund manager's assets under management and inquire as to any significant capital changes (up or down).

The activities described above should be documented and maintained in management's files.

As they do with the initial due diligence, some colleges, universities and other highly endowed institutions may outsource ongoing monitoring activities to a third party. If this is the case, the investor entity must develop appropriate monitoring controls and related documentation over its third-party service provider to make sure that its monitoring activities are complete and effective.

---

1 When effective (fiscal years beginning after November 15, 2007), the new disclosure requirements of Statement of Financial Accounting Standard No. 157, *Fair Value Measurements* ("FAS 157"), will likely provide the investor entity with additional transparency and information relating to the investee fund's fair valuation policies and exposures.
2 Some investee fund managers or fund administrators may have a SAS 70 report on their internal controls. SAS 70 is a standard issued by the AICPA, titled "Reports on the Processing of Transactions by Service Organizations." SAS 70 sets forth the professional standards used by an auditor to assess the internal controls of a service organization and issue a report.

2. Documentation and other evidence to support due diligence programs

It would be prudent for management to expect – and prepare for in advance – the external auditor's request for supporting documentation related to the investor entity's due diligence and valuation practices. Good internal controls include strong documentation related to initial due diligence, ongoing monitoring and financial reporting controls. The following table summarizes some examples of the documentation that may be maintained to provide evidence of certain management controls. To the extent that management does not have sufficient information on its underlying investments, and/or sufficient evidence of such information, the auditor needs to consider the reporting implications.

Area	Illustrative documentation
Selection, evaluation and approval of investee fund managers	• Written due diligence memos, with appropriate review and approvals indicated • Formal due diligence checklists/questionnaires, with appropriate review and approvals indicated • Written minutes (or summaries) of meetings where investment decisions were made
Periodic visits or phone calls to investee fund managers	• Written documentation of visits to or discussions with investee fund managers
Investment policy for asset allocations and valuations	• Written policy that has been adopted/approved by the Investment Committee • Written evidence that policy exceptions were presented to the committee for acknowledgement
Review of audited financial statements	• Written checklist that may address: (a) reconciliation of audited financial statements to recorded balance, (b) roll-forward of audited balance from investee fund's year end to investor entity's year end, and (c) comparison of actual returns to benchmarks, and explanations of significant variances
Review of valuations prepared by investee fund managers, including review of portfolio holdings, key methodologies, inputs and assumptions used	• Written notes on valuations or separate memo documenting understanding of the investee fund manager's process and conclusions • Memo explaining rationale for acceptance of investee fund manager's valuations or adjustments deemed appropriate

3. Knowledge, experience and training of personnel, and adequacy of systems

An important consideration – especially for colleges, universities and other highly endowed institutions – is the required resources to select, monitor, value and report alternative investments, along with the related governance structures in place to oversee these efforts on behalf of the investor entity. As mentioned above, many investor entities have very experienced, dedicated teams, while others (primarily colleges, universities and other highly endowed institutions) may rely on third parties to perform initial and ongoing due diligence. Regardless of which approach is used, the investor entity should maintain a sufficient complement of investment, accounting and finance personnel with an appropriate level of knowledge, experience and training commensurate with the nature, extent and complexity of the investor entity's alternative investment portfolio. The team dedicated to alternative investments should have deep investment experience and extensive experience evaluating and monitoring alternative investments, including the unique tax, legal and regulatory issues.

Equally important are the systems used in the monitoring, oversight, and reporting of alternative investments. Also, given the complexity and risks associated with alternative investments, adequate communication and training are essential.

4. Coordination and communication between parties

To ensure an efficient and effective process, all parties should open the lines of communication and take the time to understand the roles and responsibilities of the other parties, including:

- Independent auditors: What audit procedures will they perform and how does the complexity, liquidity and volatility of the alternative investments impact the nature, timing and extent of those procedures?

- Investee fund managers: What controls and processes have they established, documented and shared with their investors?

- Internal constituents: Is there proper coordination and communication between the personnel within an investor entity who perform and document the due diligence and those who perform accounting and financial reporting for such investments? Do the members of the Audit Committee (if applicable), Investment Committee, front/investment office and back/controller's office fully understand how their roles and responsibilities align?

- Other external parties (e.g., valuation specialists, investment consultants), if applicable: What are their responsibilities and how do they satisfy them? What information is shared with the investor entity, in what form and how often?

5. Financial reporting controls, including valuation

Valuation is one of the two key issues discussed in the Interpretation and AICPA Practice Aid. The AICPA Practice Aid notes that a readily determinable fair value does not exist for many alternative investments. Despite the difficulty of estimating a fair value for alternative investments, they must generally be stated at their fair value, and management is responsible for determining such fair value. The AICPA Practice Aid states that "management of the investor entity is responsible for the valuation of alternative investment amounts as presented in the investor entity's financial statements" and "this responsibility cannot, under any circumstances, be outsourced or assigned to a party outside of the investor entity's management." This means that although management may look to the investee fund manager for the mechanics of the valuation, management of the investor entity must be able to independently evaluate and either accept or challenge the investee fund manager's valuation. In order to take responsibility at this level, management must have an effective process and controls in place, as well as a sufficient understanding of the investee fund's investment strategies, operations, underlying investments, and valuation policies and procedures.

The timing and extent of the investor entity management's understanding is based on its assessment of risk of material misstatement of the financial statements. The extent of management's fair valuation process and related controls should reflect the significance of the alternative investments to the investor entity's financial statements as a whole, the nature of the underlying investments and their risk assessment. In lower-risk situations, such as for alternative investments invested in readily marketable securities (e.g., bank common/commingled trust funds), an effective valuation process ordinarily requires a less sophisticated process and related controls than a higher-risk portfolio of illiquid and complex alternative investments.

An investor entity with an effective valuation process would obtain and review the investee fund's financial reports (e.g., independently audited financial statements, monthly statements). Ideally, the investee fund's reports would include a detailed list of the underlying investments and their fair values, along with other risk metrics. In the absence of detailed data, the investor entity can request other summarized data, such as condensed portfolio data, sector data, etc., that the investee fund may be willing to provide.

Management of the investor entity must do more than simply obtain the detail of the underlying investments to support its assertion regarding the valuation of the alternative investments. However, the investor entity's valuation process need **not** include recalculation of estimated fair values for the alternative investments. Management of the investor entity should understand the characteristics of the underlying investments and the valuation process used by the investee fund manager for the investments held at the balance sheet date. Management of the investor entity should perform an independent, separate valuation only if it becomes aware of erroneous or incomplete assumptions or methodology.

The following points summarize some sound practices related to the financial reporting and valuation for all types of alternative investments, including fund-of-funds:

- Compare the unaudited net asset values (NAV) received by the investor entity at the investee fund's year-end date (often December) to the information included within the investee fund's audited financial statements. Identify and investigate any significant differences.
- Track the timeliness of NAV statements provided by the investee fund manager during the year.
- For hedge funds, consider whether the fund's estimated NAVs received are consistent with the final NAVs received from the investee fund manager or administrator. Identify and investigate any significant differences.

- Obtain the investee fund's Schedule K-1 (for investee funds structured as partnerships, or taxed as such) and review for any federal and state tax liability. Also, compare the capital account information reflected on the Schedule K-1 with the capital account information provided by the investee fund manager and recorded by the investor entity. Identify and investigate any significant differences.

- Compare the investee fund's NAV statements with the value included on the statement provided by the investor entity's custodian, to the extent applicable. Identify and investigate any significant differences.

- On a regular basis, ask the investee fund manager, via phone calls or on-site visits, about any changes in the fund's valuation polices and procedures, including the valuation methodologies, key inputs and assumptions.

- Request and review changes to valuation policies and procedures. Ask whether the investee fund manager employs a consistent valuation process throughout the year.

- Compare the investee fund manager's valuation policies and procedures across different funds in the fund's peer group to identify potential differences in methodologies or key inputs. Ask the investee fund manager to explain any differences in methodologies or inputs.

- When valuations change significantly, find out what caused the change and consider the reasonableness of the explanation. This can be particularly relevant for private equity funds with a discrete number of private investments whose values do not tend to fluctuate period to period.

- Compare cash distributions to previously reported values throughout the year.

- Inquire periodically as to the composition of the investment portfolio and obtain exposure levels, portfolio attribution, large positions, degree of leverage, etc. (primarily for hedge funds).

- For hedge funds, inquire and understand movements to/from "side pocket accounts" maintained by the fund and any related valuation changes for "side pocket investments." (Note: See Appendix B for further discussion of side pockets.)

Valuation may present the single biggest challenge of alternative investments. Therefore, a robust financial reporting and valuation monitoring process that is well documented is essential, and becomes increasingly important as the size and complexity of the portfolio of alternative investments increases. Investor entities should expect their independent auditors to focus on valuation issues. It would be a good idea to discuss with the auditor – sooner rather than later – what audit evidence the auditor will expect from the investor entity to support the adequacy and reasonableness of the portfolio's valuation.

Other financial reporting controls

In addition to exercising its responsibility for determining the fair value of alternative investments, management should take other actions to coordinate the financial statement preparation and prepare for its annual audit. These actions include, but are not limited to, the following:

- Coordinate financial reporting responsibilities between the front and back offices. For colleges, universities and other highly endowed institution, coordinate between the "investment office" and the "controller's office."

- Consider financial reporting controls and related accounting policies over key investment transactions, including investment income, realized gains and losses, and unrealized gains and losses.

- Understand and assess the implications associated with the investee fund's basis of accounting and significant accounting policies and procedures pertaining to the valuation of alternative investments.

- Monitor the level of ownership in each investee fund to determine the proper accounting method (for certain types of investor entities).

- Ensure disclosures related to alternative investments not only meet GAAP standards, but also enhance the transparency of an entity's financial statements given the increasingly high expectations about transparency that exist in the current environment.

B. Management's risk assessment

The AICPA Practice Aid focuses on the existence and valuation assertions associated with alternative investments. Management of the investor entity is responsible for the existence and valuation of the alternative investments presented in the investor entity's financial statements. To exercise this responsibility, the investor entity's management must have a sufficient understanding of the underlying investments in order to design and maintain an effective process and related controls over its alternative investments.

An auditor's approach is based on an assessment of the risk of material misstatement of the financial statements. While management's risk assessment is based on its assessment of the inherent risk of material misstatement in its financial statements, it encompasses other factors as well. One of the challenges that investor entities and their auditors have experienced in addressing the new auditing guidance set forth in the AICPA Practice Aid has been understanding each other's assessment of risk for their respective purposes. Clearly this is an essential element to an efficient and effective audit process.

To design an efficient and effective risk assessment process that addresses the unique risks associated with alternative investments, management must consider all relevant factors. It is clear that several types of alternative investments with varying structures and strategies, each with their own attributes and characteristics, present unique risks. Accordingly, a "one-size-fits-all" approach to assigning risk attributes to alternative investments may not be appropriate.

So, how does management consider all of these factors? In many cases, management has developed its own assessment of risk across its alternative investment portfolio to facilitate its due diligence and ongoing monitoring of its investee funds. There are several quantitative and qualitative approaches that have been used in practice to address this issue. For example, the investor entity may categorize or stratify its portfolio of alternative investments into different risk categories (e.g., "low," "moderate" and "high" risk categories) and/or assign each investee fund a risk rating, score or grade based on specified criteria. Management would then design procedures and controls appropriate for each risk category to provide adequate comfort given the relative risk rating (e.g., more robust procedures and controls for the "high" risk category). This approach involves considerable judgment and requires extensive experience with alternative investments in order to balance all relevant factors for each investment.

Appendix A provides an illustrative AU332 risk assessment and related considerations that capture certain risk factors being considered in practice, including considerations related to the following areas:

Management, governance and service providers
- Quality and experience of fund management
- Role and effectiveness of fund governance
- Quality of service providers

Strategy, structure and key terms
- Nature, complexity and liquidity of strategy
- Nature of the fund's liquidity terms
- Complexity of structure and key terms

Transparency and reporting
- Nature and quality of transparency
- Quality of financial reporting

Internal controls
- Adequacy of infrastructure, personnel and general internal controls
- Design and effectiveness of valuation policies and procedures
- Quality of risk monitoring
- Impact of regulatory compliance matters
- Impact of legal and tax matters

This information is presented for illustrative purposes only, and is not intended to be an all-inclusive list of risk factors that management should consider.

Given the focus in the AICPA Practice Aid on transparency and the nature, complexity and liquidity of the investee funds and their underlying investments, these factors are discussed in more detail below.

Nature and quality of transparency provided by the investee fund manager

Among the factors management should consider in performing its risk assessment is the nature and quality of transparency provided by the investee fund manager. An effective process for supporting fair value estimates of its alternative investments requires the investor entity's management (directly or through agents acting on its behalf) to gather sufficient information on the investment strategy and the underlying investments and to understand the policies and procedures used by the investee fund manager and/or an outside service provider, such as a fund administrator, to value the underlying investment portfolio. In many instances, the investor entity's management may not be able to obtain full transparency into the underlying investment portfolio, including a detailed list of the underlying investment portfolio held by the alternative investments. However, the issue of transparency can also be viewed broadly to encompass all forms of information or access provided by the investee fund manager, including the information and activities described earlier.

Nature, complexity and liquidity of underlying investments of the investee funds

In assessing the risks associated with an investor entity's alternative investments, management should consider the nature of the underlying investments held by the investee funds. Generally, more actively traded, liquid securities held by an investee fund generate the highest level of confidence regarding the valuation and existence assertions at both the investor and investee levels. This is consistent with FAS 157. Conversely, the more complex, illiquid or esoteric the investee fund's investments are, the more effort the investor entity may need to put forth to gain comfort over the investee fund's valuation and existence assertions. The auditor's efforts operate in the same manner as that of the investor entity. The audit effort needed to support the valuation and existence assertions is greater for a more complex or illiquid investee fund than for a less complex and more liquid fund. Therefore, management's risk assessment should consider the complexity of the underlying investments and the policies relating to valuation for each major asset class.

Management may also consider how the ultimate investments are held by the investee fund. The complexity of the structures used by investee funds may affect the degree of transparency provided to or available for the auditor and the investor entity's management with respect to the underlying investment portfolio. For example, information on the underlying investments may be more limited for investments held through multi-tiered fund structures, like master-feeder or fund-of-funds structures, or through various special-purpose vehicles. Such structures may result in further challenges in assessing the existence or valuation assertions.

Typically, there should be a general correlation between the liquidity of an investee fund's investment portfolio and the liquidity terms of the investee fund itself (i.e., redemption provisions). Investor entity management, as part of its initial due diligence in evaluating potential investee funds and ongoing due diligence in monitoring existing investee funds, should consider risks associated with a potential mismatch of liquidity terms between an investee fund's investments and the liquidity terms of the investee fund. Due diligence procedures should also consider the potential for "style drift" for each investee fund and the effect it may have on the matching or mismatching of liquidity.

If we are to assume correlation of liquidity, as described above, management should give special consideration to the investee funds that hold non-public, illiquid investments such as private equity funds, special opportunity funds, real estate funds and other real asset or natural resource funds. Since these funds hold assets that are generally illiquid and for which no ready market exists, such assets are generally carried at the investee fund manager's estimate of fair value. This yields a higher level of judgment relating to the valuation assertions.

Nature, complexity and liquidity of the investee funds themselves

In performing its risk assessment, management should consider the liquidity of the investee fund itself, and assess the risks associated with any potential mismatch of liquidity between the investee fund's investment portfolio and the liquidity terms of the fund itself.

As noted earlier, the AICPA Practice Aid defines alternative investments to include hedge funds, private equity funds, real estate funds, venture capital funds, commodity funds, offshore fund vehicles, fund-of-funds, as well as bank common/collective trust funds. Some alternative investments, such as bank common/collective trust funds and certain offshore funds, may be highly liquid (e.g., daily liquidity) with underlying investment portfolios consisting mostly of marketable securities. Accordingly, these types of alternative investments may not require significant judgment by the investor entity's management in the assessment of fair value and provide a lower risk of material misstatement to the overall financial statements, on a relative basis. As noted in the AICPA Practice Aid, alternative investments that are themselves invested in marketable securities require a less sophisticated fair value process. Therefore, this publication focuses primarily on hedge funds and private equity/venture capital funds because they are more likely to hold complex and/or illiquid investments and may provide limited, if any, liquidity.

Hedge funds

In general, key structural and operational issues associated with hedge funds complicate their capital structures and related liquidity terms, which may affect fair value considerations of the investor entity. Such issues include, but are not limited to:

- Legal structures
- Liquidity of the underlying investment portfolio
- Timing of cash flows and net asset value determinations
- Prevalence and mechanisms associated with performance-based fee arrangements (e.g., incentive allocations)

For example, the use of a corporate form for most offshore funds (as opposed to a limited partnership form for most domestic funds) imposes certain complexities on the capital structure. In addition, multiple classes of shares or partnership interests with varied terms, as well as master-feeder or other multi-tiered structures, also contribute to the complexity of the fund and issues related to liquidity and fair value.

Investors in domestic and offshore hedge funds can generally withdraw amounts from, or redeem interests in, hedge funds on a monthly, quarterly, semi-annual or annual basis, as the case may be for each fund, subject to certain notice and timing requirements. Such terms (commonly referred to as the "liquidity terms") are governed by the respective investee fund's governing documents (e.g., limited partnership agreement, confidential offering memorandum and articles of association). In particular, the use of "side pocket accounts" may affect the risk assessment. Other liquidity terms include initial lock-ups, the ability to withdraw with penalties (i.e., redemption fees), notice periods, holdbacks and gates. Each of these liquidity terms are described in more detail in Appendix B. Other key terms that may affect the determination of fair value for an investor entity's interest in an investee fund are summarized in Appendix C. Management of an investor entity should be familiar with the various fund terms that may affect the risk assessment with respect to an investee fund, with a particular focus on the investee fund's liquidity terms.

Private equity funds

Redemption upon liquidation or termination of the entity is generally the case for investment fund structures traditionally used for private equity funds (comprising buyout, venture capital, mezzanine and other similar strategies). These entities are referred to as "limited-life funds" pursuant to the AICPA's Statement of Position 03-4, *Reporting Financial Highlights and Schedule of Investments by Nonregistered Investment Partnerships: An Amendment to the Audit and Accounting Guide Audits of Investment Companies* and AICPA Statement of Position 95-2, *Financial Reporting by Nonpublic Investment Partnerships*. Some closed-end hedge funds employing certain investment strategies (e.g., special opportunities, distressed debt, and so-called "PIPEs," or private investments in public equities) may also be structured in a similar way. These funds typically do not provide for limited partner-initiated redemptions. Rather, by the terms of their offering documents, these funds have limited lives, often 8 to10 years, with the ability for the general partner to extend the life for a specified period of time (e.g., 2 years). Therefore, unless an investor entity's interest is sold in the "secondary market," such funds have limited opportunities, if any, for investor entities to withdraw before the fund is terminated. As a result, interests in private equity funds are less liquid than interests in hedge funds because investors in hedge funds generally have the ability to redeem their interests at their discretion, subject to applicable liquidity terms.

Also, unlike hedge funds, which are generally open to the acceptance of new capital, private equity funds do not continuously raise capital. Rather, investor entities "commit" a specified amount of capital upon inception of the fund (i.e., committed capital), which is then generally "drawn down" over a specified period of the fund's life (i.e., the investment period) either on a "just-in-time basis" (i.e., as needed by the general partner to make investments or fund the payment of fees and expenses) or at specified intervals. Both the investor entity and its auditor should be aware of the amount of future commitments, not only for disclosure, but also for understanding the projected liquidity of the overall investments in the portfolio.

Private equity funds have, as a predominant operating strategy, the return of the proceeds from the disposition of investments to investor entities. Therefore, upon the disposition of an investment, the proceeds will generally be distributed to the investor entities (including both the limited and general partners), subject to a limited ability of the general partner to "recycle" (i.e., reinvest) the capital under certain circumstances. Distributions can be in the form of cash or securities.

Finally, unlike hedge funds, private equity funds do not routinely acquire (directly or indirectly) market-traded securities or derivatives as part of their investment strategy. Rather, they generally invest in the equity and/or debt securities of private companies.

Funds that specialize in purchasing the existing interests of an investor entity in a closed private equity fund are referred to as "secondary funds." This type of fund may aim to exploit an existing investor entity's need for liquidity or desire to avoid future draws on unfunded commitment balances by purchasing these interests, often at a price that is different than the capital balance attributable to the interest. The divergence between the purchase price of the interest and the purchased capital balance (which is often a discount to the investee fund's NAV but may also be a premium) creates unique valuation considerations for these secondary funds. Because many of these transactions purchased at a discount have a "fire sale" attribute to them, the purchase price actually may not be fair value. Conversely, if the purchase price was derived from negotiations between the buyer and seller after robust due diligence by the buyer, and there is no "fire sale" element to the transaction, the purchase price may be indicative of fair value. Therefore, the investor entity's management must carefully consider the nature of each transaction and the specific facts and circumstances of each transaction when determining fair value. In each case, the investor entity should document the nature and circumstances surrounding the transaction to support the fair value assertion.

3 | Implications for investee fund managers

The challenges of increased investor due diligence, new auditing requirements, a growing interest in demonstrating operational soundness and stability, and other factors have all combined to force management of investor entities and investee fund managers to grapple with the issues of transparency and more intensive due diligence. As a result, investee fund managers should expect an increase in the nature and extent of due diligence by investors and requests for greater transparency. As described in this document, the request for greater transparency will not come just from management of the investor entity – it will also come from the investor entity's auditor. With respect to such requests for greater transparency, investee fund managers should consider the following:

Anticipate requests and plan response

Investee fund managers should anticipate and prepare for confirmation requests from investor entities' auditors. As described earlier, such requests should include a request for portfolio-level detail. Formulating a policy and approach to such requests will likely require investee fund managers to make an evaluation between:

- Providing certain information they generally consider proprietary
- Meeting investors' expectations by fulfilling these requests
- Addressing legal and compliance considerations relating to providing information to some but not all investors

Carefully consider response

As discussed earlier, the auditor's request for confirmation of the investee fund's holdings on a security-by-security basis is required by the Interpretation, and uncertainty about whether the investee fund manager will provide the requested

information does not obviate the auditor's requirement to obtain sufficient appropriate audit evidence. As a result, by and large, it should be expected that auditors will send confirmation requests that include requests for portfolio-level detail similar to those set forth in the AICPA Practice Aid.

To help satisfy the accounting and reporting needs and expectations of their investors, we encourage investee fund managers to carefully consider their responses to these new confirmation requests. Other than the request for portfolio-level detail, the other information requested in the confirmation should not be too controversial or difficult for an investee fund manager to provide. To facilitate the audit of the investor entity, we encourage investee fund managers to respond to these requests for such information in a timely fashion, even if a response to the request for portfolio-level detail is sent separately.

We also encourage investee fund managers to carefully consider these confirmation requests and respond in a manner that balances the needs of their investors and their own policies and obligations with respect to transparency and confidentiality. Many investee fund managers have formulated responses that appear to have met this balance by providing the requested portfolio-level detail and/or providing other adequate information about the investee fund and its investment portfolio. Based on our experience to date, such other information has taken a variety of forms, including, but not limited to, one or more of the following:

- Condensed portfolio detail
- Performance and/or risk reports
- Exposure levels at the asset class, geography, industry and/or position level
- Liquidity analysis of the investment portfolio
- Valuation procedures, in general or by asset class

Some investee fund managers have responded with a standard reporting package, while others address each request separately. Some have even considered scheduling conference calls or hosting web-casts for investors during which they discuss valuation policies and procedures and other matters.

While the portfolio-level detail remains the requirement pursuant to the AICPA Practice Aid, the type of information described above may also be helpful or necessary for the auditor to address the valuation and existence assertions and to corroborate information the investor entity has represented or directly provided to the auditor with respect to the nature, complexity and liquidity of an investee fund.

"One size does not fit all"

It is important for investee fund managers to recognize that requests for greater transparency from their investor entities and from their investor entities' auditors will likely not be consistent, at least for some time. Such inconsistency could result from continued uncertainty about applying the requirements set forth in the AICPA Practice Aid (which this document hopes to alleviate), and some could result from other reasons relating to the application of the considerable judgment required in this process. For example, different investor entities investing the same amount in the same investee fund may approach their due diligence responsibilities differently because of various factors, including different views about risk, different levels of sophistication with respect to their due diligence, different resources, etc. Also, auditors auditing an investment held by different investor entities in the same investee fund may also have different approaches and expectations with respect to the nature and level of transparency needed to satisfy their respective audit requirements. These different expectations and approaches could be driven by various factors, including:

- Different risk assessments by the investor entity and/or their auditor for various reasons, including the significance of the alternative investment to a given investor entity

- The design and effectiveness of the investor entity's procedures and controls

- Different audit approaches

Fund-of-funds, in particular, may face significant challenges with respect to the requirements of the Interpretation and the AICPA Practice Aid because they are both an investor entity (investing in investee funds) and an investee fund for their own investor entities.

4 | Implications for the auditor

A. Auditor's risk assessment

The AICPA Practice Aid focuses on the existence and valuation assertions associated with alternative investments. The auditor's approach is based on an assessment of the risk of material misstatement of the financial statements. As stated in AU Section 312.11, the auditor's consideration of materiality is a matter of professional judgment – and materiality judgments involve both quantitative and qualitative considerations. The risk of material misstatement includes assessing inherent risk and control risk.

With respect to investments in alternative investments, an auditor's risk assessment depends on the particular facts and circumstances, including, but not limited to, the following risk factors, each of which is discussed in more detail below[1]:

1. Significance of alternative investments to the investor entity's financial statements
2. Nature and extent of the investor entity's process and related internal controls associated with the alternative investments
3. Nature and extent of information available to the investor entity to support its valuation process and valuation conclusions (including the availability of portfolio detail and audit reports)
4. Nature, complexity and liquidity of the underlying investments of the investee funds
5. Nature, complexity and liquidity of the investee funds themselves

1. Significance of alternative investments to the investor entity's financial statements

In assessing the risks to the investor entity's financial statements related to alternative investments, auditors need to consider the size of the portfolio devoted to alternative investments and the assessment of materiality at the overall financial statement level or in relation to financial statement assertions for classes of transactions, account balances and disclosures. However, with respect to an investor entity's interests in alternative investments, the relative size is not the only factor used to determine the audit strategy. Auditors also should consider the complexity of the strategies of these investments, the complexity of the entities or legal structures that hold the investments, the level of transparency into the underlying investments, the level of oversight by management and the Investment Committee, and other factors. These other risk considerations are addressed in more detail below.

---

1 The AICPA Practice Aid includes items (1) through (4), although we have re-sequenced them to reflect the order in which we believe they should be considered. The above list also includes item (5) which was not explicitly included in the AICPA Practice Aid. While we believe there is often an implicit correlation between the nature, complexity and liquidity of the underlying investments (item (4) above) and that of the funds themselves, we have included item (5) to ensure that auditors appropriately focus on this issue as well.

2. Nature and extent of the investor entity's process and related internal controls

In performing the risk assessment of the investor entity's valuation assertion, the auditor should consider the process used by the investor entity's management in developing its fair value estimates and the controls established relative to those estimates. See Section 2 for further discussion of investor entity management's controls and procedures.

In many cases, other parties play a role in the valuation and/or due diligence process. For example, the investor entity's management will often look to the investee fund manager for the mechanics of the valuation. In addition, depending on the extent of the investor entity's investment activities and the relative sophistication of its internal investment process and resources, the investor entity may use the services of a third-party investment consultant to initially select alternative investments (often within the context of its overall investment portfolio) and/or monitor such investments. As stated in the AICPA Practice Aid, management's "responsibility cannot, under any circumstances, be outsourced or assigned to a party outside of the investor entity's management." Therefore, while management of the investor entity may initially rely on the investee fund manager for the valuation of the underlying investments and the determination of its interest in the investee fund, management is not bound by such valuations. Management must have sufficient information to evaluate the investee fund's valuation and either accept or independently challenge it, as appropriate. Also, while management of the investor entity may engage a third-party consultant to select and monitor its alternative investments, it needs to design controls, including monitoring controls, to ensure that its outsourced investment monitoring and due diligence are effective.

As discussed above, regardless of whether other parties are involved in the valuation and/or due diligence process, management must have a sufficient understanding of the nature of the underlying investments, the portfolio strategies of the alternative investments, and the methods and significant assumptions used by the investee fund managers to value the underlying investments. To do this, management must maintain a sufficient complement of personnel with an appropriate level of knowledge, experience and training commensurate with the risks associated with its alternative investments. In addition, management should document its understanding of the nature of the underlying investments and the associated assumptions and methodologies used by the investee fund managers to value underlying investments.

As part of the overall risk assessment, the auditor uses professional judgment in assessing control risk (i.e., the risk that a potential material misstatement will not be prevented or detected on a timely basis by the entity's internal control). The auditor's assessment of control risk is based on an evaluation of the effectiveness of an entity's internal control to prevent or detect material misstatements in the financial statements. Since this assessment should generally be applied in the context of a particular process, it should be applied when obtaining an understanding of processes and controls, and when evaluating and validating internal controls around alternative investments. This may require that the auditor understand, evaluate and, if appropriate, validate varying controls over different classes or types of alternative investments held by the investor entity. As stated above, the controls to be tested may include those listed in Appendix 2 to the AICPA Practice Aid. As previously noted, however, that list is not intended to be all-inclusive or to be used as a checklist by the investor entity's management or the auditor. Management must design controls appropriate to its organization and the nature and extent of its alternative investments.

The assessment of control risk determines the nature and extent of controls comfort, if any, from the effective operation of internal controls. The nature of controls testing relates to the purpose and type of audit procedures. The extent of controls testing relates to the quantity and quality of audit evidence needed to demonstrate that controls operated effectively throughout the period of reliance. The level of comfort obtained from testing the controls drives an auditor to determine the nature and extent of substantive procedures to be performed.

If the auditor believes that controls are unlikely to be effective as they relate to existence or valuation of alternative investments, or believes that evaluating their effectiveness would be inefficient, the auditor would assess control risk for those assertions at the maximum, resulting in obtaining little or no controls comfort from the effective operation of internal control. Conversely, if the auditor assesses control risk at a low level, then significant controls comfort can be obtained by evaluating and validating the effectiveness of the design and operation of internal controls. Assessing control risk below the maximum level requires that the auditor:

- Identify specific controls relevant to specific assertions
- Test controls
- Conclude on the assessed level of control risk

In order to rely on controls around alternative investments, an auditor must also validate, through testing, the design and operating effectiveness of the related internal controls, including those in the information technology environment.

3. Nature and extent of information available to the investor entity

Management of the investor entity is responsible for the valuation of the alternative investments presented in the investor entity's financial statements. To exercise this responsibility, the investor entity's management must have a sufficient understanding of the underlying investments in order to design and maintain an effective process to support fair value estimates of its alternative investments. The timing and extent of management's procedures is based on its assessment of the inherent risk of material misstatement in its financial statements. In higher risk situations, management should have a better understanding of the underlying investments and the process used to value such investments. Management must also have sufficient information to understand, evaluate and either accept or independently challenge the investee fund's valuation policies and application thereof.

Management of the investor entity must also have a sufficient understanding of the nature of the investee fund's underlying investments, the portfolio strategy employed and the policies and procedures used by the investee fund manager and/or an outside service provider, such as a fund administrator, to value the underlying investment portfolio, including the inputs, methods and key assumptions used. Such understanding should be documented in the investor entity's files.

An effective process for supporting fair value estimates of its alternative investments requires the investor entity's management (directly or through agents acting on its behalf) to have sufficient information on the underlying investments. Therefore, an auditor needs to assess the nature and extent of information available to management and the documentation and support of such information in management's files. Good internal controls include strong documentation related to both initial and periodic ongoing due diligence. To the extent that management does not have sufficient information on its underlying investments, and/or sufficient evidence of such information, the auditor needs to consider the internal control and financial statement reporting implications.

4. Nature, complexity and liquidity of underlying investments of the investee funds

In assessing the risks associated with an investor entity's alternative investments, the auditor should consider factors including, but not limited to, the nature of the underlying investments held by the investee funds, the policies relating to valuation for each major asset class, and the manner in which investments are held by the investee fund.

As discussed in Section 2, the auditor's efforts operate in the same manner as that of the investor entity. Generally, more actively traded, liquid securities held by an investee fund generate the highest level of confidence regarding the valuation and existence assertions. This is consistent with FAS 157. The audit effort needed to support the valuation and existence assertions is greater for a more complex or illiquid investee fund than for a less complex and more liquid fund.

The investor entity's auditor should also consider management's policies relating to obtaining an understanding and evidence of the composition of the investee fund's investment portfolio and the valuation policies relating thereto (e.g., what are the valuation inputs and methodologies, how much of the portfolio is fair valued, how often is the portfolio priced). The auditor, in developing a risk assessment, must also consider how the ultimate investments are held by the investee fund. The complexity of the structures used by investee funds may affect the degree of transparency provided to or available for the auditor and the investor entity's management, with respect to the underlying investment portfolio. For example, information on the underlying investments may be more limited for investments held through multi-tiered fund structures like master-feeder or fund-of-funds structures, or through various special-purpose vehicles. Such structures may result in further challenges in assessing the existence or valuation assertions.

As discussed in Section 2, there should be a general correlation between the liquidity of an investee fund's investment portfolio and the liquidity terms of the fund itself (i.e., redemption provisions). As part of its risk assessment, the auditor should consider the potential for liquidity mismatch between an investee fund's investments and the liquidity terms of the investee fund itself, as well as the potential for "style drift" for each investee fund and the effect it may have on liquidity.

5. Nature, complexity and liquidity of the investee funds themselves

In performing its risk assessment over an investor entity's portfolio of alternative investments, the auditor should consider the liquidity of the investee funds themselves, with a particular focus on hedge funds and private equity funds. When assessing the risk of the investment, management of the investor entity and the auditor should understand the nature and extent of the investee fund's liquidity terms. For the following reasons, funds that provide less liquidity (i.e., less frequent redemption rights) may be considered higher risk than funds with greater liquidity:

- Investor entities are not as readily able to redeem their interests in the fund.

- There is an expected correlation between the liquidity terms of the fund itself and the liquidity of the investee fund's underlying investment portfolio.

Therefore, investee funds with longer lock-up periods and/or notice periods may suggest that the investee fund is less liquid – and therefore higher risk – than funds with shorter or no lock-up periods. This is because investors in funds with shorter or no lock-up periods generally have the ability to redeem their interests more frequently. Also, since investor entities lose any redemption rights with respect to the portion of the underlying investments designated in "side pocket accounts" (as explained in Appendix B), the use of such mechanisms may create inherent difficulties in assessing fair value. Therefore, it is important to determine if investments held in the side pocket accounts are material to the investor entity's overall capital balance, and for management to understand the nature of the fair value policies and procedures over the related side pocket investments. Further, the imposition of the "gate" could indicate significant redemptions from the fund. Depending on the liquidity of the underlying investments in the fund, this could affect the amount and timing of the investor entity's redemptions from an investee fund and, therefore, affect the investor entity's assertion related to fair value (i.e., consider whether the net asset value of the investment should be discounted).

Some of these terms could affect the investor entity's net realizable value with respect to an investee fund. For example, the investor entity and the auditor should be aware of situations where the holdback period (described in Appendix B) has ended and proceeds have either not been received from the investee fund or have been received but not for the full amount. This could indicate an issue associated with the net realizable value of the receivable from the investee fund with respect to such holdback amount.

When assessing the risk of the investment, the auditor (and management of the investor entity) should ensure they understand the nature and extent of the investee fund's liquidity terms in combination with other factors. For example, since private equity funds have limited opportunities, if any, for investor entities to withdraw before the fund terminates (other than through a sale in the "secondary market"), interests in private equity funds may be considered less liquid than interests in hedge funds. Therefore, simply from a liquidity perspective, private equity funds may be considered higher risk. Other factors, however, such as the possibility of a sale in the "secondary market" and/or the higher level of transparency often provided by private equity fund managers to their investors may serve to mitigate the higher risk. Private equity fund managers tend to provide significant transparency to investors because their portfolios consist of positions that were "privately negotiated" with little access to the transactions through the public market.

Summary of auditor's risk assessment

As noted throughout this section, with respect to investments in alternative investments, the auditor's risk assessment depends on the particular facts and circumstances, including, but not limited to, the following risk factors:

- Significance of alternative investments to the investor entity's financial statements
- Nature and extent of management's process and related internal controls associated with alternative investments
- Nature and extent of information available to management to support its valuation process and valuation conclusions
- Nature, complexity and liquidity of the underlying investments of the investee funds
- Nature, complexity and liquidity of the investee funds themselves

In determining the nature, timing and extent of audit procedures, the auditor must consider all of these factors. It is clear that several types of alternative investments with varying structures and strategies, each with their own attributes and characteristics, present unique audit risks. Accordingly, a "one-size-fits-all" approach to auditing an investor entity's interests in various alternative investments may not be appropriate. To design efficient and effective audit procedures that address the unique risks associated with each investment, all relevant factors must be considered. As with management's risk assessment, there are several approaches to addressing this issue. One approach would be to categorize or stratify the investor entity's portfolio of alternative investments by the auditor's perceived risk assessment into "low," "moderate" and "high" risk categories. The auditor would then design procedures for each category to provide adequate comfort given the relative risk rating (e.g., more robust audit procedures for the "high" risk category). For example, based on the risk assessment, the auditor may categorize the portfolio of alternative investments as follows:

Low risk	Moderate risk	High risk
• Lower relative risk than other categories	• Moderate relative risk compared with other categories	• High relative risk compared with other categories
• Heavier reliance on management's process and controls	• Moderate reliance on management's process and controls	• Low reliance on management's process and controls
• Some substantive testing of valuation and existence assertions	• More substantive testing of valuation and existence assertions	• Heavy substantive testing of valuation and existence assertions

This approach, which involves considerable judgment by the auditor, should consider all relevant factors for each alternative investment. For example, if the auditor considered the liquidity of the alternative investment as the only relevant factor in categorizing risk, all closed-ended private equity funds would default to a "high" risk rating. If the auditor considered other factors, such as the transparency of portfolio holdings and quality of quarterly investment summary disclosures, the risk assessment for those private equity funds may change to "moderate" or "low."

Also, given the varying terms, structures and strategies within different types of alternative investments, it is likely that the alternative investments within a general category (e.g., hedge funds, private equity funds) may be placed into different risk categories. For example, a hedge fund that holds highly liquid, marketable securities and provides monthly liquidity may be categorized as "low" risk, while another hedge fund that holds liquid and illiquid investments and has a longer lock-up period may be considered "moderate" or "high" risk. The same could apply for funds that employ a similar investment strategy but are structured differently.

In addition, a fund-of-funds investment might be categorized initially as "high" risk given the inherent liquidity issues and transparency constraints with respect to the ultimate underlying investments. If, however, the fund-of-funds manager has effective procedures and strong internal controls and periodically provides detailed or summary information on portfolio funds, the risk assessment might change to "moderate" or "low" risk.

As discussed in Section 2, in many cases, management may have developed its own stratification of risk across its alternative investment portfolio to facilitate its due diligence and ongoing monitoring of the investee fund managers. Though the factors management considered in their stratification effort may vary from those of an auditor, the auditor should understand management's approach and any significant differences that could influence their ultimate risk categorization of the investments. An efficient approach may be for the auditor to obtain and assess management's risk assessments, corroborate the information, and then design appropriate audit procedures around each category.

B. Addressing the existence and valuation assertions

As with any audit area, an auditor's approach is based on an assessment of the risk of material misstatement of the financial statements. Accordingly, the auditor needs to consider the quantity and quality of audit evidence to be obtained when assessing risks and designing audit procedures. There is a direct relationship between the risk of misstatement and the quantity of audit evidence needed – the greater the risk, the more audit evidence is required. Also, the quantity and quality of audit evidence are interrelated because the higher the quality of audit evidence, the less quantity of audit evidence may be required.

The evaluation of the quality of such evidence is subject to the auditor's professional judgment. The AICPA Practice Aid highlights that the quantity and quality of the audit evidence necessary generally increases as:

- The percentage of alternative investments to total assets and the total investment portfolio increases
- The nature, complexity and volatility of the underlying investments increases

Refer to Exhibit I and related discussion in the AICPA Practice Aid for further information.

In general, a direct relationship also exists between the quality of the audit evidence and the nature and extent of the information provided by the investor entity and/or the investee fund manager as of a date closest to the investor entity's balance sheet date. As the quality and extent of information as of the investor entity's year end increases, so does the quality of the audit evidence available. Because of certain inherent issues associated with alternative investments, auditors may face challenges in obtaining the same quality and quantity of audit evidence across an investor entity's portfolio of alternative investments. The evaluation of the quality and quantity of audit evidence is subject to the auditor's professional judgment. Table 4A is a non-all-inclusive list of the various types of audit evidence an auditor may receive and an illustrative assessment as to its quality.

Table 4A

Information available	Quality
US GAAS/GAAP audited financial statements of the investee fund, including detailed schedule of investments, as of the investor entity's balance sheet date	Highest
US GAAS/GAAP audited financial statements of the investee fund, including condensed schedule of investments, as of the investor entity's balance sheet date	High
Unaudited detailed list of the investee fund's underlying investments as of the date of the investor entity's balance sheet date, particularly to the extent the investments are highly liquid	High
Non-US GAAP audited financial statements of the investee fund, including detailed schedule of investments, as of the investor entity's balance sheet date, along with reconciliation to US GAAP	Moderate/High
Unaudited investee fund's condensed schedule of investments as of the date of the investor entity's balance sheet date	Moderate
Unaudited detailed listing of the investee fund's underlying investments as of a date other than the investor entity's balance sheet date	Moderate
Audited financial statements of the investee fund, including a detailed or condensed schedule of investments as of a date other than the investor entity's balance sheet date	Moderate
Confirmation with the investee fund manager or with a third-party administrator of the investor entity's interest in the investee fund (e.g., number of units held or percentage ownership, and value of the investor entity's proportionate share of net assets/partners' capital) as of the investor entity's balance sheet date	Moderate/Low
Limited visibility into the underlying investments	Low

Existence assertion

The existence assertion addresses whether the alternative investments exist at a given date. The occurrence assertion addresses whether the alternative investment transactions reported in the financial statements actually occurred.

Confirmation process

The AICPA Practice Aid provides guidance on the confirmation process that auditors should incorporate into their audit approach. According to the AICPA Practice Aid, simply confirming investments in the aggregate does not constitute adequate evidence with respect to the existence assertion. Rather, the AICPA Practice Aid states that, if the auditor concludes that the nature and extent of audit procedures should include confirming the existence of the entity's investments, confirmation of the holdings of the alternative investments on a security-by-security basis typically would constitute adequate audit evidence with respect to the existence assertion. Appendix 1 to the AICPA Practice Aid includes an illustrative confirmation for alternative investments. This confirmation is illustrative only and may be enhanced or modified if appropriate. For example, for private equity funds, it may be appropriate to also confirm the investor entity's share of committed capital and the unfunded capital commitment as of the reporting date. It may also be appropriate to create different confirmations for an investee hedge fund (domestic and offshore funds) or an investee private equity fund.

If the confirmation request is not returned to the auditor or the details of the underlying investments are not otherwise provided, the AICPA Practice Aid states that the auditor should perform alternative procedures to assess the existence of the alternative investments. Even if the auditor obtains a detailed confirmation of the investee fund's holdings, the AICPA Practice Aid states that the auditor may need to perform additional procedures, depending on the significance of the alternative investments to the investor entity's financial statements. Considerable auditor judgment is required to determine whether the auditor has sufficient evidence to satisfy the existence assertion.

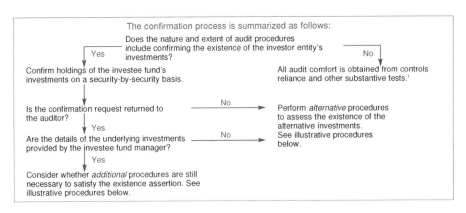

The confirmation process is summarized as follows:

Does the nature and extent of audit procedures include confirming the existence of the investor entity's investments?

Yes → Confirm holdings of the investee fund's investments on a security-by-security basis.

No → All audit comfort is obtained from controls reliance and other substantive tests.[1]

Is the confirmation request returned to the auditor?

No → Perform *alternative* procedures to assess the existence of the alternative investments. See illustrative procedures below.

Yes → Are the details of the underlying investments provided by the investee fund manager?

No → Perform *alternative* procedures to assess the existence of the alternative investments. See illustrative procedures below.

Yes → Consider whether *additional* procedures are still necessary to satisfy the existence assertion. See illustrative procedures below.

---

1 It would be unusual for the nature and extent of audit procedures to not include confirming evidence of the investor entity's alternative investments.

APPENDIX E

Illustrative alternative or additional procedures

Alternative or additional auditing procedures include, but are not limited to, the following:

1. Observe management site visits or listen to telephone calls to investee funds (or review documentation of such calls or visits).

Observation: Depending on the timing of management's site visits or telephone calls to investee funds and the willingness of the investee fund manager to allow participation by the auditor, auditors may or may not be able to actually observe such visits or calls. However, management of the investor entity, as part of its due diligence process, should maintain adequate records of such visits or calls, which auditors can review.

2. Review executed partnership, trust, limited liability corporation or similar arrangements.

Observation: The ability and extent to which executed documents help satisfy the existence assertion depends on factors such as the nature of the investee fund and the aging of the investment. For example, the limited partnership agreement for a private equity fund may include a list of each limited partner and their corresponding capital commitment. Reviewing executed copies of such documents may provide evidence as to the existence assertion, especially when the investment is relatively new. However, if an investment in a private equity fund is aged (i.e., greater than one year), reviewing the partnership agreement would give the auditor less evidence of the ownership of that alternative investment as of a current reporting date.

The limited partnership agreement for a hedge fund does not typically provide an investor list. Rather, each limited partner separately executes a limited partnership agreement and related subscription document upon admission to the hedge fund. Limited partners may execute additional subscription documents or other documents upon subsequent subscriptions to the fund. Limited partners may also execute redemption requests upon providing notice of their intention to redeem from an investee fund.

The auditor might obtain adequate audit evidence by reviewing executed documents, along with confirmation of related capital activity, with the investee fund manager or with a third-party fund administrator, and vouching the related cash.

3. Inspect other documentation supporting the investor entity's interest in the fund (e.g., confirmation of subscription, periodic statements, tax forms).

Observation: Upon subscription to a fund, the investee fund manager or fund administrator may provide a "confirmation" of the investment made. Typically, the investee fund manager or fund administrator also provides periodic statements reflecting an investor entity's interest in the fund, related capital account or number of shares/units held. Such information may be useful audit evidence for the existence assertion, especially when it is supplied to the investor entity directly by a third-party fund administrator. Alternative investments structured as domestic partnerships (or taxed as such) would also be required to provide limited partners with a Schedule K-1, which reports the components of taxable income, the capital account balance and related activity, as well as the percentage of interest of such investor entity in the fund. Auditors need to keep in mind that, like most alternative investments, funds structured as domestic partnerships predominantly have a December 31 year end. For such information to be most useful to the auditor of the investor entity, management of the investor entity with a different year end should reconcile such calendar year tax information to the audit period and year end of the investor entity.

4. Review periodic investor/partner statements from the investee fund or administrator/custodian reflecting investment activity and compare such activity with the investor entity's records.

Observation: As noted above, the investee fund manager or fund administrator typically provides periodic statements reflecting an investor entity's interest in the fund, related capital account or number of shares/units held. Comparing such documentation reflecting investment activity to the records of the investor entity may provide the auditor with valuable audit evidence, especially when such information is supplied directly to the investor entity by a third-party fund administrator.

5. Review annual audited financial statements.

Observation: In most cases, alternative investments are required to have an annual audit. The timing of the audit depends on factors primarily driven by the investee fund's fiscal year end and the nature of its underlying investment portfolio. The vast majority of alternative investments have a December 31 year end. Some offshore hedge funds, however, may have a different year end, often June 30. Reviewing annual audited financial statements (or, to a lesser extent, quarterly or semi-annual unaudited financial statements) may be useful in satisfying the existence assertion, especially when the financial statements include additional information detailing an investor entity's interest in the fund. Considerations related to the use of such financial statements are discussed in further detail later in this section.

6. Vouch relevant cash receipts and disbursements.

Observation: Comparing cash activity reflected in the records of the investor entity with the corresponding cash movements reflected in bank or brokerage statements generally provides the auditor with valuable audit evidence.

Valuation assertion

The valuation assertion addresses whether alternative investments have been included in the financial statements at the appropriate values. This guidance addresses alternative investments required to be carried at fair value.

Illustrative procedures

The auditor's consideration of the valuation assertion typically begins with understanding the process used by the investor entity's management to develop its fair value estimates and the controls established relative to those estimates.

As discussed earlier, management of the investor entity is responsible for the valuation of the alternative investment amounts presented in the investor entity's financial statements. The AICPA Practice Aid states that this responsibility **cannot be outsourced or assigned** to a party outside of the investor entity's management. While management can look to other parties for the mechanics, review, accounting or oversight of the valuation – such as the investee fund manager, administrator/custodian or a third-party investment consultant – management must have sufficient information to evaluate the investee fund's valuation, and either independently challenge it or accept it, as appropriate. In certain circumstances, challenging the investee fund's valuation may cause the investor entity to modify it in some way.

APPENDIX E

The investor entity's auditor needs to develop a solid understanding of the investor management's process and controls to determine the estimated fair value of its alternative investments in order to assess how they affect the nature, timing and extent of the auditing procedures. The AICPA Practice Aid suggests that the auditor test management's fair value estimates using one or more of the following approaches as of the balance sheet date:

a. Confirm the alternative investment

b. Review and test the investor entity's process and related data

c. Use audited financial statements

d. Review recent transactions

These approaches are described in more detail below. To the extent that the investor entity's management estimates the fair value of a significant portion of its alternative investments as of an interim date, management of the investor entity needs to obtain sufficient information to record such investments at fair value as of its balance sheet date. In those cases, the auditor must test both the investor entity's estimation process as of the interim date and the investor entity's roll-forward process to the reporting date.

The auditor must also consider how much management of the investor entity relies on the information reported to it by the investee funds. If management of the investor entity relies significantly on the investee fund manager's valuations and valuation process, management must first ascertain whether it is appropriate to do so by gathering as much information about each of the investee fund managers as possible. Much of this information is obtained and analyzed as part of management's initial and ongoing due diligence procedures described in the AICPA Practice Aid and discussed in Section 2.

The auditor should ensure that it understands where within the investor entity's organization the due diligence and monitoring process takes place. The auditor should not only review the procedures performed by operational and accounting personnel, but also focus on the functions performed by areas such as portfolio management, risk management and the legal department. In some cases, the responsibility for the due diligence programs and related documentation is dispersed within an investor entity's organization. It is also helpful for the auditor to understand the type of data that is presented to management, Valuation Committees and/or the board of directors at the investor entity with respect to alternative investments.

Where management of the investor entity has determined that they are NOT comfortable relying on an investee fund's reported value, management must arrive at its own estimate of fair value. This is typically done with the help of the underlying investee fund manager because the information about the portfolio investments that would facilitate the valuation process is often not totally transparent or available to the investor entity. For example, if the investee fund reports on a tax basis (rather than US GAAP), the investor entity should contact the investee fund manager to obtain the necessary information to arrive at fair values in accordance with US GAAP for the investee fund's investment portfolio.

The approaches described in the AICPA Practice Aid for the auditor to test management's fair value estimates are each stated below, with additional guidance provided on the use of financial statements and the review of recent transactions.

a. Confirm the alternative investment

The AICPA Practice Aid states that if the auditor determines that the nature and extent of auditing procedures should include testing the measurement of the investor entity's investment, simply receiving a confirmation from the investee fund of its underlying investments, either in the aggregate or on a security-by-security basis, does not, in and of itself, constitute adequate audit evidence with respect to the valuation assertion. The extent of additional procedures is directly related to the assessed risk of material misstatement of the financial statements.

b. Review and test investor entity's process and related data

A confirmation on a security-by-security basis may provide the auditor with corroborating evidence to support the data used or considered by the investor entity's management in its valuation process. However, if detailed information, such as a description of each investment, ownership percentage, shares owned and estimated value is not available, then the auditor should look to other information that management of the investor entity used in its valuation.

Such other information may include detailed descriptions of the investee fund process to determine fair value and the investor entity's assessment of that process. It may also include a review of Valuation or Investment Committee minutes or other memoranda or summaries that document key valuation assessments and judgments made in the process.

Often, management uses a wide variety of information to assess valuation. This includes management's understanding and supporting documentation related to the valuation controls at the investee fund manager, as well as information it receives on a periodic basis. As part of its ongoing due diligence, the investor entity may receive full transparency to the investee fund's underlying portfolio or something less, such as material positions. Alternatively, they may receive other information, such as exposure reports or benchmarking data, which they may use to assess the reasonableness of the returns provided by investee fund managers. For instance, a fixed-income hedge fund may not provide an investor with full transparency to the fund, but may give the investor key data with respect to the portfolio that the investor may in turn use to track the fund against observable benchmarks. Such data includes the duration of the portfolio, weighted average maturity, weighted average coupon, portion of the portfolio that is hedged, etc. The investor entity may then use this information to derive expectations related to the investee fund, which are then compared to actual returns.

Another example would be an investee fund invested in over-the-counter derivatives. The investee fund may provide enough information related to the portfolio, such as its sensitivity relative to the benchmark (e.g., the delta of the portfolio) that it could be tracked against an observable market. In the absence of sufficient audit evidence, especially when the year end of the investee fund does not coincide with that of the investor entity, auditors may consider testing these analytical procedures by performing independent analytical procedures using publicly available information or testing the assumptions used.

c. Use audited financial statements

The investor entity should provide the auditor with the most recent financial statements of each investee fund and the accompanying audit report. The investor entity should also provide the auditor with the reconciliation of such financial statements with the investment balance recorded by the investor entity. In reviewing these financial statements and related reconciliations, the auditor should consider the factors discussed below.

Obtain and review available financial statements

In general, coterminous financial statements of the investee fund that are reported on the same basis of accounting as those of the investor entity and which have been audited by an auditor whose report is satisfactory to the investor entity's auditor, for this purpose, may constitute sufficient evidential matter.

Upon reviewing the investee fund's financial statements, however, the auditor may conclude that additional evidence is needed because of factors such as:

- Unfamiliarity with, or questions surrounding, the professional reputation and standing of the investee fund's auditor

- Significant differences in fiscal year ends between the investor entity and the investee fund

- Significant differences in the basis of accounting between the investor entity and the investee fund resulting in significant differences in the accounting principles applied

- Questions regarding the audit opinion for the investee fund and/or its accounting policies

- Timing of the investor entity's audit that precludes receipt of the audited financial statements of the investee fund

- Other factors that cause management of the investor entity discomfort with relying on an investee fund manager's estimate of value

APPENDIX E

The following decision tree is a tool to help the auditors of investor entities as they consider the use of financial statements of investee funds.

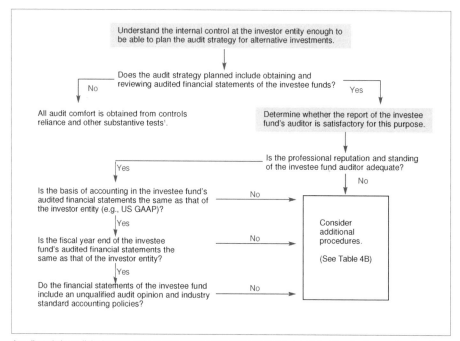

As reflected above, if the investor entity and the investee fund have the same year end and basis of accounting, then the audited financial statements of the investee fund and the accompanying auditor's report may provide significant audit evidence regarding the valuation of the investment. To the extent that the investor entity and the investee fund have different year ends and/or a different basis of accounting, the auditor may need to perform additional procedures.

---

1 It would be unusual for the audit strategy to not include obtaining and reviewing the most recent audited financial statements of the investee funds.

IMPLICATIONS FOR THE AUDITOR

If, because of the issues listed above (or others), the auditor needs more evidential matter, the auditor should perform additional procedures to gather the additional evidence. The nature, timing and extent of these additional procedures is a matter of professional judgment after considering factors such as the materiality of the investment in relation to the financial statements of the investor entity. These procedures may include those listed in Table 4B below.

Table 4B

Factors impacting use of audited financial statements	Illustrative additional procedures
Professional reputation and standing of the investee fund's auditor	• Investigate the professional reputation and standing of the investee fund's auditor. • Request that the investor entity apply, or have the auditor apply, appropriate procedures to the financial statements and/or the underlying records. • Request that the investor entity call or visit the other auditor to discuss audit procedures followed and the results thereof. Review the audit program and/or working papers of the other auditor, to the extent permissible.[1] While it may be appropriate for auditors to observe such visits (or to review documentation of the calls or visits), the investor entity retains primary responsibility.
Significant differences in fiscal year ends	• Obtain and review interim financial information supplied by the investor entity related to the investee fund and test their tracking analyses. • Obtain from the investor entity any roll-forward or analytical procedures over the investment balance from the date of the investee fund's year end to the date of the investor entity's year end.
Significant differences in basis of accounting	• Obtain a reconciliation of the reported amounts to US GAAP. Such reconciliation should be prepared by the investor entity or obtained by the investor entity from the investee fund manager and reviewed by the investor entity. • Obtain documentation from the investor entity assessing differences in the basis of accounting and the effect on the investment balance. For investments not held by the investee fund at fair value, review the independent assessment of fair value provided by the investor entity's management.[2]
Qualified opinion and/or unusual accounting policies	• Review financial statements of the investee fund to assess the potential effect of a qualified opinion or unusual accounting policies. • Obtain documentation from the investor entity assessing the potential effect of a qualified opinion or unusual accounting policies.

---

1 To the extent that the investee fund's auditors have policies that prevent an investor from contacting them directly, investor entity auditors need to consider alternative procedures.

2 This is typically done with the help of the investee fund manager whenever possible. For example, if the investee fund reports on a tax basis (rather than US GAAP), management of the investor entity should contact the investee fund manager to obtain the necessary information to arrive at fair values for the investments held by the investee fund. For real estate funds, for instance, the investee fund manager may have independent appraisals. Management of the investor entity may obtain and review the appraisals to support its fair value assertions.

Reconcile financial statements to investment balance

In addition to assessing the adequacy of the audited financial statements of the investee funds based on the factors set forth above, the auditor should obtain management's reconciliation of the investee fund's financial statements with the investor entity's recorded investment balance.

Management's ability to reconcile the investee fund's audited financial statements to the investor entity's recorded investment balance depends on various factors, such as the nature of the information provided in the financial statements and the investee fund's capital structure. In certain situations, it may be easy for the investor entity to reconcile the recorded investment balance with information in the investee fund's audited financial statements. In other situations, it may be difficult. Consider the following examples:

- **Supplemental information:** In some cases, the audited financial statements include supplemental information containing individual investor capital balances and related activity. In such situations, the investor entity should compare the recorded investment balance with the corresponding capital balance presented as supplemental information to the investee fund's audited financial statements and reconcile any differences.

- **Unitized capital structures:** In the case of hedge funds that maintain unitized capital structures (e.g., most offshore funds structured as corporations), the audited financial statements should present the net asset value (NAV) per share for the various classes or series outstanding at year end. The investor entity may decide to compare such NAVs reflected in the audited financial statements with those used by the investor entity to record its investment balance.

- **Analytical procedures:** In other cases, it may be more difficult for management to reconcile the audited financial statements for the investee fund as a whole with the investor entity's recorded investment balance. In those cases, the investor entity may decide to perform analytical procedures over the investment balance for reasonableness. For example, it may be possible for the investor entity to reconcile its investment balance to the product of the total capital/net assets of the investee fund reflected in the audited financial statements and the investor entity's percentage interest. Such percentage interest can be obtained from information provided by the investee fund manager and/or the percentage interest reflected for the investor entity on the Schedule K-1 it receives from an investee fund structured as a limited partnership (i.e., most domestic funds).

- **Private equity funds:** With respect to investments in private equity funds, management's reconciliation of the audited financial statement to the recorded investment balance may be more difficult because the economics of private equity funds may be unique. For instance, partnership agreements may require priority returns be made to limited partners before the general partner receives distributions of capital, after which the general partner may receive amounts in excess of its capital commitments (commonly known as carried interest). The investor entity's management must have a very good understanding of the partnership agreement and its effect on fair value as of the balance sheet date. The investor entity's analysis should generally incorporate a hypothetical liquidation approach (i.e., what amount would the investor entity be entitled to under the distribution terms of the investee fund agreement if the investee fund were to liquidate all of its investments at the balance sheet date). The investor entity must also be cognizant that some financial statements of private equity funds may not allocate unrealized gain/loss to the capital accounts of the limited partners. Lack of allocation of such amounts may result in large differences associated with capital balances for the partners. The investor entity must ensure that its analysis incorporates unrealized gain/loss amounts. Finally, it is always important for the auditor to read investor letters that accompany the annual financial statements because they may identify anticipated transactions or other information that may be relevant to the determination of fair value.

d. Review recent transactions

Under Statement of Auditing Standard No. 101, the auditor's substantive tests of fair value measurements involve examining subsequent events and transactions that confirm or disconfirm the estimate. The investor entity may liquidate a portion of its alternative investment as of a date close to the investor entity's fiscal year end to support the valuation of its investment. The auditor needs to consider how often these settlements occur and the procedures used to value them, including whether there are holdbacks or whether the transactions are between willing buyers and sellers.

Recent transactions not indicative of fair value

Sometimes a recent transaction should not be considered in the valuation considerations because it may not indicate fair value. Such an example often arises in the secondary private equity market where an investor purchases a limited partner's existing interest and remaining commitment in a private equity fund. This often results from the seller's need for liquidity, inability to fund future commitments or desire to reduce exposure to private equity. The seller may sell its interest in a private equity fund to the buyer at a deep discount or at a premium to the fund's NAV. Consequently, the sale or transfer price between the buyer and the seller may not indicate a true fair value.

Another example is a "run on the fund," where funds have been forced to liquidate because of various circumstances, such as poor performance combined with expired lock-up periods or lack of "gates." This could become a situation of duress for the investee fund. In an effort to meet its redemption requests, the fund may be forced to liquidate securities in a "fire sale" situation. Such a forced liquidation or sale could result in values lower than those recorded on the books and records of the investee fund. Alternatively, the fund may sell its highly liquid investments first, leaving very illiquid investments in the portfolio. The auditor must consider those remaining investments if the investor entity remains in the fund. The investor entity must be aware of the activities occurring at the investee fund to ensure no circumstances can create a situation of duress that may affect the valuation of its investment. If indicators of duress arise, the investor entity requires additional effort to determine fair value.

Full and partial redemptions

On or close to the investor entity's fiscal year end, there may be full or partial redemptions of interests in investee funds. For a full redemption, as noted in Appendix B, the investee fund may hold back a portion of the investor entity's balance pending the issuance of the independent auditor's report of the investee fund. These amounts are generally recorded as receivables on the investor entity's books, and may range from 5 percent to 10 percent of the full redemption amount. After the auditor's report is released, the investee fund will then remit the remaining balance, with the ultimate balance perhaps being more or less than the balance recorded at year end. The investor entity's auditor's procedures should include vouching such amounts received and comparing adjustments to the amounts recorded at the balance sheet date.

Full redemptions can be indicative of value near the balance sheet date. For instance, close to year end, an investor entity may request a full redemption from an investee fund. The balance related to its investment may be materially consistent with the balance recorded at year end. Through its monitoring controls and other documentation, the investor entity should be able to assert the reasons for the difference between the year-end balance and the redemption amount. The combination of the cash received from the redemption and other documentation supporting the investor entity's assertion, with respect to the difference between the balance sheet value and redeemed value, may constitute sufficient audit evidence for the valuation assertion.

It is more difficult in a non-unitized fund environment (i.e., investment partnership) to gain significant comfort with respect to the valuation assertion from a partial redemption because there is no point of measurement for the investor entity. For example, if an investee fund reported an investor account balance of $5,000,000 and the investor entity requested $3,000,000 in redemption proceeds, the redemption provides less support for the valuation assertion with respect to the remaining $2,000,000. Accordingly, the auditor for the investor entity would have to gain additional audit evidence for both the existence and valuation assertions. With respect to unitized funds (i.e., most offshore funds), some audit comfort may be achieved because the number of units and dollar value per unit are known. But this depends on the circumstances associated with the transaction.

Summary of addressing the existence and valuation assertions

As discussed above, the auditor's approach is based on an assessment of the risk of material misstatement of the financial statements and must consider the quantity and quality of audit evidence to be obtained when assessing risks and designing further audit procedures.

Because alternative investments use varying structures and strategies, each with their own attributes and characteristics, they present unique audit risks. Accordingly, a "one-size-fits-all" approach to auditing an entity's interests in various alternative investments may not be appropriate or possible.

An effective and efficient process may involve the following:

1. Obtain management's risk assessment over its portfolio of alternative investments.

2. Review and assess such risk assessment and corroborate/test the information reflected.

3. Design efficient and effective procedures that address the unique risks associated with each investment, either individually or by assigned risk category, after considering all relevant factors.

Because of certain inherent issues associated with alternative investments, either individually or by assigned risk category, auditors may face challenges in obtaining the same quality and quantity of audit evidence across an investor entity's portfolio of alternative investments. The evaluation of the quality and quantity of audit evidence necessary to satisfy existence and valuation assertions is subject to the auditor's professional judgment.

Appendix A | Illustrative AU332 risk assessment and AU332 risk assessment considerations

The following illustrative AU332 risk assessment is provided as an example only. It depicts one approach management of investor entities might use to assess and summarize risk to determine the nature and extent of due diligence pursuant to the requirements of the AICPA Practice Aid. This example is not intended to be all-inclusive of every risk factor that management should consider.

	Risk rating[1]		
	Fund A	Fund B	Fund C
General information			
Fund type (e.g., hedge, private equity, real estate, fund-of-funds)			
Investment strategy			
Investor's original investment date			
Investor's investment balance at [date]			
Fund's net assets/partners' capital			
Amount			
As of date			
Fund manager's assets under management			
Amount			
As of date			
Fund's fiscal year end date			

---

1 Investor entities can use different approaches to assess the risk associated with their portfolio of alternative investments. Such approaches can be quantitatively driven based on the assignment of a risk score (i.e., 1 = lowest risk, 5 = highest risk) or more qualitatively driven.

ILLUSTRATIVE AU332 RISK ASSESSMENT

		Risk rating[1]		
		Fund A	Fund B	Fund C
Risk assessment areas[2]	**Management, governance and service providers**			
	Quality and experience of fund management			
	Role and effectiveness of fund governance			
	Quality of service providers			
	Strategy, structure and key terms			
	Nature, complexity and liquidity of strategy			
	Nature of fund's liquidity terms			
	Complexity of structure and key terms			
	Transparency and reporting			
	Nature and quality of transparency			
	Quality of financial reporting			
	Internal controls			
	Adequacy of infrastructure, personnel and general internal controls			
	Design and effectiveness of valuation policies and procedures			
	Quality of risk monitoring			
	Impact of regulatory compliance matters			
	Impact of legal and tax matters			
	Other factors			
Composite Risk Rating/Score/Grade				

Prepared by:	Date:
Reviewed by:	Date:

---

1 Investor entities can use different approaches to assess the risk associated with their portfolio of alternative investments. Such approaches can be quantitatively driven based on the assignment of a risk score (i.e., 1 = lowest risk, 5 = highest risk) or more qualitatively driven.

2 See accompanying pages for items to consider when assessing the risk associated with an investee fund.

AU332 risk assessment considerations

The following summarizes various considerations that management can use when addressing the risk areas in the AU332 risk assessment. These risk assessment considerations are for illustrative purposes only and are not intended to be all-inclusive of every risk factor that management should consider.

Management, governance and service providers

Quality and experience of fund management

- Is this a new or established investment manager?
- What is the quality and experience of management?
- Does the investment manager demonstrate that he or she is specifically qualified to execute the strategy in the market in which the investee fund invests?
- Is there evidence from similar endeavors of the ability of the principals to work together?

Role and effectiveness of fund governance

- Is there an Advisory Committee composed of certain limited partners or others? Is it effective?
- Is there a Board of Directors? If so, are there independent members? Is it effective?

Quality of service providers

- Are the auditors a reputable firm with the requisite knowledge and experience given the nature and complexity of the fund?
- Who is the prime broker? Will they use multiple prime brokers?
- Are the attorneys a well-established firm with appropriate industry experience?
- Is the administrator/accounting agent (if outsourced) experienced and well-established?

Strategy, structure and key terms

Nature, complexity and liquidity of strategy

- What is the nature, complexity and liquidity of the investment portfolio?
- Consider the following:
  - Investment strategy
  - Performance history
  - Concentrations and exposures
  - Asset classes (e.g., equities, fixed income, derivatives, private equity)
  - Volatility
  - Volume of transactions
  - Leverage and use of derivatives
- What is the risk and complexity of the financial instruments in the portfolio?
- Consider the following:
  - Market prices are readily available from active markets with significant transparency and reliability (e.g., stocks, bonds, options, futures).
  - Prices can be obtained from multiple sources such as dealers, brokers and intermediaries based on active markets with reasonable transparency, reliability and objectivity (e.g., certain high-yield bonds, forward contracts, matrix pricing of municipal bonds).
  - Prices can be obtained but the prices are not completely transparent, and the quality and reliability vary. The information is generally obtainable from dealers, although there may be wide spreads in prices (e.g., asset-backed securities, mortgage-backed securities, CDOs).
  - Prices are not observable in the market but can be derived from observable market data or estimated from historical performance or comparable data. The derivation or estimation requires a level of judgment (e.g., structured products, private equity).

Nature of fund's liquidity terms

- What is the liquidity of the investee fund?
- Consider the following:
  - Subscription frequency (e.g., monthly, quarterly, annually, commitments)
  - Redemption frequency (e.g., monthly, quarterly, annually, closed end)
    - Gates
    - Early redemption charges
    - Side pockets
    - Holdbacks
    - Lock-ups
- To what extent is the liquidity of the investee fund's portfolio consistent with the liquidity provisions of the investee fund itself?

Complexity of structure and key terms

- What is the complexity of the investee fund structure and key terms?
- Consider the following:
  - Management fee
  - Incentive fee/allocations
  - Carried interest
  - Hurdle rate/preferred return
  - High-water mark
  - Clawback provisions
  - Loss carryforward
  - Master-feeder
  - Multi-tiered
  - Side-by-side
  - Fund-of-funds
  - Side letters
  - Special-purpose vehicles
  - Opt-out provisions

Transparency and reporting

Nature and quality of transparency

- What is the nature, extent and timeliness of the investee fund manager's reporting (e.g., monthly, quarterly, annual statements; written correspondence in the form of newsletters, discussion of holdings and performance)?
- What level and quality of transparency is provided by the investee fund manager (e.g., full access to portfolio positions, access to books and records, access to portfolio managers and key accounting and operational personnel)?

Quality of financial reporting

- Are the accounting policies and procedures consistent with industry practice? Under what basis of accounting are the financial statements of the investee fund prepared (e.g., US GAAP, International Financial Reporting Standards, Tax)? Is it the same basis as the investor entity?
- Is the investee fund's year end coterminous with the investor entity's reporting year end?
- Has the investee fund received anything other than an unqualified audit opinion in the past three years?
- Do the financial statements contain a portfolio of investments? Is it condensed or detailed? Does it contain enough information to assess geographical or industry concentrations?
- Are there unusual accounting policies or disclosures, including related-party disclosures?

Internal controls

Adequacy of infrastructure, personnel and general internal controls

- What is the quality of the fund accounting and operational personnel? Does the investee fund manager have a sufficient complement of accounting and finance personnel with the requisite skills, experience and training to provide for the investee fund's needs?

- What is the financial condition of the investment management firm?

- Is there a good relationship between management, the board of directors and the investors?

- Are there written policies and procedures commensurate with the size, nature and complexity of the funds trading strategies? If yes, how frequently are such policies reviewed and approved by senior management?

- Does the investment manager have the necessary infrastructure to execute, process and account for the transactions?

- Does the fund manager maintain adequate oversight over outside service providers such as prime brokers, custodians, administrators, investment consultants, sub-advisors, etc.? Are such firms reputable and experienced?

- Is the fund's strategy a core or ancillary strategy of the manager? Is this a new strategy?

- Are all trading strategies determined, approved and reviewed by senior management?

- Is there a SAS 70 or other attest engagement performed over the control environment by external auditors? If service providers are used (e.g., fund administrator), is there a SAS 70 over their control environment? If applicable, what is the nature of the SAS 70 report?

- Is there an internal audit function within the complex and, if so, does that internal audit department include the investee fund operations within the scope of its review each year?

Design and effectiveness of valuation policies and procedures

- Does the firm have comprehensive written valuation policies and procedures that address the key methodologies and related inputs, by asset class, and the roles and responsibilities of the key parties in the valuation process?

- What is the degree of independence in the valuation process?
  - Role of front office
  - Role of back office
  - Role of service providers (e.g., third-party valuation experts)
  - Role of Valuation Committee

- Does a Valuation Committee exist and is it effective? Does it consist of any independent members?

- If valuation models are utilized, are:
  - They standard?
  - They consistently applied?
  - The key assumptions reasonable and reliable?
  - Third-party experts involved?

- Are there adequate information technology controls, including a disaster recovery plan?

Quality of risk monitoring

- Are there risk limitation policies?
- What types of monitoring, reporting, escalation and resolution processes exist?
- Are "stress tests" performed on a regular basis?
- Are the concentrations of risk in the portfolio routinely measured against the trading covenants/restrictions outlined in the fund's governing documents (asset class, industry, geography, etc.)?
- What is the nature of the policies and procedures around the cash management function?
- What are the sources of liquidity available to the fund?
- What policies and procedures exist around measuring the fund's exposure to potential defaults by the fund's counterparties?
- Do policies and procedures exist to measure the fund's exposure to leverage? Are they operating as prescribed?
- What policies and procedures exist to measure the fund's exposure to operational risk (data entry errors, system failures, valuation errors, fraud)?

Impact of regulatory compliance matters

- Is the advisor or the investee fund subject to SEC, CFTC, DOL, FSA or other regulations?
- If so, have there been any examinations by the regulatory bodies?
- What were the results?
  - Any investigations, sanctions or enforcement proceedings?
  - Any threatened or pending litigation?
- Does the investee fund manager maintain procedures for tracking and meeting large position reporting requirements?
- Is the investee fund manager's compliance with regulatory requirements independently reviewed? How often?
- Is there an effective chief compliance officer? Have his/her reviews resulted in any material findings that would affect the investee fund?
- Has senior management instituted a training program for all employees with respect to ethics and compliance procedures?
- Does management of the investee fund have a robust anti-money laundering program in place?

Impact of legal and tax matters

- Does the complex have an effective in-house legal function that is recognized as part of senior management?
- Are all agreements with all relevant counterparties formally documented with legally binding agreements?
- Has management established formal written document retention policies?
- Are there any lawsuits or litigation involving the general partner, its principals, employees or prior funds that would impact the investment manager or the fund?
- Are there any conflicts of interest with regard to the investee fund, as well as activities of the principals?
- Has the fund broken any covenants relating to any credit facilities or other counterparty arrangements? If yes, has the fund obtained appropriate waivers from the counterparty/credit provider?
- Is there an effective tax function and related internal controls?
- Are there significant uncertain tax positions?

Appendix B | Liquidity terms

Lock-up Period

A lock-up period refers to the initial amount of time a limited partner or shareholder is required to keep his or her money in a hedge fund before redeeming it. When the lock-up period is over, the limited partner or shareholder is free to redeem his or her interests in the fund on any liquidity date, subject to the other liquidity terms described in the fund documents. Whether a hedge fund demands a long lock-up period depends a great deal on the quality and reputation of the hedge fund as well as the liquidity of the underlying investment portfolio. Investors may be able to redeem during a lock-up period after they pay a "redemption fee," often 3 percent to 5 percent of the amount requested to be redeemed.

Notice Requirement

Following the expiration of any applicable lock-up period, a limited partner or shareholder may, upon specified prior written notice (generally 45 days to 120 days) to the general partner or manager (a "Redemption Notice"), elect to redeem all or a portion of his or her interest in a hedge fund as of the last day of a calendar quarter or month (the "Redemption Date"). Redemption requests are generally irrevocable once delivered and are unconditional. Redemption requests that purport to be revocable or conditional can generally be ignored or treated as irrevocable and unconditional, at the discretion of the general partner or investment manager.

Payment and Holdback

When the general partner or investment manager receives a Redemption Notice, the hedge fund will redeem the interests of a limited partner or shareholder as specified in the Redemption Notice, at the redemption price as of the applicable Redemption Date. The fund will distribute all or a substantial portion (i.e., 90 percent) of the redemption price with respect to the interests being redeemed within a specified number of business days (e.g., 30) following the applicable Redemption Date. Any balance (i.e., the remaining 10 percent) is distributed within a specific timeframe, often following the release of the fund's audited financial statements for the year in which the Redemption Date falls. Sometimes (but not always) the redeeming limited partner or shareholder is entitled to interest on the unremitted balance. Holdback amounts protect the general partner or investment manager from adjustments made to the net asset value of the fund as a result of an audit of the financial statements.

Side Pockets

Some hedge funds have an investment strategy that allows the fund to invest in illiquid securities, yet investors are still allowed periodic redemption. In such cases, a common mechanism used is a "side pocket," whereby, at the time an investment is made in such an illiquid security, a proportionate share of a limited partner's capital account, relative to the entire capital balance of the fund, is assigned to a separate memorandum capital account or "side pocket account" for that limited partner. This side pocket account generally does not incur a performance fee until the illiquid security is sold or otherwise deemed liquid. Typically, limited partners lose redemption rights to their side pocket accounts, and even a full redemption request is fulfilled only with that capital ascribed to his or her "basic" capital account (i.e., the non-side pocket capital account). Only after the security is sold (or otherwise deemed liquid) by the fund is the amount moved back to each applicable limited partner's basic capital account. Side pocket accounts are often referred to as "designated accounts" or as "special investment accounts."

Suspension or Postponement of Redemption

Pursuant to the hedge fund's governing documents, the general partner or investment manager can suspend or restrict the determination of net asset value and/or the right of any limited partner or shareholder to redeem his or her interests (whether in whole or in part). The general partner or investment manager can implement this restriction for certain reasons, including the aggregate amount of redemption requests, certain adverse regulatory and tax consequences and other reasons that may cause the inability to promptly and accurately calculate the fund's net asset value. The most common example is the use of a "gate," whereby redemption requests are deferred because the aggregate amount of redemption requests as of a particular Redemption Date exceeds a specified level, generally ranging from 15 percent to 25 percent of the fund's net asset value.

Appendix C | Other key terms

Hedge funds

Key terms	Potential implications

Classes of Shares or Partnership Interests

Offshore hedge funds may issue interests in the form of a single class of shares or multiple classes of shares. Partnerships may also have different ownership classes or interests. Multiple-class funds have unique operational and accounting issues. The terms of the fund documents dictate how income, expenses, gains and losses are to be allocated to determine the net asset value for each class or interest. In addition, specific classes may have class-specific expenses or be entitled to specific items of income (e.g., "new issue" income). Finally, fee waivers may exist for certain classes of shares.

The investor entity should understand the terms of its ownership interest and ensure that the class of shares or partnership interest that is reported by the investee fund manager on its investor statement is consistent with the subscription documents maintained in its files.

High-Water Mark

A high-water mark ensures that an incentive fee/allocation (see below) is made only to the extent that the net asset value of an investor's interest exceeds the highest net asset value as of any previous incentive fee/allocation period. In general, a high-water mark is the capital balance of an individual partner/shareholder after the last incentive fee/allocation was charged. This balance is then adjusted for any contributions or withdrawals during the period to establish a new high-water mark. The agreement or offering memorandum defines the high-water mark and dictates how the incentive fee/allocation is calculated.

The investor entity should be aware of the high-water mark provision in the fund documents and if its investment exceeds the high-water mark for a given period. If the investment balance exceeds the high-water mark, the investor entity should ensure that its net asset value is calculated net of the incentive fee/allocation.

Incentive Fee/Allocation

Incentive fee/allocation is performance-based compensation in which the investment manager or general partner receives a specified percentage (often 20 percent) of net income. These amounts are accounted for in accordance with the offering memorandum/partnership agreement, sometimes as an expense (income statement) as in the case of a corporate structure or as a special allocation of partnership profits (statement of changes in partners' capital) to the general partner in the case of a partnership. The amount of the allocation should be shown in the statement of operations or in the statement of changes in partners' capital, and the method of computing such allocations should be disclosed.

When determining fair value, the investor entity should ensure that its capital balance is reported net of the incentive fee/allocation.

Key terms	Potential implications

Loss Carryforward

A loss carryforward is a technique or provision in the partnership agreement or offering document that applies the current year's net operating losses to future period profits when calculating the incentive fee/allocations. These provisions protect the investor entity by ensuring the general partner or investment manager makes up the shortfall of losses before he or she is entitled to any incentive fee based on profits. Accordingly, if the investee fund has earned profits in the current period, the general partner or investment manager may not be entitled to an incentive fee/allocation because there may be pre-existing loss carryforwards from prior periods. Typically, unused carryforwards are reduced pro rata for redemptions made while they are outstanding.

The investor entity must be aware of loss carryforward provisions that exist in investee fund partnership agreements and the impact, if any, to the fair value of its investment.

Master-Feeder Funds

Certain funds will have structures under which they invest in other affiliated funds. A feeder fund is a fund that conducts virtually all of its investing through another fund (called the master fund). The master fund conducts all investing activities. Each feeder fund's statement of assets and liabilities shows an investment in the master fund, which is usually the sole or principal investment of the feeder fund.

A schedule of portfolio investments is generally not presented at the feeder level. Accordingly, the investor entity should obtain the feeder fund's and the master fund's financial statements to ascertain the capital structure and associated net asset value of its investment and understand the nature, complexity and liquidity of the underlying portfolio investments.

New Issue Eligibility

New issue securities are defined by the National Association of Securities Dealers Inc. (NASD) as equity securities being sold through an initial public offering. Resulting profits or losses from new issue securities are not allocated to the capital accounts of those investor entities considered to be restricted persons. In many cases, separate share classes will be created for shareholders who are eligible and ineligible to participate in new issue income.

The investor entity should be aware of its eligibility and whether it has subscribed to the appropriate class of shares. Accordingly, when analyzing the fair value of its investment, the investor entity should ensure that new issue income has been properly included or excluded from its capital account balance.

Key terms	Potential implications

Open-End Fund

An open-end fund is an investment company that is ready to offer or redeem its shares or partnership interests periodically. Open-end funds provide for liquidity to investor entities. The frequency of contributions or redemptions is dictated by the fund's documents. Contributions and redemptions can be monthly, quarterly, semi-annually, annually, etc. The amount of liquidity provided to investor entities in a particular fund is usually consistent with the liquidity and risk associated with the underlying portfolio (i.e., the more liquid the investments in the portfolio, the greater the liquidity generally provided to the investors).

The investor entity should be aware of the liquidity provisions associated with the fund in which it invests. If the investee fund is less liquid, the investor should have a better understanding of the nature, complexity and risks associated with the underlying investments.

Side Letters

In general, a side letter is a private agreement between a general partner and a limited partner, relating to the limited partner's investment in a partnership, which provides the limited partner with rights that are not otherwise available to the limited partners under the fund agreements. A side letter typically appears as a unilateral letter agreement delivered by the general partner to the limited partner, although it can be drafted as a traditional, two-party agreement. Side letters may provide for certain agreements outside of the partnership agreement, such as management fee waivers, co-invest or opt-out provisions.

Side letters are not part of the fund agreements; therefore, those within the investor entity responsible for monitoring of and accounting for the investment must know if side letters exist between the investor entity and the fund because the side letter may have a direct impact on the calculation of the investor entity's investment in the investee fund.

Special-Purpose Vehicle (SPV)

Special-purpose vehicles (SPV) are usually created for a single, well-defined and narrow purpose. The SPV can take any number of legal forms: corporation, partnership, trust, unincorporated entity or a multi-user structure (such as a protected cell company). In certain cases, SPVs are referred to as a "bankruptcy-remote entity," with operations limited to the acquisition and financing of specific assets. Sometimes, funds will own interests in SPVs, which will in turn own interests in specific investments.

Just as the investor entity must understand the terms and conditions associated with an investee fund, it must also understand the terms and conditions associated with the SPV and its effect on the liquidity and fair value of the investee fund.

Private equity funds

Key terms	Potential implications

Capital Commitments

A capital commitment is a general or limited partner's obligation to provide a certain amount of capital to a fund. Commitments are usually made up front at the time capital is raised. Profits and losses may be allocated in accordance with capital commitments or unfunded capital commitments rather than capital contributed to the fund.

The investor entity should consider its ability to meet its obligations under its capital commitment. Disclosure should be made in the financial statements with respect to the investor entity's obligation.

Carried Interest

This term denotes the split of profits to the general partner. This is the general partner's compensation for carrying the management responsibility plus all the liability for serving as general partner, as well as providing the needed expertise to successfully manage the investments in the fund. Carried interest is somewhat analogous to incentive fee/allocation for a hedge fund. There are many variations of this profit split, both in its size and how it is calculated and accrued. The carried interest terms will affect the balance of the capital account for both the general partner and limited partners, depending on the terms of the agreement.

Carried interest incorporates a "waterfall" calculation based on the terms of the agreement. The investor entity should be aware that in certain cases the carried interest is considered more of a distribution concept than an allocation concept. The investor entity must ensure that the investee fund considered a hypothetical liquidation model when calculating its capital account (i.e., if the fund were completely liquidated on the reporting date, how would the proceeds be distributed to the general partner and the limited partners?). In most cases, but not all, this allocation is reflected in the capital statement already – on a hypothetical liquidation basis – and disclosed as such.

Clawback

A clawback obligation represents the general partner's promise that, over the life of the fund, the managers will not receive a greater share of the fund's distributions than they are entitled to. Generally, this means that the general partner cannot keep distributions representing more than a specified percentage (e.g., 20 percent) of the fund's cumulative profits. When triggered, the clawback requires that the general partner return to the fund an amount equal to what is determined to be "excess" distributions. Clawbacks can present issues with respect to valuation when the value of the portfolio falls below a specific threshold. Issues arise because carried interest distributions have often already been made to the general partner, thus requiring that amounts be returned to the fund by the general partner. The calculation of the amount of clawback obligation is dictated by a number of technical, often highly negotiated, provisions in the fund's limited partnership agreement. These provisions look at the aggregate amount of distributions received by the general partner over the life of the fund, but typically exclude both amounts received in respect of the general partner's capital contribution (usually 1 percent) and the taxes payable by the general partner on all carried interest distributions. More complex provisions exist as well. When applying the waterfall calculation concept, clawback provisions must be taken into consideration. Also see Carried Interest above.

When a clawback is triggered, it may affect the investor entity's interest in the investee fund. Certain clawback provisions may result in a negative general partner balance or a receivable from the general partner. The investor entity must assess the impact of the clawback on its own investment balance and consider the credit risk associated with the general partner's obligation to refund the clawback to the partnership. Also see Carried Interest above.

Key terms

Potential implications

Closed-End Fund

A closed-end fund is an investment company that has a fixed number of shares outstanding or a fixed amount of capital commitments from investors, which it does not stand ready to redeem. This structure is very common to private equity funds because the underlying investments are illiquid. As such, the fund has no liquidity to provide for redemptions to investors. Accordingly, investors are "locked in" and must wait until the fund can sell its investments in order to convert the fair value of the investment into cash that can then be distributed under the terms of the agreement.

The investor entity should be aware of the liquidity provisions associated with the fund in which it invests. If the investee fund is less liquid, the investor entity should have a better understanding of the nature, complexity and risks associated with the underlying investment portfolio.

In-Kind Contributions and Distributions

Certain agreements may provide for capital contributions or distributions in the form of securities or investments in other funds. The valuation of these transactions, for purposes of allocations/distributions under the agreement, may be non-GAAP. For instance, for a private equity fund, a distribution may be based on a value determined using a 10-day average, unlike GAAP, which would require the securities to be fair valued on the date of distribution.

The investor entity should be aware of the accounting policies used by the investee fund and ensure that its accounting policy conforms with GAAP.

Opt-out Provisions

Certain investment partnership agreements will allow partners to "opt out" of a particular investment by providing a written notice or written opinion to the effect that a limited partner's participation in such investment would have a detrimental effect due to legal, regulatory, or other requirements. Accordingly, the limited partner would be excluded from participation in that type of investment within the fund's portfolio.

Gains and losses associated from the restricted investment should not be reflected as part of the fair value of the investor entity's interest in the investee fund.

Key terms	Potential implications

Preferred Return and Catch-Up Amount

The preferred return is the internal rate of return that a fund must achieve before its general partner can receive a carried interest. When the fund achieves the preferred return as defined in the fund documents, the general partner is usually entitled to receive a carried interest (see definition above). In many cases, the general partner is entitled to a "catch-up amount" whereby all or a specified large percentage of profit is allocated to the general partner after the preferred return is achieved until the general partner has received cumulative profits equal to the carried interest percentage (e.g., 20 percent).

See *Carried Interest* discussed earlier.

Priority Allocation

Certain funds may incorporate priority returns to the general partner or other partner that result in economics for a partner or shareholder that are other than a pro rata share of income or loss. For example, this could take the form of management fees waived by the general partner in exchange for a priority allocation of a gain associated with a particular investment.

Priority allocations must be taken into consideration when applying the waterfall provisions of a private equity partnership agreement in determining the fair value of an interest in that partnership.

Practice leaders

Mark Casella
Assurance Partner
National Alternative Investment Funds
Practice Leader
646.471.2500
mark.j.casella@us.pwc.com

John A. Mattie
Assurance Partner
National Education and Not-for-Profit
Practice Leader
617.530.4251
john.a.mattie@us.pwc.com

Principal authors

Michele Godvin
Assurance Partner
Alternative Investment Funds
206.398.3801
michele.l.godvin@us.pwc.com

Mike Greenstein
Assurance Partner
Alternative Investment Funds
646.471.3070
michael.s.greenstein@us.pwc.com

Tim Grady
Assurance Partner
Alternative Investment Funds
617.530.7162
timothy.grady@us.pwc.com

Lee Ann Leahy
Assurance Partner
National Education and Not-for-Profit
617.530.4554
leeann.c.leahy@us.pwc.com

About PricewaterhouseCoopers

PricewaterhouseCoopers is a leading provider of professional services for alternative investment funds and for colleges and universities. Our goal is to help our clients turn their complex business issues into opportunities and measurably enhance their ability to build value, manage risk and improve performance.

For more information about our alternative investment funds services, call us in the US at 646.471.2500 or visit our Web site at http://www.pwc.com/alternatives. For more information about our higher education services, call us in the US at 1.888.272.3236 or visit our Web site at http://www.pwc.com/education.

PricewaterhouseCoopers (www.pwc.com) provides industry-focused assurance, tax and advisory services to build public trust and enhance value for our clients and their stakeholders. More than 130,000 people in 148 countries across our network share their thinking, experience and solutions to develop fresh perspectives and practical advice.

"PricewaterhouseCoopers" refers to the network of member firms of PricewaterhouseCoopers International Limited, each of which is a separate and independent legal entity.

www.pwc.com

Behind the numbers*

Understanding the Higher Education
and Not-for-Profit Balance Sheet

*connectedthinking

PRICEWATERHOUSECOOPERS 🅿

What is a Statement of Financial Position?

Also known as the balance sheet, the statement of financial position is a snapshot of the financial condition of an organization at a particular point in time, usually at the end of its fiscal year. The statement of financial position presents total assets, liabilities and net assets as well as totals for each of the three classes of net assets.

The statement of financial position is designed to give readers important information about an organization's financial health. For example: What are its assets worth? Will it be able to pay its debts? Can it afford to provide students with need-based financial aid? The ability to answer such questions with some degree of precision is very important, and the statement of financial position is the source for much of the knowledge.

However, many find it difficult to understand the statement of financial position of a college, university, or not-for-profit organization. Where should the reader begin? How can he or she understand the financial story it tells?

The objective of this point of view is to provide some insight on what's behind the numbers for board members and other financial statement readers.

We want to:

· Discuss how to analyze the statement of financial position

· Deepen the reader's understanding of the statement by learning how assets and liabilities are recorded

What information is shared?

The statement of financial position provides readers with information about an organization's: 1) **liquidity,** 2) **financial flexibility,** and 3) **financing needs.** Assets that can be realized in one year or less are current assets, and liabilities that are due in one year or less are current liabilities. Current assets and liabilities are the most liquid. The first thing to look at is whether the current assets are larger than the current liabilities. The larger the current assets relative to the current liabilities, then the more liquid the organization is. Having sufficient liquidity to meet near-term debts, but not too much, is the goal. (A very high ratio of current assets to current liabilities might indicate that the organization should invest more of its current assets in longer term investments for greater return.)

Generally speaking, the greater an organization's investments, including its endowment, and the lower its debt, the more **financial flexibility** it has. Organizations with significant endowments can afford to supplement their revenues from tuition and fees with endowment income that eases the pressure on the annual budget. Simply stated, such organizations have more choices.

There are different ways to look at **financing needs.** Debt enables organizations to add significant fixed assets (e.g., new dorms, classrooms, research facilities) to the campus, increasing the organization's net worth, but also committing it to large expenditures for debt principal and interest for many years. While endowment income increases financial flexibility, debt reduces it. Debt enables an organization to grow, but it comes with a price tag. (In recent years, however, interest rates have been very low, so more organizations have been taking advantage of them.)

Recorded values

A challenge is that one line item in the statement of financial position may be stated on a different basis of accounting than another. In fact, there are four different ways to state an asset or a liability: 1) **historical cost,** 2) **net realizable value,** 3) **current market value,** and 4) **present value of future cash flows.** Understanding this will deepen a reader's understanding of this financial statement.

1) **Historical cost** is defined as the amount of cash, or its equivalent, paid to acquire an asset, per Statement of Financial Accounting Concepts No. 5 (CON 5), *Recognition and Measurement in Financial Statements of Business Enterprises* (paragraph 67). Property, plant and equipment are generally presented at historical cost on the statement of financial position.

2) **Net realizable value,** or settlement value, is defined as the nondiscounted amount of cash, or its equivalent, into which an asset is expected to be converted in due course of business less direct costs. For example, accounts receivable are usually presented at net realizable value (net of uncollectible amounts) on the statement of financial position.

3) In 1995, the Financial Accounting Standards Board (FASB) issued Statement No. 124 (FASB 124), *Accounting for Certain Investments Held by Not-for-Profit Organizations*, which had a significant impact on financial statements. FASB 124 requires not-for-profit organizations to record their marketable securities up to the **current market value.** Current market value is defined as the amount of cash, or its equivalent, that could be obtained by selling an asset in orderly liquidation. Upon implementation of FASB 124, marketable securities, including unrealized gains, which until this point were disclosed in footnotes to the statement of financial position, were moved up and reflected on the statement itself at market value.

4) The fourth basis is the **present value of future cash flows.** Again, per CON 5, the present (or discounted) value of future cash flows is the present or discounted value of future cash inflows into which an asset is expected to be converted in due course of business less present values of cash outflows necessary to obtain those inflows. The initial recording of a multiyear pledge is at the current present value of future cash flows as is required by FASB 116, *Accounting for Contributions Received and Contributions Made.*

WHAT IS A STATEMENT OF FINANCIAL POSITION?

In Table 1, we have provided a summary, showing the basis for each amount on the statement of financial position and a sample statement of financial position in Appendix 1. For those of you who want more detail, we provide additional information about each line item in Appendix 2. For now, note how the line items on the statement of financial position are valued in one of four ways.

Table 1: Accounting basis

Current Assets:	
Cash	Current market value
Collateral held for loaned securities	Current market value
Accounts receivable, net of allowance	Net realizable value
Prepaid expenses	Historical cost
Long-term assets:	
Deposits paid	Historical cost
Contributions receivable, net	Net realizable value
Investments:	
Marketable securities	Current market value
Alternative investments	Current market value
Real estate	Current market value or historical cost
Notes receivable, net:	
Mortgages from faculty	Net realizable value
Student loans	Net realizable value
Property, plant and equipment:	
Land	Historical cost
Buildings	Historical cost
Equipment	Historical cost
Less: accumulated depreciation	Historical cost
Total assets	All four bases
Liabilities	
Current liabilities:	
Accounts payable	Net realizable value
Accrued liabilities	Net realizable value
Long-term liabilities:	
Security lending obligation	Current market value
Split-interest obligations — held in-house	Net realizable value
Split-interest obligations — held by third party	Present value of future cash flows
Bonds and notes payable	Net realizable value
Government advances for student loans	Net realizable value
Funds held for others	Net realizable value
Conditional asset retirement obligation	Present value of future cash flows
Total liabilities	
Net Assets	
Unrestricted	All four bases
Temporarily restricted	Net realizable value or present value of future cash flows
Permanently restricted	Historical cost, or net realizable value, or present value of future cash flows
Total net assets	All four bases
Total liabilities and net assets	All four bases

Current developments

Due to a wide diversity in practice of applying fair market valuation standards for those balances that are to be reported at fair market value, the FASB has recently issued its Statement No. 157 (FASB 157), *Fair Value Measurements*. FASB 157 is designed to standardize the process for determining fair market value and apply consistent definitions. It is effective for fiscal years beginning after November 15, 2007 and interim periods within those fiscal years.

FASB 157 defines fair value as: "the price that would be received to sell an asset or paid to transfer a liability in an orderly transaction between market participants at the measurement date" (par. 5). FASB 157 does not require that all assets and liabilities be recorded at fair value. It only applies to assets and liabilities that are currently required to be reported at fair value. It does not require other assets or liabilities, such as fixed assets or bonds payable, to be recorded at fair value.

The FASB also recently issued its Statement No. 159 (FASB 159), *The Fair Value Option for Financial Assets and Financial Liabilities*. It allows organizations to state certain financial assets and financial liabilities at fair value without having to apply complex hedge accounting provisions.

Will financial statements be stated fully at fair values? The standard-setting community is moving in that direction, but we do not believe that it will change in the short term.

The key balances on the statement of financial position are investments, fixed assets, debt and net assets.

Interpreting the statement of financial position

The largest asset of a higher education or not-for-profit organization is usually either its investments (including endowment) or its fixed assets. Investments are generally recorded at fair market value on the financial statements. Readers of financial statements (as well as bond rating agencies, donors and others) can rely on this number as the current value (as of the date of the statement) of the organization's investments. Also, readers can find more detailed information about the investments in the footnotes to the financial statements.

Let us show some examples where the recorded value may not accurately reflect the true value to the organization.

Fixed assets are recorded at historical cost less accumulated depreciation. An organization could have fully depreciated its facilities, but still be using them. Does this mean the assets have no value to the organization? Absolutely not.

Historic buildings might be fully depreciated, and they also may be among the most prized at an organization because of their historical significance. The real value of institutional facilities might be their replacement values for insurance purposes rather than the historical cost, less accumulated depreciation, on the statement of financial position. Also, in many cases, an organization's land has appreciated in value.

Debt (i.e., bonds or notes payable), which is used to fund construction and renovation of an organization's facilities, is often the largest line item under liabilities. Bonds or notes payable represent the original amount borrowed. Assuming a fixed rate borrowing, the interest rate is established at the time of the borrowing and this rate may be higher or lower than rates that would have to be paid if the borrowing were made as of the date of the statement of financial position. The present value of future cash flows is not recorded, but rather only the amount of the remaining original debt.

WHAT IS A STATEMENT OF FINANCIAL POSITION?

Net assets are comparable to equity or retained earnings for a for-profit company.

The three categories are:

- **Permanently restricted net assets** include funds with donor-imposed restrictions, such as endowment funds. Permanently restricted net assets are valued at a combination of historical cost, net realizable value, and the present value of future cash flows.

- **Temporarily restricted net assets** have donor-imposed restrictions that can be satisfied by the passage of time or by actions of the organization. Once the restrictions are satisfied, these funds become unrestricted net assets. Temporarily restricted net assets are valued at net realizable value or the present value of future cash flows.

- **Unrestricted net assets** include board-designated funds and other funds that do not have donor restrictions. Unrestricted net assets are valued at historical cost, net realizable value, the present value of future cash flows, and market value.

Other questions to consider on the statement of financial position include the following:

- What is the quality of the organization's receivable balances, including accounts receivable and pledges receivable? With respect to pledges receivable, note how much is due to be collected in the next year, which should be disclosed in the footnotes.

- Are property, plant and equipment almost or fully depreciated? Older fixed assets could indicate the need for large upcoming capital expenditures and you would need to consider the financial flexibility of the organization to determine their ability to meet this challenge.

- Does the organization have a large portfolio of alternative investments? Although alternative investments have generated sizable returns in the last few years, they are risky and difficult to value. Alternative investments might be over- or undervalued on the statement of financial position.

It's also important to consider items that are not on the statement of financial position but are crucial to an organization's financial health. For example, deferred maintenance is not on any of the financial statements. However, an organization has a responsibility to remediate the existing deferred maintenance. For some organizations, it is possible that this estimated obligation may exceed certain (or all) liabilities currently recorded on the statement of financial position.

Unrestricted net assets

A relatively simple indicator of an organization's financial strength that can be gleaned from its statement of financial position is the overall growth in net assets, and in each category of net assets. An increase in overall net assets indicates that an organization is adding to its reserves. The increase must be greater than inflation if an organization is to achieve real growth of its financial resources.

Unrestricted net assets include property, plant and equipment less any related debt. To get a better idea of the net assets that are "readily available" for financial flexibility, subtract net property, plant and equipment, and consider the remaining amount. A sample statement of position can be found in Appendix 1 on page 8.

Unrestricted net assets include moneys that may be designated internally by either the board or management for specific current purposes or future needs of the organization. For example, the board might designate some funds in unrestricted net assets to function as endowment funds. In other words, the board is setting these funds aside to enhance its long-term stability. What is left after subtracting board-designated funds? The remaining amount is available to the organization for current needs.

Two ratios that might be helpful for analyzing debt and investment performance are:

· The ratio of total debt to expendable net assets measures the relationship of outstanding debt to expendable net assets. It includes all unrestricted net assets (less net investment in plant assets) as well as temporarily restricted net assets that are expected to be available to meet the organization's obligations, operating and otherwise.

· The total return on long-term investments ratio measures the total return on an organization's investments, including investment income plus the realized and unrealized gains on the investment portfolio.

The importance of footnotes

The footnotes provide information that is critical to better understand the financial statements, including the statement of financial position. In fact, financial statements say under each statement, "The accompanying notes are an integral part of these financial statements."

The first footnote often describes how the organization is organized. The second footnote usually summarizes the organization's accounting policies, including the bases of accounting. One footnote usually provides information about the organization's investments while others discuss its debt and fixed assets.

The footnotes discuss the assumptions being used to arrive at certain amounts. For example, a pledges receivable footnote would discuss the discount rates being used (or the range of rates being used) to discount the multiyear pledges. A footnote for split-interest agreements would provide the rates being used in the calculation, as well as the mortality table(s) being used. This information is useful in comparing like-kind organizations or to determine if the amounts recorded have current market assumptions behind them.

Generally Accepted Accounting Principles (GAAP) require the footnote disclosure of certain fair values (notes payable/receivable and bonds payable). However, GAAP does not currently require the fair value disclosure of fixed assets. With fixed assets representing a significant component of the total assets, there could be a material amount of unreported appreciation in the footnotes. (But then one would need to consider whether this amount would be relevant for anything. It is unlikely the organization would sell its fixed assets, so would recording fixed assets at fair value be useful?)

Conclusion

Due to different bases of reporting and the use of
judgments and estimates, reading and understanding
an organization's financial statements is more of
an art than a science. This is also why the shift in the
industry is to the full recording of legal obligations
and continued encouragement for full transparency in
the footnotes.

A well-prepared set of financial statements and footnotes
can provide the reader with a good understanding
of the organization as of a particular point in time, or of its
activities over a period of time.

As one becomes more familiar with financial statements
and footnotes, the underlying assumptions will
become more apparent and outdated assumptions will
be identified more quickly, allowing the reader to
mentally determine if the asset or liability is really over-
or understated.

Appendices

Appendix I: Sample statement of financial position

Assets	(000's)
Cash	$1,611
Collateral held for loaned securities	50,332
Accounts receivable, net of allowance	1,988
Prepaid expenses	386
Deposits paid	128
Contributions receivable, net	18,694
Investments:	
Marketable securities	259,783
Alternative investments	60,882
Real estate	4,372
Notes receivable, net:	
Mortgages from faculty	15,730
Student loans	15,438
Property, plant and equipment:	
Land	7,884
Building	280,730
Equipment	25,343
Less: accumulated depreciation	(73,799)
Total assets	$669,502
Liabilities:	
Accounts payable	$10,558
Accrued liabilities	12,580
Security lending obligation	49,345
Split-interest obligations – held in-house	12,406
Split-interest obligations – held by third party	3,894
Bonds payable	50,000
Government advances for student loans	11,477
Funds held for others	1,243
Conditional asset retirement obligation	10,000
Total liabilities	161,503
Net assets:	
Unrestricted	365,168
Temporarily restricted	15,333
Permanently restricted	127,498
Total net assets	507,999
Total liabilities and net assets	$669,502

APPENDICES

Appendix 2: Basis for line items

Cash – represents the amount of funds within the organization's bank account(s). Cash is always considered at market value.

Collateral held for loaned securities – is considered at current market value as it is generally 102 percent (depending on the organization's agreement with their investment custodian) of certain marketable securities (which are at current market value).

Accounts receivable, net – the allowance for uncollectible amounts has the organization stating this balance at the net realizable value. These receivables could be very current (made just before fiscal year-end) or greater than a year old, but in either case, the net realizable value is reflected. These receivables—even if long-term—are not recorded at the present value of future cash flows.

Prepaid expenses – historical cost is the basis as the amounts recorded reflect the amount remitted to the third party for a future benefit. The prepaid period may be in excess of one year, so there really may be some embedded additional future value to be derived, but this additional benefit is not recorded in the financial statements.

Deposits paid – similar to prepaid expenses, these are recorded at the amount originally remitted. Most often these amounts relate to such items as last month's rent for a rental or lease agreement.

Contributions receivable, net – at the time a contribution receivable (pledge) is obtained, a current (market) discount rate is assigned to the pledge. Then using the estimated future cash flows a net present value of the pledge is calculated using a then current discount rate and recorded. However, at each subsequent fiscal year-end, the cash flows may be adjusted to reflect any changes made by the donor, but the discount rate utilized to calculate the "present value" is not changed. So for a multiyear pledge, future reflected amounts are calculated using a noncurrent (or stale) discount rate. This receivable is then further reduced by any allowance for uncollectible amounts. Depending on current market conditions, the amount of the net contributions receivable could be over- or understated as compared to its "true" present value of future cash flows if current discount rates were used.

Marketable securities – FAS 124 requires that marketable securities be reflected on the statement of financial position at their current market value as of the date of the statement of financial position.

Alternative investments – recently there has been an increased emphasis (especially by the AICPA) to have these items recorded at their current market value. Many organizations have attempted to work with their investment managers to obtain market values for these assets, but it is very common to have a hybrid valuation method. This is because alternative investments may not have audited financial statements as of the organization's fiscal year-end. So the organization may have to take the market value as of the most recent audited financial statements of the alternative investment and then "roll forward" the value to add in any capital contributions remitted by the organization or subtract any capital distributions received by the organization since the date of the alternative investment's audited financial statements. Additionally, management of the organization may have additional interim information from the investment manager that will be taken into account when arriving at a "current market value."

Real estate investments – the recorded amount for this asset will depend on the organization's accounting policy. These assets could be recorded at historical cost or at current market value. Recording at current market value would require the organization to obtain an annual appraisal or other similar analysis. In practice, it is more common for appraisals to be obtained every few years and in the off years review the local real estate market for any impairments. If no impairments are found in these off years, the value of the real estate investments is generally not changed.

Notes receivable, net – for amounts lent to both faculty and students, the amount originally recorded is the actual amount provided to the borrower. Subsequent to that, the amount is reduced only by payments received and any further reduction is due to any allowance for estimated uncollectible amounts. These receivables are generally long-term and are not recorded at the present value of future cash flows. So in comparing these long-term receivables to contributions receivable—we find that contributions receivable are generally shorter in term and discounted back to a present value at the time of original recording, whereas the longer term notes receivable are at net realizable value.

APPENDIX F

Basis for line items, cont.

Property, plant and equipment – these amounts are recorded at historical cost, the amount originally paid for the asset (or the fair value at the date the asset was donated). Depreciation is usually calculated on a straight-line basis and represents a "write off" of the assets (excluding land) over the estimated useful life of the asset. For most organizations, fixed assets represent the largest undervalued amount on the statement of financial position. Many organizations acquired their land and buildings numerous years ago and due to the increase in real estate values over the past years, a large amount of (unreported) equity could be owned by the organization. But then, one must ask the question—does unreported equity really mean anything?—the organization is unlikely to sell its fixed assets, so this increase in value will never be actually recognized.

Accounts payable – the recorded amount represents the amount that will be remitted to the organization's vendors to settle its financial obligations. These are generally short-term in nature and could also be seen as "market value."

Accrued liabilities – the recorded amount could be a combination of a few different methodologies. One of the largest components is generally accrued vacation. Accrued vacation is calculated based on the employees' wage base at the end of the fiscal year. However, the employee may not take their vacation until after raises are given, thus increasing the actual amount that is actually paid out to the employee. Another component could be deferred compensation agreements. These are adjusted to the present value of future cash flows, but as a component of accrued liabilities are generally not that significant.

Security lending obligation – this is the offsetting amount for the asset, Collateral held for loaned securities. This is the amount of securities (at their market value) that are "pledged" to others through the arrangement with the investment custodian.

Split-interest obligations – held in-house—when these agreements are obtained, a then-current discount rate is assigned to the individual agreement. During the life of the agreement, the discount rate utilized for calculating the obligation does not change, even if outside market conditions change. Additionally, if the obligation calculation is based on a particular investment portfolio, the investment portfolio's value is updated to the current market value, but the assigned discount rate for the calculation is not changed.

Split-interest obligations – held by third party—unlike split-interest obligations held in-house, the components to these calculations are updated on an annual basis. Both the investment portfolio value and the discount rate utilized are updated to reflect current market conditions.

Bonds and notes payable – if any premium or discount were involved at the time the bonds or notes payable were issued, these amounts would also be recorded in the statement of financial position. The bonds or notes payable represents the original amount borrowed. Assuming a fixed rate borrowing, the interest rate is established at the time of the borrowing and this rate may be higher or lower than rates that would have to be paid if the borrowing were made as of the date of the statement of financial position. The present value of future cash flows is not recorded, but rather only the amount of the remaining original debt.

Government advances for student loans – this represents the amount obtained from the federal government to establish a Perkins loan program—effectively it is "seed" money. The amount on the statement of financial position represents the net sum (total amount received less any returned funds) received by the organization over the years of the program. If the federal government were to cancel the program, this is the amount that would need to be returned. The amount recorded is the net realizable amount as this balance could be offset by loans assigned back to and accepted by the government, loans forgiven by the government, etc. As the date that such funds may need to be returned is not known, it is not possible to arrive at a present value of future cash flows.

Funds held for others – is generally comprised of funds held for on-campus organizations (associated student body, clubs, etc.) in which the organization is essentially serving as a bank. These funds are increased and decreased throughout the year.

Conditional asset retirement obligations – this amount represents the present value of future cash flows and all of the components of this calculation are updated annually to reflect market conditions.

APPENDICES

Rick Wentzel

Rick is an audit partner in PricewaterhouseCoopers' Education & Nonprofit practice and is based in our Los Angeles office. He specializes in accounting and auditing services for colleges and universities and not-for-profit organizations. Prior to joining PwC, Rick worked as Director of Finance for a large Los Angeles area not-for-profit where he rebuilt the business office and strengthened the internal controls. He also served as Controller at Occidental College where again he rebuilt the business office, implemented a set of internal controls, redesigned the financial reporting and implemented SFAS 116 & 117.

Rick regularly teaches several of PwC's courses on auditing standards and accounting principles as well as compliance audits for not-for-profit entities and is a frequent speaker at industry events.

About PricewaterhouseCoopers

PricewaterhouseCoopers (www.pwc.com) provides industry-focused assurance, tax and advisory services to build public trust and enhance value for its clients and their stakeholders. More than 140,000 people in 149 countries across our network, share their thinking, experience and solutions to develop fresh perspectives and practical advice.

www.pwc.com/education

*APPENDIX G

Fair value option considerations*

A guide for not-for-profit organizations (New)

*connectedthinking

PRICEWATERHOUSE(COOPERS 🙖

APPENDIX G

This publication has been prepared for general information on matters of interest only, and does not constitute professional advice on facts and circumstances specific to any person or entity. You should not act upon the information contained in this publication without obtaining specific professional advice. No representation or warranty (express or implied) is given as to the accuracy or completeness of the information contained in this publication. The information contained in this material was not intended or written to be used, and cannot be used, for purposes of avoiding penalties or sanctions imposed by any government or other regulatory body. PricewaterhouseCoopers LLP, its members, employees and agents shall not be responsible for any loss sustained by any person or entity who relies on this publication.

The content of this publication is based on information available as of September 15, 2008. Accordingly, certain aspects of this publication may be superseded as new guidance or interpretations emerge. Financial statement preparers and other users of this publication are therefore cautioned to stay abreast of and carefully evaluate subsequent authoritative and interpretive guidance that is issued.

APPENDIX G

Introduction

Historically, an organization's ability to use fair value accounting has been limited to a handful of assets and liabilities. Issued in February 2007, FASB Statement No. 159 (FAS 159), *The Fair Value Option for Financial Assets and Financial Liabilities*, expands the ability to select fair value as the basis of measurement for certain financial assets and liabilities, referred to as the fair value option (FVO). This guide introduces key concepts of FAS 159 using a case-study approach to assist management and audit committees of not-for-profit organizations (NPOs) in understanding the implications of this important standard.

Bob Garner is CFO of ABC Health System (ABC), a not-for-profit organization. ABC is comprised of ABC Hospital and its subsidiary, ABC Nursing College (the College). As a health care organization, ABC prepares its financial statements in accordance with the requirements of the AICPA Audit and Accounting Guide, *Health Care Organizations* (AAG-HCO)[1]*;* however, ABC also issues separate subsidiary financial statements for the College that are prepared in accordance with the AICPA Audit and Accounting Guide, *Not-for-Profit Organizations* (AAG-NPO).

ABC participates in a 50-50 joint venture with DEF Health System (an unrelated organization) to operate MRI Inc., a mobile MRI business. ABC also has interests in the net assets of two financially-interrelated[2] foundations (Foundation X and Foundation Y). ABC does not control these foundations (thus, they are not consolidated); however, they were established to receive contributions that solely benefit ABC.

ABC's fiscal year ends on September 30. FAS 159 is effective for fiscal years beginning after November 15, 2007. Since FAS 159 requires adoption as of the beginning of the year, ABC would have to adopt FAS 159 on October 1, 2008 in order to elect to measure any of its eligible assets and liabilities at fair value. In light of this relatively short window, Bob's challenge is to quickly gain an understanding of the standard's key provisions; determine what assets and liabilities are eligible; and establish the key considerations for determining whether FVO election(s) would be advantageous.

Understanding the key provisions

FAS 159 provides an opportunity for ABC to measure many financial assets and liabilities at fair value that are currently measured using other bases of accounting. Bob determines the following:

- The FVO is a one-time election for eligible assets and liabilities on ABC's balance sheet at the time it adopts FAS 159. If ABC does not elect the FVO for those assets and liabilities at that time, it will not have another opportunity to do so (unless those assets or liabilities are subsequently affected by certain remeasurement events).

- The FVO is irrevocable. If ABC elects the FVO for any asset or liability, it remains in effect for as long as ABC holds that asset or liability.

- The FVO can only be adopted for financial assets and liabilities. Generally speaking, financial assets and liabilities are those that can be settled in cash or with other financial instruments; all other assets and liabilities are considered nonfinancial (e.g., property and equipment, obligations to deliver goods or services).

- FAS 159 permits application of the FVO on an instrument-by-instrument basis, with some exceptions. [3] Therefore, ABC can elect the FVO for certain instruments but not others within a group of similar items (e.g., for a single alternative investment, rather than for all alternative investments).

- ABC will be required to measure fair values based on the framework established in FASB Statement No. 157 (FAS 157), *Fair Value Measurements*.

---

[1]   With conforming changes as of March 1, 2008.

[2]   As defined in paragraph 13 of FASB Statement No. 136 (FAS 136), *Transfers of Assets to a Not-for-Profit Organization or Charitable Trust That Raises or Holds Contributions for Others.*

[3]   See paragraph 12 of FAS 159.

UNDERSTANDING THE KEY PROVISIONS

- Any adjustments required for the adoption would be reported by ABC as a cumulative-effect adjustment to the opening balances of the appropriate net asset classes.

- Because ABC is a not-for-profit healthcare organization, all subsequent changes in fair value for the elected items would be reported within ABC's performance indicator (as defined in the AAG-HCO). This is not a consideration for the College's separate financial statements since the College does not report a standardized performance indicator.

- To address comparability concerns, FAS 159 requires extensive disclosures related to any asset or liability for which the FVO is elected. Organizations that elect the FVO must either report separate line items in the balance sheet for fair value and non-fair-value amounts, or aggregate the fair value and non-fair-value amounts and parenthetically disclose the carrying amounts on the balance sheet. In addition, such organizations must disclose the amount of gain or loss related to changes in fair value, including where they are reported in the statement of operations/activities. Items for which the FVO is adopted also are subject to FASB Statement No. 157 *(FAS 157) Fair Value Measurements* FAS 157's disclosure requirements related to recurring fair value measurements.

Identifying eligible assets and liabilities

Whether it would be beneficial for ABC to adopt the FVO for any of ABC's financial assets or liabilities depends on the nature of the specific assets and liabilities that are eligible.

ABC's most recent interim balance sheet (summarized) appears as follows:

ABC Balance Sheet
(in thousands)

Assets			Liabilities		
Investments:			Split-interest obligations—held in-house	$	22,000
Trading securities	$	10,000	Derivative liabilities		19,000
Available-for-sale securities		215,000	Government loan liability		75,000
Alternative investments—equity method		140,000	Bonds payable		250,000
Alternative investments—cost		75,000	Lease obligations		50,000
Alternative investments—fair value*		55,000	Other liabilities		150,000
		495,000	**Total liabilities**		566,000
Investments in joint ventures		22,000	**Net Assets**		
Contribution receivable, net		2,500	Unrestricted		232,500
Student loan receivable, net		90,000	Temporarily restricted		257,500
Derivative asset		4,000	Permanently restricted		125,000
Split-interest—held by third party		7,500	**Total net assets**		615,000
Interests in financially-interrelated organizations		50,000			
All other assets		510,000			
Total assets	$	1,181,000	**Total liabilities and net assets**	$	1,181,000

* Represents ABC Nursing College's investments

APPENDIX G

Bob's analysis of which financial assets and liabilities on ABC's balance sheet would potentially be eligible for FVO elections appears as follows:

Potentially eligible for FVO	Not eligible for FVO
• Available-for-sale securities	• Investments in consolidated subsidiaries
• Alternative investments	• Employee benefit-related obligations
• Noncontrolling interests in joint ventures or partially-owned related entities	• Financial assets and financial liabilities recognized pursuant to leases (e.g., lease obligations)
• Contributions receivable (e.g., multi-year promises to give cash)	
• Obligations arising under split interest agreements for which ABC serves as trustee	
• Interest in net assets of financially-interrelated organization	
• Student loan receivables	
• Long-term debt (e.g., bonds payable)	
• Derivative assets (e.g., interest rate swaps)	

Key considerations for eligible items

For each eligible financial asset and liability, Bob next must identify the key considerations in evaluating whether electing the FVO would be advantageous.

Marketable securities

Observation: NPOs that do not report a standardized performance indicator would derive no benefit from electing the FVO for marketable securities since their reporting in the statement of activities would not change.

ABC has $225 million of marketable equity and debt securities that are accounted for under FASB Statement No. 124 (FAS 124), *Accounting for Certain Investments Held by Not-for-Profit Organizations*. For those securities classified as trading ($10 million), Bob determines that there would be no reason to make a FVO election, as trading securities are already carried at fair value with changes reflected within the performance indicator. However, for those classified as available-for-sale ($215 million), election of the FVO may simplify recordkeeping and result in more symmetrical accounting for gains and losses. This is because realized gains and losses (including other-than-temporary impairment losses (OTTI[4]) must be reported within the performance indicator,[5] while unrealized gains and losses must be excluded from the performance indicator. If ABC has significant unrealized losses on marketable securities that are deemed to be other-than-temporary, such losses are required to be recognized within the performance indicator as realized losses, while all unrealized gains remain below the performance indicator. Election of the FVO would change this reporting to require all gains and losses (both unrealized and realized) to be reported above the performance indicator. Investments designated under FAS 159 in effect will be accounted for similar to FAS 115/124 "trading" securities.

---

[4] Based on the guidance in FASB Staff Position FAS 115-1/124-1 (FSP FAS 115-1/124-1), The Meaning of Other-Than-Temporary Impairment and its Application to Certain Investments.

[5] AAG-HCO, par. 4.14.

KEY CONSIDERATIONS FOR ELIGIBLE ITEMS

Bob also evaluated the merits of making the election for marketable securities reported in the College's stand-alone financial statements. Unlike its parent health system, the College is not required to report a standardized performance indicator and, thus, does not have the same OTTI considerations related to its marketable securities (since realized and unrealized gains are not segregated). Therefore, Bob determined there would be little benefit for the College to elect the FVO for its marketable securities, as no change in the presentation of gains or losses in the statement of activities would result.

> **Observation**: For healthcare organizations, electing fair value measurement for alternative investments could be challenging, since many of those investments are not readily marketable and there is limited transparency into the underlying holdings.

Alternative investments

ABC owns noncontrolling investments in several alternative investment partnerships and LLCs (e.g., private equity funds, hedge funds, etc.). The method of accounting used for those investments is based on the extent of ABC's ability to influence the investee. If ABC can exercise significant influence over the investee, the equity method[6] of accounting is used; if it cannot, the cost method is used.

Currently, the accounting for ABC's $140 million portfolio of equity method investments is relatively straightforward. Bob simply records ABC's share of each security's income/loss (the "equity pickup") based upon the audited (or in some cases, interim) financial statements received from the investment company or fund. For many of ABC's alternative investments that apply investment company accounting,[7] measurements obtained using the equity method have closely approximated their pre-FAS 157 fair values (based on net asset values (NAVs)), so there is little if any balance sheet difference between equity method carrying value and fair value. However, once FAS 157 is adopted, Bob knows that the fair values may be different than carrying value under the equity method, particularly if the investments have liquidity restraints or other restrictive covenants that may affect measurements under the FAS 157 framework.

> **Observation:** Under the FAS 157 framework, organizations making the FVO for investments in LPs and LLCs that have restrictive terms such as lockups, holdbacks, or side pockets (i.e., liquidity constraints), must consider whether an adjustment (i.e., a discount) to NAV is required for those constraints when determining fair values.

Similar considerations apply with respect to ABC's $75 million portfolio of cost-method alternative investments. Bob estimates that that portfolio has an aggregate fair value of approximately $110 million based upon net asset values (NAVs). Thus, ABC's balance sheet is potentially undervalued by approximately $35 million relative to those investments. Currently, the statement of operations reflects only the dividend and interest income earned rather than mark-to-market adjustments each period. Additionally, the accounting, recordkeeping, and internal control requirements associated with cost-method investments are much less complex than they are for either equity method or fair value investments.

Therefore, in determining whether electing the FVO for ABC's alternative investments would be beneficial, Bob will need to evaluate whether the time and effort (and, in some cases, expense) required to determine the fair value of each investment and to explain the increased volatility in the statement of operations (particularly in relation to cost-method investments) to users of the financial statements would outweigh any benefits to be derived from fair value measurement in the form of balance sheet enhancement. Further, carrying those investments at fair value would require ABC to assess its system of internal control over financial reporting for investments in order for Bob to be able to appropriately estimate and monitor fair value.

---

[6] Based on the guidance in Accounting Principles Board (APB) Opinion No. 18, The Equity Method of Accounting for Investments in Common Stock; AICPA Statement of Position 78-9, Accounting for Investments in Real Estate Ventures; EITF Issue No. 03-16, Accounting for Investments in Limited Liability Companies; and FASB Staff Position SOP 78-9-1, Interaction of AICPA Statement of Position 78-9 and EITF Issue No. 04-5.

[7] In accordance with the AICPA Audit and Accounting Guide, Investment Companies.

APPENDIX G

Bob also evaluated the merits of making the election for alternative investments reported in the College's stand-alone financial statements. The College's $55 million portfolio of alternative investments already are reported at fair value under the option allowed in Chapter 8 of AAG-NPO (which allows such investments to be carried at fair value only if that election is made for all alternative investments). Similar to the considerations for the College's marketable securities, Bob determines that there appear to be no potential benefits associated with electing the FVO for the alternative investments. If the College did not follow this option and instead carried alternative investments at cost or equity, the considerations discussed above for ABC Health System would apply to the College's investments as well.

Joint ventures/operating investments

ABC accounts for its participation in the MRI joint venture using the equity method of accounting. Bob estimates that the fair value of ABC's 50% interest is roughly $50 million, based upon a recent offer made by a third-party to acquire ABC's interest. The difference between the fair value of $50 million and the carrying value of $22 million is primarily due to the fact that certain significant assets (e.g., property, plant and equipment) of the venture are carried at historical cost, rather than at fair value. Therefore, making the FVO election for the joint venture would initially boost ABC's balance sheet by $28 million. However, instead of recording ABC's share of the venture's income/loss ("equity pickup") each period thereafter, Bob would have to estimate the fair value of the 50% venture interest and reflect the entire mark-to-market adjustment through income.

The benefits of electing the FVO for operating investments such as joint ventures will vary depending on the facts and circumstances surrounding the investment. Similar to alternative investments, Bob need to evaluate whether the time, effort, and expense required to estimate the fair value of the venture under the FAS 157 fair value framework would outweigh any benefits resulting from the balance sheet enhancement. Estimating fair value will require Bob to gather inputs at each measurement date based on looking to comparable public entities, recent transactions, and/or cash flow analysis, any or all of which may be difficult to perform or costly to obtain. In particular, obtaining market comparables or looking to transactions of similar organizations poses unique challenges in the NPO environment, since many transactions involving NPOs do not involve fair value exchanges.

Contributions receivable

ABC's balance sheet reflects net unconditional multi-year promises to give cash (i.e., contributions receivable) totaling $2.5 million. Under FASB Statement No. 116 (FAS 116), *Contributions Received and Contributions Made,* unconditional promises to give are initially recorded at fair value. ABC measures the fair value of the unconditional promises to give using the present value of the future cash flows, discounted using a risk-free rate (as required by AAG-NPO for periods prior to adoption of FAS 157).[8] In conformity with paragraph 12 of APB Opinion No. 21 (APB 21), *Interest on Receivables and Payables,* the discount rate determined at the time a pledge is initially recognized is not revised subsequently. Since market discount rates change period-to-period and the discount rate used is not adjusted each period to reflect these changes, the subsequent measurements of the unconditional promise to give do not represent fair value.

---

[8] When ABC adopts FAS 157, AAG-NPO's requirement to use a risk-free rate of return is superseded by the requirement to use FAS 157's present value techniques, including the discount rate adjustment technique, in which the rate should be based upon the rate a market participant would demand (e.g., endowment or investment return). The period associated with the discount rate should be consistent with the term of the promise to give. For instance, a two-year promise to give will likely be valued using a different discount rate than that used for a ten-year promise to give.

KEY CONSIDERATIONS FOR ELIGIBLE ITEMS

In order to comply with APB 21's requirement that the discount on pledges be amortized between the date the promise is initially recognized and the date the cash is received, Bob maintains spreadsheets of all of ABC's long-term pledges, all with varying discount rates based on the year of receipt. Bob determines that an election to measure some or all of ABC's pledges at fair value on a recurring basis (through the FVO) may simplify recordkeeping, because all pledges for which the FVO is elected would be remeasured each period using a discount rate reflective of the term of the pledge (i.e., the discount rate in effect at each measurement date), rather than the individual discount rates in effect at the date of each gift. However, Bob must weigh the advantages of simplified recordkeeping against the additional administrative burden associated with FAS 159, in particular the increased disclosure requirements that are required under FAS 157. If the FVO is not elected, ABC will not have any FAS 157 pledge-related disclosures since pledges are only initially recognized at fair value. If the FVO is elected, however, pledges will become recurring fair value measurements, which must be included in FAS 157 tabular disclosures each year. If the measurement of pledges is determined to require Level 3 inputs (as is likely to be the case), disclosure requirements would be even more extensive.

Split-interest agreements

ABC is a party to a number of split-interest agreements. These agreements come in several forms (e.g., charitable lead annuity trusts, charitable remainder annuity trusts, charitable lead unitrusts, etc.). At present, ABC serves as trustee for split-interest agreements with trust assets of $50 million[9] and trust obligations (to lead or remainder beneficiaries) of $22 million. ABC also has $7.5 million of beneficial interests in split-interest trusts administered by third-party financial institutions.

Whether ABC serves as trustee will dictate whether the FVO election is available for split-interest trusts. If a third-party institution (rather than ABC) serves as the trustee, ABC's beneficial interest in the trust is already required to be measured at fair value on a recurring basis[10] and, thus, the FVO would not be useful. When ABC is the trustee, however:

- ABC recognizes the assets contributed to the trust at fair value, recognizes a liability to the beneficiaries of the lead or remainder interests based on the present value of the estimated payments to be made over a fixed period or their estimated remaining lives, and recognizes the difference as contribution revenue when the agreement is initially executed.

- The trust agreements generally require ABC to invest the trust assets in marketable securities, which are measured at fair value on a recurring basis (as discussed on page 3).

- The trust's liabilities payable to other beneficiaries are measured at fair value only at the time of initial recognition. In subsequent measurements, the present value calculation retains the same discount rate as was used at initial recognition and, thus, are not fair value measurements.

---

[9] Included in the $215 million of marketable securities reported in ABC's balance sheet.

[10] In accordance with paragraph 15 of FAS 136.

Consequently, the FVO election would be available for measuring the trust obligations in circumstances where ABC serves as trustee under the agreement. Similar to the considerations for promises to give, electing this option may simplify recordkeeping, as ABC would remeasure its obligations at fair value each period by adjusting the discount rates to reflect market conditions (as is currently done for beneficial interests in trusts administered by third parties). However, Bob must weigh the advantages of simplified recordkeeping against the additional administrative burden associated with fair value disclosures, especially the increased disclosure requirements that will be required for recurring fair value measurements under FAS 157. Additionally, recurring fair value measurement of the liability must also incorporate considerations associated with nonperformance risk. If the FVO election is not made, there are no additional disclosures required by FAS 157, since the liability is only initially measured at fair value. If the FVO is elected, however, the liability would be subject to recurring fair value measurements and thus, would need to be included in the FAS 157 tabular disclosures each year. If the fair value measurement is determined to involve Level 3 inputs, the recurring disclosures required would be even more extensive.

Interests in net assets of financially-interrelated organizations

ABC reports its interests in the net assets of its financially-interrelated foundations (Foundation X and Foundation Y) of $50 million in accordance with FAS 136, periodically adjusting those interests for ABC's share of the changes in the Foundations' net assets using a method similar to the equity method of accounting. Because this method does not involve fair value measurement, Bob wishes to consider the merits of electing the FVO for those assets.

In evaluating the pros and cons of electing fair value measurement, Bob determined that the nature and complexity of a particular foundation's mix of assets and liabilities would directly impact the level of difficulty associated with determining that foundation's fair value and would likely determine the extent to which ABC would be inclined to pursue the FVO election.

Bob's FVO analysis related to these interests revealed the following:

Foundation X is comprised entirely of marketable securities (carried by the foundation at fair value) and cash. Historically, the carrying value of ABC's interest has been equivalent to the pre-FAS 157 fair values of the Foundation's assets. Although ABC's asset is its interest in the net assets of Foundation X and not the Foundation's underlying assets themselves, Bob believes it is reasonable to assume that the fair value of ABC's interest would, on an ongoing basis, approximate the fair value of the underlying assets. This is because (a) all of Foundation X's holdings are marketable securities (measured at fair value) or cash, and (b) ABC has the ability to influence the timing and amount of the distributions it receives from Foundation X.[11]

Despite the ease of estimating fair value for this interest, Bob determines that little if any benefit would be gained from electing the FVO, as there is little difference between the carrying value of the interest and its fair value. Further, electing the FVO would cause the entire change in fair value of the interest to be included in ABC's performance indicator, potentially subjecting the statement of operations to additional volatility.[12] At present, since ABC has the ability to influence the amount and timing of distributions from Foundation X, the portion of the change in fair value of the interest attributable to unrealized gains and losses on Foundation X's investments is excluded from the performance indicator. (In other words, ABC is able to "look through the foundation" and report the investment activity in the same geographic classifications as it would if it held the investments directly.)

---

[11] See AICPA Technical Practice Aid 6400.42 for a discussion of how a healthcare organizations that can influence the timing and amount of distributions from a financially-interrelated foundation should report changes in its interest in the net assets of that foundation that are attributable to unrealized gains and losses on the foundation's marketable securities.

[12] This would not be a concern for NPOs that do not report a standardized performance indicator.

KEY CONSIDERATIONS FOR ELIGIBLE ITEMS

Foundation Y has a more complex balance sheet comprised of investments (some of which are readily marketable, others which are not), property and equipment, and a capital lease obligation. Similar to the considerations noted above for ABC's investment in a joint venture, because Foundation Y has balance sheet items that are not measured at fair value (e.g., the alternative investments, fixed assets, and capital lease obligation), the fair value of ABC's interest in Foundation Y's net assets may differ significantly from its carrying value. Despite the fact that measuring the interest at fair value potentially could impact ABC's balance sheet, there are drawbacks, such as the time, effort and, in some cases, expense required to determine fair value on an ongoing basis. As was the case with Foundation X, electing the FVO would cause the entire change in fair value of the interest to be included in ABC's performance indicator, thus resulting in additional volatility in the statement of operations.

Student loans

The College's student loan receivables (currently reported at their net realizable value of $90 million) are financial assets eligible for the FVO. The effect of measuring these loans at fair value instead of net realizable value will result in volatility in the loans' fair value due to differences between market interest rates and stated interest rates on the loans. Thus, if volatility is a concern (e.g., because it could require additional efforts to explain to financial statement users), ABC would need to evaluate whether those concerns would outweigh the benefits.

Additionally, $75 million of the College's student loans were funded with Perkins Loan program funds. [13] Funds received from the Federal government for this purpose are accounted for as advances (a financial liability also eligible for the FVO). Because there may be legal restrictions limiting the College from transferring the assets and/or liability associated with the Perkins Loan program, this would need to be considered in determining fair value. In addition, if ABC elected the FVO for both the assets and the liability, there may be little if any meaningful impact on the financial statements (that is, any fair value adjustments associated with the gross-up in the balance sheet would offset, so that there is no impact on the statement of activities other than perhaps adjustments to the liability for nonperformance risk).

Long-term debt and interest rate swaps

Fixed-rate debt

Observation: Derivatives not used in a hedging relationship (e.g., options, futures, etc.) are already carried at fair value and marked-to-market each period. The changes in fair value are recorded within the performance indicator. Therefore, there would be no reason to elect the FVO for non-hedging derivatives.

As an issuer of $150 million of fixed-rate municipal bonds, ABC is exposed to the risk that changes in interest rates could negatively impact the fair value of its bonds. To mitigate this risk, ABC entered into an interest rate swap that effectively converts the fixed-rate liability into a variable-rate liability. ABC has designated the swap as a fair value hedge of the debt in accordance with FASB Statement No. 133 (FAS 133), *Accounting for Derivatives Instruments and Hedging Activities*. In this type of hedge, the change in the fair value of the derivative is offset by a portion of the change in the fair value of the hedged debt.

Accounting for hedges under FAS 133 is complicated. The FVO provides ABC an opportunity to reduce the efforts required in hedging the risk of changes in the fair value of its debt. FAS 133 already requires the swap to be carried at fair value in the balance sheet (at present, a $4 million asset); by electing the FVO for the fixed-rate debt, ABC may be able to achieve a "natural hedge" (i.e., changes in fair value of the debt will be offset by changes in the fair value of the swap) without having to apply the often onerous hedging requirements of FAS 133.

---

[13] This is a federal government program which provides funding to higher education institutions to enable them to make low-interest student loans available.

However, while the FVO potentially could provide some relief from the rigors of FAS 133 hedge accounting, additional volatility could result. A perfect offset of the changes in fair value between the debt and the derivative will not occur in a "natural hedge" due to the following factors:

- In a FAS 133 fair value hedge, only that portion of the long-term debt attributable to the risk being hedged (e.g., interest rate risk) must be reported at fair value. However, if the FVO is elected for the hedged debt, the entire debt issue must be recorded at fair value.

- Under FAS 133, any changes in fair value of the hedged debt attributable to ABC's changes in credit standing are ignored if the interest rate risk is the designated item. Under the FVO, however, ABC would be required to reflect the impact of changes in its credit standing/nonperformance risk in determining the fair value of its debt. The swap's fair value will be affected by credit standing/nonperformance risk of the swap counterparty (i.e., the financial institution that is party to the contract). Therefore, since the swap is in an asset position, the fair value will reflect the credit standing/nonperformance risk of the counterparty while the fair value of the debt will reflect ABC's credit standing/nonperformance risk. In this case, the fair value changes of the two financial instruments may not offset, creating potential ineffectiveness.

Other pertinent considerations related to electing the FVO include:

- Once elected, the FVO is irrevocable; the debt would have to be measured at fair value throughout the life of the issue. ABC's fixed-rate bonds mature in 30 years; thus, Bob potentially would be committing to fair value measurement for a very lengthy period. Under the FAS 133 fair value hedging rules, Bob can elect to discontinue application of hedge accounting (and therefore, of fair value measurement of the debt) at any time.

- Currently, deferred financing costs are treated as part of the carrying value of ABC's debt, and are amortized over the life of the debt as part of the effective interest cost. FAS 159 requires removal from the balance sheet of any differences between the carrying value and the fair value of items for which the FVO is elected. Thus, all of ABC's unamortized issuance costs associated with the fixed-rate debt would need to be written off as part of the cumulative effect adjustment at transition when the election is made. If the FVO were subsequently elected for any new debt issuances, the associated deferred financing costs would need to be expensed immediately.

- In addition to providing the long-term debt disclosures currently required by FASB Statement No. 107, *Disclosures about Fair Value of Financial Instruments*, election of the FVO would require ABC to provide the ongoing disclosures required for recurring fair value measurements under FAS 157, as well as FAS 159 disclosures.

Variable-rate debt

Observation: Electing the FVO for variable-rate debt held by non-healthcare NPOs would not be beneficial. Because those NPOs are not permitted to use cash flow hedge accounting, their changes in net assets already are subject to volatility associated with swings in the fair value of the swap, just as they would be if the FVO were elected. Thus, even though there would be no financial statement impact associated with electing the FVO, the NPO would assume the burden of having to provide ongoing FAS 157 disclosures for recurring fair value measurements.

ABC also has $100 million of variable rate debt that pays LIBOR +2%. ABC is exposed to the risk that the interest rate on its bonds (and therefore ABC's interest costs) could increase. To mitigate this risk, ABC entered into a variable-to-fixed interest rate swap (currently in a liability position of $19 million) which effectively converts the variable-rate liability into a fixed-rate liability. ABC has designated the swap as a cash flow hedge in accordance with FAS 133.[14] In a cash flow hedge, the effective portion of changes in the fair value of swap are excluded from the performance indicator until such time as the forecasted transaction affects earnings, thus shielding ABC from some or all of the volatility associated with changes in fair value of the swap.

---

[14] FAS 133 cash flow hedge accounting is available to not-for-profit health care organizations because they report a standardized performance indicator. NPOs that do not report a standardized performance indicator cannot utilize cash flow hedge accounting.

KEY CONSIDERATIONS FOR ELIGIBLE ITEMS

Bob determined that electing the FVO for ABC's variable rate debt would not likely be practicable. Changes in the fair value of variable rate debt are reflected as changes in the variable interest rate, not as changes in the amount of liability reported in the balance sheet.[15] Thus, adopting the FVO would subject ABC's operating results to volatility associated with swings in the fair value of its swap, with no offsetting impact of changes in the fair value of the debt other than adjustments for changes in the underlying credit/nonperformance risk of ABC.

Other considerations

Other broader considerations that Bob must keep in mind with respect to FVO elections include:

- Situations identified by the AICPA's Center for Audit Quality in which making a FVO election could be deemed inappropriate if the election is not considered substantive.[16]

- The extent to which changes to internal controls would be required for accounts for which the FVO is elected.

- The potential impact of FVO elections on restrictive covenants (e.g., in debt agreements).

- The expanded disclosures that are associated with the FVO. In addition to robust disclosure requirements under FAS 159, ABC will also have to comply with FAS 157's disclosure requirements for recurring fair value measurements.[17]

---

[15] Variable rate debt by its nature is issued and trades in the market at par, with changes in the interest rate reflecting changes in the market for the debt.

[16] An Alert was issued by the Center for Audit Quality Alert in April 2007 (CAQ Alert No. 2007-14), when some companies were early adopting FAS 159. Certain proposed applications of FAS 159 that were deemed inappropriate were observed during the period of early adoption. Such applications would similarly not be considered acceptable upon adoption by ABC in fiscal 2009.

[17] Appendix B of FAS 159 includes an example of a disclosure that integrates FAS 159's disclosure requirements with the requirements in both FAS 157 and FAS 107. The example is for illustrative purposes only and does not present the only method to comply with the disclosure requirements.

Key questions

Prior to making any FVO elections, Bob must consider the following:

- Would increased volatility in its statement of operations be a concern? For example, would that increased volatility have implications for any restrictive covenants (e.g., associated with debt agreements)?
- Is creating symmetry in the accounting for gains and losses on FAS 124, available-for-sale investments, important to ABC (i.e., eliminating OTTI)?
- How significantly would simplifying recordkeeping for investments, contributions, split-interest agreements, etc. benefit ABC?
- Would the benefits of "natural hedges" outweigh the downsides?
- Overall, do the potential benefits of electing the FVO outweigh the burden associated with the expanded disclosure requirements that would be required?
- By changing the measurement basis to fair value, what implications would applying FAS 157/159 have for ABC and for the audit?

SUMMARY OF CONSIDERATIONS

Appendix—Summary of considerations

The following table summarizes the significant pros and cons associated with electing the fair value option for assets and liabilities discussed in this guide.

Asset or liability	Pros	Cons
Trading securities	• None, as mark-to-market adjustments are already reported within the performance indicator.*	• None, as mark-to-market adjustments are already reported within the performance indicator.*

Available-for-sale securities	• Simplified record keeping.
	• Symmetrical reporting of gains and losses (realized and unrealized would both be reported within the performance indicator*).
	• Eliminates the necessity of evaluating other-than-temporary impairments.
	• Unrealized gains will be included within the performance indicator.*
		• Increased volatility within the performance indicator* will require:
		  - Assessment of impact on internal budgeting and forecasting, contractual arrangements (e.g., debt covenants, compensation arrangements, etc).
		  - Communication/disclosure to users of financial statements to improve their ability to interpret the affects of volatility.

Alternative investments carried under the equity method or at cost	• More faithful representation of value on balance sheet.	• Increased volatility within the performance indicator* will require:
		  - Assessment of impact on internal budgeting and forecasting, contractual arrangements (e.g., debt covenants, compensation arrangements, etc).
		  - Communication/disclosure to users of financial statements to improve their ability to interpret the affects of volatility.
		• Requires internal control assessment to ensure adequate controls are in place to support fair value assertions.
		• Time, effort and cost associated with fair value measurement.
		• Increased disclosure requirements.

Alternative investments carried at fair value**	• None, as they are already carried at fair value.	• None, as they are already carried at fair value.
Contribution receivable—Multi-year promises to give cash	• Some simplification of record keeping.	• Time, effort and cost associated with fair value measurement. • Increased disclosure requirements.

---

*   Performance indicator as defined in AAG-HCO.

**   Applies only to "other investments" carried at fair value under Chapter 8 of AAG-NPO.

APPENDIX G

Asset or liability	Pros	Cons
Noncontrolling interest in joint venture (or partially owned entities)	• More faithful representation of value on balance sheet.	• Increased volatility within the performance indicator* will require: - Assessment of impact on internal budgeting and forecasting, contractual arrangements (e.g., debt covenants, compensation arrangements, etc). - Communication/disclosure to users of financial statements to improve their ability to interpret the affects of volatility. • Requires internal control assessment to ensure adequate controls are in place to support fair value assertions. • Time, effort and cost associated with fair value measurement. • Increased disclosure requirements.
Obligations under split-interest agreements—NPO serves as trustee	• Some simplification of record keeping.	• Increased volatility within the performance indicator* and/or temporarily restricted net assets will require: - Assessment of impact on internal budgeting and forecasting, contractual arrangements (e.g., debt covenants, compensation arrangements, etc). - Communication/disclosure to users of financial statements to improve their ability to interpret the affects of volatility. • Requires internal control assessment to ensure adequate controls are in place to support fair value assertions. • Time, effort and cost associated with fair value measurement. • Increased disclosure requirements.
Interest in net assets of financially-interrelated organization	• More faithful representation of value on balance sheet.	• Increased volatility within the performance indicator* and/or temporarily restricted net assets will require: - Assessment of impact on internal budgeting and forecasting, contractual arrangements (e.g., debt covenants, compensation arrangements, etc). - Communication/disclosure to users of financial statements to improve their ability to interpret the affects of volatility. • Requires internal control assessment to ensure adequate controls are in place to support fair value assertions. • Time, effort and cost associated with fair value measurement. • Increased disclosure requirements.

* Performance indicator as defined in AAG-HCO.
** Applies only to "other investments" carried at fair value under Chapter 8 of AAG-NPO.

SUMMARY OF CONSIDERATIONS

Asset or liability	Pros	Cons
Long-term debt and derivatives (e.g., interest rate swaps)	• May eliminate need to pursue FAS 133 hedge accounting.	• Increased volatility within the performance indicator* and/or temporarily restricted net assets will require: - Assessment of impact on internal budgeting and forecasting, contractual arrangements (e.g., debt covenants, compensation arrangements, etc). - Communication/disclosure to users of financial statements to improve their ability to interpret the affects of volatility. • Requires internal control assessment to ensure adequate controls are in place to support fair value assertions. - Time, effort and cost associated with fair value measurement. • Increased disclosure requirements. • Changes in the fair value of the debt will not be fully offset by changes in a swap.
Student loans	• More faithful representation of value on balance sheet.	• Increased volatility within the performance indicator* and/or temporarily restricted net assets will require: - Assessment of impact on internal budgeting and forecasting, contractual arrangements (e.g., debt covenants, compensation arrangements, etc). - Communication/disclosure to users of financial statements to improve their ability to interpret the affects of volatility. • Requires internal control assessment to ensure adequate controls are in place to support fair value assertions. • Time, effort and cost associated with fair value measurement. • Increased disclosure requirements.

*   Performance indicator as defined in AAG-HCO.
**   Applies only to "other investments" carried at fair value under Chapter 8 of AAG-NPO.

Authors

Michael George

A senior manager in PricewaterhouseCoopers' national office, Michael provides accounting consulting services to the assurance practice within the healthcare, not-for-profit, and governmental industries. Prior to joining the national office, Michael provided assurance and consulting services to a variety of healthcare and not-for-profit clients in PwC's New York Metro Health Industries Practice.

David Merriam

A senior manager in PricewaterhouseCoopers' national office, Dave consults with engagement teams on accounting issues affecting a variety of industries, with a specialization in the healthcare and higher education industries. Prior to his current role, he served a wide variety of healthcare and higher education clients in PwC's Health Industries Practice in Boston and New England.

Martha Garner

Martha Garner is a managing director in PricewaterhouseCoopers' national office, where she consults with engagement teams and clients on complex and difficult accounting and financial reporting issues affecting healthcare, higher education, not-for-profit, and governmental clients. She is actively involve in standard-setting activities affecting those sectors, serving on numerous FASB, GASB, and AICPA standard-setting task forces and committees.

The following PwC personnel also contributed to the content or served as technical reviewers of the guide:

Tom McGuinness

John Horan

Kenneth Dakdduk

Robert Valletta

John Mattie

Steve Luber

Jeffrey Thomas

Brian Huggins

AUTHORS

pwc.com

Index

INDEX